Bergen
– A Cultural Guide

Hey Love!
This is a few
years old and
new stuff has
popped up, but
still good idea
of what this
city offers!

Love,
Anne

Bergen
– A Cultural Guide

Norvall Skreien

KUNNSKAPSFORLAGET

© Kunnskapsforlaget
  H. Aschehoug & Co (W. Nygaard) A/S and
  Gyldendal Norsk Forlag ASA, Oslo 1999

Translated by Mette-Line Myhre
Editors: Turi Enge and Øystein Eek
Consultants: Professor Anders Bjarne Fossen and
 Journalist Lotte Schønfelder
Graphic co-ordinator: Randi R. Joveng
Design and typesetting: Norvall Skreien
Coverdesign: Scandinavian Design Group, Oslo
Photos: Norvall Skreien, unless otherwise stated.
Bergen City Map: Unimap A/S, Drøbak, © Kunnskapsforlaget
Typesetting: 9/10 New Century Schoolbook, 8/9 Futura
Printed and bound by John Grieg AS
First published 1999
First print: 3000

This book is published with support from the Bergen Municipality,
Bergensbanken, Det Nyttige Selskab and Grieg Shipping.

ISBN 82-573-0990-7

Mayor of Bergen, Ingmar Ljones, on Bergen
– A Cultural Guide

In the days to come culture will become a major focal point in Bergen. Its official status as one of Europe's leading cultural cities is a great honour. But with honour comes an obligation to present our cultural treasures to our many guests from near and far. However, it is just as important that both our heritage and modern art are discovered and cherished by those of us who live in this unique city.

On behalf of this cultural city it is a great privilege to warmly recommend this book as an outstanding guide to the city's many attractions. The overwhelming amount of information is so clearly presented that it is a pleasure to acquire the knowledge conveyed.

Ingmar Ljones
Mayor of Bergen

9

■ A FEW WORDS BEFORE WE BEGIN

"Because the inhabitants of Bergen are a collection of all kinds of nations, you will see that they differ from the other Norwegians in manner of speech, customs and habits."
Ludvig Holberg

Welcome to Bergen – soon to be 1000 years old, but still a lively European cultural centre, known for its hospitality! Thank you for displaying your confidence, expressed by keeping this book in hand, and for your interest thus shown in the history, art and culture of the city. You are hereby invited on a city tour, to learn of its pioneers and to visit past events as well as modern attractions. The words will lead the way, accompanied by a considerable number of illustrations.

The route, laid out in alphabetical order, is easy to follow. The trip from A to Å will be a long one, but there will be plenty of stations, or chapters, to stop at along the way. You, the reader, can simply choose how long each stop will last. The individuals appearing at many of the stops have been chosen because the city itself has emphasised their importance, either by naming a street after them or by raising a monument or memorial in their honour. At the back of the book there is a list of useful addresses and telephone numbers of cultural institutions. There is also a list of literary sources which may provide you with further information.

As a journalist in Bergen since 1955, I have had a front row seat in the cultural life of this city. Many of those who have experienced the fiery, almost Mediterranean temperament of the people of Bergen would say that I was privileged. The atmosphere between the city's seven surrounding mountains changes as quickly as the weather, from heavenly to hellish, says the former mayor, Bengt Martin Olsen. The people are also a generous lot. Bergen has probably produced more patrons than any other city. The 'Latinos of the north' are accustomed to caring about their city. I hope this book will show you why they have every reason to do so.

Along the way you will run into several words and names which include the Norwegian vowels Æ, Ø and Å. The letter Æ sounds like 'a' in 'bad'. The letter Ø resembles 'ea' as in 'earn', while the letter Å sounds like 'o' in 'north' or 'oo' in 'door'.

Many fine consultants deserve thanks for their valuable assistance. I would especially like to thank Dr. Inger Elisabeth Haavet, Journalist Lotte Schønfelder, Professor Anders Bjarne Fossen and Editorial Director Øystein Eek.

My thanks to the municipality of Bergen and "Det Nyttige Selskab" for their financial support of this project.

Finally, I would like to wish you all a pleasant journey!

■ A PORTAL TO THE CULTURE OF BERGEN

Mon Plaisir – my pleasure – was what the Bergen businessman, Michael D. Prahl, called his remarkable garden pavilion in Mulen. Shaped like a Greek temple with ionic pillars, the pavilion is a lovely symbol both of the genuine cultural exuberance among the people of Bergen, and of the city's openness to the rest of the world and its close ties with the cultural spirit of Europe. It seems natural to choose this temple of joy and vision as the portal to a guide on the art and culture of Bergen.

Culture and art have given inspiration to generations of people in the city. There is many a striking testimony to this. They surround each 'Bergensian's' daily activities. There is a Norwegian saying, "You do not realise how much you own until you move". Many a family has had this experience. But the truth of this expression can be seen in a wider context.

It was only after Bergen was promoted to the elite division of the European cultural cities that most of the city's inhabitants began to realise how rich in culture their city really was. Just as a family on the move packs up their bags and baggage, the city of Bergen will have to take stock of their valuable belongings before entering the distinguished society of the great cultural cities. The cultural diversity in this city surrounded by seven mountains can, however, make it difficult to see the forest for the trees.

The list of famous names, or should we say 'stately trees', is a lengthy one. Bergen is the birthplace of such great figures as Ludvig Holberg, Ole Bull, J.C. Dahl and Edvard Grieg. Here Henrik Ibsen and Bjørnstjerne Bjørnson worked, and Petter Dass attended school. It was in Bergen that one of the world's oldest existing symphony orchestras was formed, and its annual International Festival is the outstanding international cultural event in Norway. Bergen's medieval district, Bryggen, is on the UNESCO list of the world's cultural monuments most worthy of preservation. Bryggen is a direct link to the formation of the very first cities of the early Middle Ages and to European culture in general.

The privilege of being surrounded by both the natural and cultural wonders of a city like Bergen is one that perhaps only a tourist can fully appreciate. For the native inhabitant of Bergen, the city's cultural landscape may at times seem like the snow-covered mountains to a snow-blind skier. Without sunglasses the contours and dimensions of the landscape are almost invisible.

A helping hand may be needed to discover the diversity, the complexity and the lavishness of the cultural scene in Bergen. This book is a helping hand, a pair of cultural sunglasses.

One man who has clearly been dazzled by the culture of Bergen is the Danish critic and literary historian, Georg Brandes. Before we embark our journey into the cultural landscape of Bergen, take a moment to read his unbiased opinion in a speech written for the city of Bergen in 1914:

"Perhaps Bergen, in regard to culture, is a refined Norwegian city. Together with the grey, rainy atmosphere and a certain delicacy of the heart, there exists a practical energy, as this gentleman (Prime Minister and shipowner Christian Michelsen) who I by great fortune have standing here at my right, exemplifies. It occurs to me that in order to do well in Norway, one would have to have been born in Bergen, or perhaps, spiritually speaking, have been baptised here in this city. Holberg allowed himself to be born in Bergen. Ole Bull and Edvard Grieg did the same, Gerhard Gran did the same. Ibsen and Bjørnson received their spiritual baptism here. The whole world has passed through Bergen. Jonas Lie, Gunnar Heiberg – and many others whom I at the moment fail to remember. As a rule, one could say, that almost everything of importance for Norway has either passed out of Bergen or passed through Bergen."

Art and culture is everywhere in Bergen. This fresco with its easily recognisable motifs from Bergen decorates a house wall on Olav Kyrres gate. The artwork was painted by Bjarne Lund and Ansgar Larssen in 1928. The owner of the property at the time was Smith-Sivertsen, a baker.

■ ALVØEN

Antiquarian industrial site

Alvøen approx. 12 km. Route 555 toward Sotra.

Alvøen manor from 1797 received its modern façade in 1835. ▼

Most people would not consider an industrial site on the west coast an idyllic spot. But there is always an exception to the rule. A rare example of this is Alvøen, where Norway's oldest paper factory was established in 1797. The industrial history of the place can be traced back to the 17th century. Today Alvøen has a special status as an area deserving of preservation.

This pleasant industrial community gives the impression of a holiday paradise on the southern coast. Over 30 small, white-painted workers' houses from the 19th century strengthen this impression. The buildings are scattered around the pleasant gardens of Alvøpollen, like wildflowers in a meadow.

From their windows, the workers had a view of the blue fjord and the inviting rock slopes of the beaches just a stone's throw away. From their homes they could also see their workplace, the large factory building at the farthest end of the fjord, and they could literally look down upon the factory owner's luxurious residence, partly hidden by lush vegetation at the end of a long tree-lined path. The house of the managing director was centrally located both by area and as a centre of activity. This building and its 15 acres including gardens and a park was donated in 1953 by Hans B. and Frieda Fasmer to the foundation "Alvøen Hovedbygning" (Alvøen Manor). Members of the Fasmer family, with its roots in Bremen, had always been the sole owners of Alvøen's industrial area.

The property was opened as a museum in 1983. At the same time the "Vestlandske Kunstindustrimuseum" (The West Norwegian Museum of Applied Arts) took over the administration. The purpose of the foundation is to preserve the buildings, the collection and the property as a cultural landmark.

Top quality and high value. It is mainly the latter most people associate with the trademark Alvøen. Owning a great deal of the final product, (namely money), was of course equivalent to wealth. Alvøen provided Norges Bank (the National Bank of Norway) with the paper for printing bills until the manufacturing of paper ended in 1981. Alvøen was the last factory in Norway to produce high quality paper towels based on 100% cloth. Some of the finer quality paper products are still being manufactured at Alvøen, though today they are based on raw materials from Holland.

The industrial history of Alvøen began long before the paper factory, however, with not quite so peaceful a objective. The first thing to be produced at Alvøen was gunpowder! In 1926 Alvøen obtained both a gunpowder plant and a flourmill. A string of new products made their entrance later, including saltpetre, linseed oil and finally, paper. For a time there was even a shipyard on the premises.

Gift from the Fasmer family

The more than 30 small, white-painted workers' houses give Alvøen the resemblance of a holiday paradise on the south coast.

Paper manufactured for Norwegian paper money

The pavilion from 1797 still adorns the gardens.

A

Valuable art

The museum at Alvøen includes a vast collection of valuable art objects, antique furniture, textiles and a large book collection. Some of the books date back to the 15th century, and contain, for example, scientific and religious literature from the Age of Enlightenment. Among these treasures are also paintings by J.C. Dahl, a valuable collection of silver from Bergen, and Chinese porcelain.

■ ANTIQUE BOOKSHOPS

Books and postcards

There are three antique bookshops in the downtown area of Bergen. They specialise in everything from books to old prints, postcards and comic books. Some offer antique objects. See the back of the book for addresses.

■ ANTIQUES

Varied and rich selection

The visitor looking for antiques will have a good chance of finding something of interest in Bergen. The shops are many and the selection is both rich and varied in price, style and the number of objects. The antique market reflects the city's rich gold and silver tradition. See the back of the book for addresses.

■ THE NORWEGIAN ARBORETUM

*"The Lace House"
(from the 1800)
had to make way
for the expansion of
Haukeland Hospital
and was moved to
the Arboretum in
1992. There it is
used as a café and
information centre.
A lacy, decorated
moulding explains
the name.*

Although the Garden of Eden may not have been located in Bergen, we do have a good substitute. Det Norske Arboret (The Norwegian Arboretum) at Milde is probably the closest thing to the biblical ideal this far north of the equator.

Ever since the collection, started by Fritz C. Rieber, was laid out in 1971, almost 3000 different kinds of plants have taken root on the 150 acre park near Fanafjord, and new plants, bushes and trees continue to arrive. HRH Harald, then Crown Prince, was given the honour of planting the first tree, an oak. As a visual experience, however, the King's oak cannot compare to the largest rhododendron collec-

tion in the Nordic countries, when it blooms each year from April to June in an explosion of colour. Of the world's 1000 wild species, about 300 of them are growing at Milde, along with an additional 400 cultivated species.

The arboretum is a foundation with links to the University of Bergen, that also includes the historic gardens by Fana folkehøgskole. Remnants of one of Norway's oldest Renaissance gardens are found here, including the 300-year-old Buksbom trees. The gardens are laid out at Store Milde gård (the Great Milde farm) which during the Middle Ages belonged to Lysekloster (Lyse Cloister).

Touring paths through the park area are up to six miles long and offer abundant opportunities for exploring nature in a west coast landscape full of exciting botanical elements from all over the world. Tropical plants are grown in the greenhouse, and it is possible, for example, to harvest ripe figs from the greenhouse fig trees.

A separate botanical garden has been created for research and study purposes in co-operation with the Muséhagen at Nygårdshøyden.

▲
Over 700 different species grow in Scandinavia's largest rhododendron garden at Milde.

Getting there:
Bus to Milde from Bergen bus station, platform 18. Parking by Mildevågen and by Vågelva. Free admission all year. Tours can be reserved for a fee.

The Arboretum is a collection of trees and bushes grown outdoors for the purposes of research, instruction and experimentation on plants in our climate.

■ ART IN BERGEN

First royal portrait in Norway

Marble head of King Øystein from Munkeliv monastery – Norway's earliest royal portrait. It is held today in the Bergen Museum.

Earliest panorama of Bergen

The earliest panorama of Bergen is a copper plate from 1575, done by Jerome Skol (Hieronymus Scholeus in Latin) for Theatrum Urbiumt, a German collection of views of the best-known cities in the world. The plate is rich in detail and has therefore been an important source of historical information. The Scholeus plate would become a model for other Bergen prospectuses over the next two hundred years.

During their excavations at Klosteret (the Cloister) in 1853, where the powerful Munkeliv Cloister stood during the Middle Ages, archaeologists found Norway's oldest royal portrait. A head of white marble with the inscription "Øystein Rex" portrays King Øystein 1 Magnusson (approx. 1088–1123), the brother of Sigurd Jorsalfarer. King Øystein founded the cloister before 1110. The marble head is also the oldest preserved sculpture which has been created in Bergen.

Examples of early art objects are otherwise often found in churches. The many sculptures and painted antependiums, or altar fronts, which decorate churches from the Middle Ages all over western Norway, were almost without exception executed by artists from Bergen. The head of the National Archives, Harry Fett, believed that Bergen had to be "counted as one of the great northern European art cities in the 14th century, along with Paris and London, and perhaps even the Italian art cities". (See ▶ Bergen Museum.)

The dominant position of the Hanseatic League during the following 200 years led to the stagnation of cultural development at home. Norwegian art drowned in the mass-produced imported goods that then flooded the market. It was not until 1558 that the traditions of art and handicrafts flourished again in Bergen. Middle-class youth were given privileges, and German craftsmen in the city were given an ultimatum: either become a citizen or go home to Germany! Art traditions prospered, largely thanks to the contributions of immigrant artists. One of the most prominent names from this period is Søffren Oelssen, who sculpted the statues of the disciples in ▶ Mariakirken (St. Mary's Church) in 1634.

The greatest painter in Bergen during the middle of the 17th century was Elias Fiigenschoug. His signature appears on the oldest known landscape painting in Norway, Halsnøy kloster (Halsnøy Cloister) from 1656. Danish immigrant Mathias Blumenthal (approx.

1719–63) concluded the 'international' period of art history in Bergen. He introduced the Rococo style to Bergen, but is best known for his colourful adornments of the Blumenthal Room, now in ▶ Rasmus-Meyer's Collection. Here, in allegorical form, he portrays the reconstruction of the city after the fire of 1756.

Lyder ▶ Sagen contributed to a new artistic 'awakening' during the 19th century. Painting as an art form had until then lived in the shadow of music and theatre in the city. Painter Johan Georg Müller and illustrator Johan F.L. Dreier were at this time the city's only professional painters. Müller, who had been educated at the Academy of Arts in Copenhagen, became J.C. ▶ Dahl's first teacher. Dreier is well known for his city prospectuses.

Artist temple at Damsgård

Urdi at Damsgård was purchased in 1894 by artist couple Olav Rusti (1850–1920) from Vanylven in Sunnmøre and German-born Frida Rusti (1861–1963). The lovely temple-like building became a meeting place for artists and New Norwegian writers. Frequent guests included Edvard Grieg, writers Per ▶ Sivle and Arne Garborg, and painters Harriet Backer, Gerhard Munthe and Erik Werenskiold. In 1989 the first Harding fiddle competition was arranged at Urdi. See ▶ Vestmannalaget. Rusti is especially well known as a portrait painter.

◀

"Spring Feelings" is the name of Fritz Røed's lovely sculpture in Mulen. The sculpture and 10,000 rhododendron bushes were given to Bergen by Rieber & Son Inc. when the firm celebrated its 150th anniversary in 1989.

A

"Reclining poet"
on *Ole Bulls plass*
was sculpted by
Hans Jacob Meyer.
The sculpture won
second prize in the
Nordahl Grieg mon-
ument competition.
On the recommen-
dation of the jury it
was purchased by
"Det Nyttige Sel-
skab" and donated
to the city in 1958.

▶

**Outstanding
painter**

Dahl would later stand out as the greatest
painter not only of Bergen, but also of Norway.
He was also the first artist to discover the rich
array of artistic motifs in western Norway and
paved the way for his younger colleagues. One
of these was Bernt Tunold (1877–1946). He
was born in Selje, but belonged to the Bergen
school of art. After Nicolai Astrup, he became
the foremost interpreter of western Norwegian
nature. Other leading painters in Bergen during the 19th century include Frants Bøe
(1820–92) and Tycho Christoffer Jæger (1818–
89), a student of J.C. Dahl.

**Portrayed
Bergen**

Nils Krantz (1886–1954) was born in Mo-
sjøen, but came to Bergen as a child, a city he
was to lose his heart to. City landscapes became his specialty. Krantz portrayed Bergen
revealing a great appreciation for the Bergen
character, in a moderate, cubist style. Examples of his work can be found in Nygård
School, which he embellished in 1926.

Ansgar Larssen from Sandnes came to Bergen as Axel Revold's assistant for the decoration of the ▶ Frescohallen (Hall of Frescos) in the Bergen Stock Exchange from 1921 to 1923. Larssen later taught his technique. The first religious fresco in Norway was carried out in 1924 by Hugo Lous Mohr in the parish house of Johanneskirken (St. John's Church). Bjarne Lund painted his enormous frescos inside the new Telegraph Building in 1927. A year later Lund collaborated with Ansgar Larssen on a fresco over Smith-Sivertsen's bakery on Olav Kyrre's Street. (Photo, page 11.) And finally, the new Handelens og Sjøfartens hus (House of Trade and Shipping) was decorated by Arne Lofthus in 1931. With that, 'fresco fever' swept the city where these monumental works of art were first introduced.

Bergen has also 'exported' many talented painters. J.C. Dahl settled in Dresden, Arne Lofthus (1881–1962) moved to Denmark, while Henrik Lund (1879–1935) and Arne Kavli (1878–1970) preferred the country's capital as their workplace. Knut Rumohr (born 1916) was born in Bergen, but left his birthplace quite early.

Hjørdis Landmark (1882–1961), a student of Harriet Backer, was noteworthy as a sensitive portrait artist with a subdued impressionist style. Other female painters to have made their hometown of Bergen proud are Gerda Knudsen (1899–1945), Borghild Berge (1898 –1976) and Else Christie Kielland (1903–93). In the latter part of the 20th century several other remarkable female artists entered the scene, such as Aagot Kramer, Eva Synnestvedt, Lise Landmark, Eva Winther-Larssen, Tit Mohr, and among the younger artists, Inger Bergitte Sæverud. Prominent male colleagues in the post-war period are Gabriel Dahl and his sons, Peer Dahl and Ole Gabriel Dahl, Eilif Amundsen, Waldemar Stabell, Inggard Rosseland, Ingvald Holmefjord, Asbjørn Brekke, Einar Rustad Hansen, Knut Glambek, Bjørn Tvedt and Per Remfeldt. The latter also displayed great talent as a creative art promotor when he was an intendant in the Bergen Art Association.

First nude sculpture

"Youth" by Ingebrigt Vik in Teaterparken is the first nude sculpture publicly displayed in Norway. It was created in 1913 and first stood by the old city hall. The sculpture is one of the artist's most significant works.

A

The people of Bergen have been generous with offers of work for artists from out of town when artistic embellishments for the city have been required. About 60 different sculptors have created the over one hundred monuments adorning the city. Many of them have come about as a result of competitions. Still, Bergen's own sculptors, Sofus ▶ Madsen, Ambrosia Tønnesen (see ▶ Hordamuseet), Hans Jacob Meyer and Bård Breivik, are responsible for the major part of the public monuments and memorials in their hometown.

Ingebrigt Vik's sculpture, "Ynglingen" (The Youth) in Teaterparken was the first nude sculpture in Bergen and probably also the first in the country when it was created in 1913. A year later his Grieg statue was erected in Byparken. Vik, who was born in Øystese in Hardanger, ran a wood carving workshop and a small factory that manufactured ceiling plaster decorations during the years 1892–1902. (See also ▶ Galleries.)

Stone sculpture in Christie Park, sculpted in Swedish granite by Bård Breivik.

You've seen this in many of my photos?

■ ASSISTENTKIRKEGÅRDEN

Cemetery for famous Bergensians

Monday, August 23rd 1880 is a date that will forever be etched in the cultural history of Bergen. The whole city dressed in black on that day and followed violin virtuoso Ole ▶ Bull to his final resting-place in the Assistantkirkegården (The Assistant Churchyard), originally named Korskirkens Assistentkirkegård. Never before had the city experienced such a funeral ceremony. Bjørnstjerne Bjørnson gave one of his great speeches at the grave, and Edvard Grieg honoured his friend and musician colleague with a wreath and a few beautiful words in Bull's memory.

The Assistentkirkegården is like a peaceful, green sanctuary between ▶ Stadsporten (the City Gates) and the train station. Because of its central location near the Stadsporten, the city council found it worthy as the gravesite for Ole Bull. The grave was meant to be easily accessible to the enormous number of admirers Bull had in the city, and it was meant as a memorial to remind travelers of Bergen's great heir. Bull's grave is what makes a visit to the old churchyard worthwhile. The churchyard has been in use since 1837, although no one has been buried there since 1919. The urn of Edvard Grieg stood in the churchyard in 1907 until the following year when it was finally placed at Troldhaugen.

Short stay for Grieg

Frederik Meltzer (1779–1855), the businessman and Eidsvoll-politician from Bergen, better known as the father of the Norwegian flag, was also laid to rest in the Assistentkirkegården. Meltzer had the idea for the cross-patterned Norwegian flag in red, white and blue, as we know it today. His suggestions for the design of the flag were approved by Parliament in 1821.

Designed the Norwegian flag

Ole Bull's grave in the "Assistent Churchyard".

B

■ NORMA BALEAN

Bergen's queen of the operetta

Private photo of the Bergen entertainer, Norma Balean. She was honoured with the royal gold medallion for achievement for her 51 successful years at the National Theatre of Bergen. Also awarded the entertainment statuette "Gledespiken". In 1977 she recorded "How good it is not to be young".

The actress Norma Balean (1907–89) earned a special place in the hearts of the people of Bergen during her 51 years as the city's queen of the operetta.

Norma Balean was born in London. When she was five years old, her mother, who was from Bergen, left Norma's English father and returned home with her daughter. Norma quickly became a genuine Bergen citizen both in thought and speech. Following her school years at U. Phils Girls' School and a short career as a clerk in a jewellery store, Norma made her way to the bright lights of the stage. It happened in 1928, by sheer accident, although sheer luck might be a more appropriate term. By chance she happened to be visiting a girlfriend, the step-daughter of orchestral conductor Sverre Jordan, when the theatre manager called to ask if he might know of any short, dark-haired girl with a good singing voice. Two weeks later, Norma made her debut as Miss Mabel in the operetta "The Circus Princess" by Emmerich Kálmán.

Norma was an enormous hit with the audience right from her debut. She was to lend her voice to the biggest roles, mostly in operettas and musicals, light comedies and vaudeville acts. But she also mastered more dramatic roles such as Ophelia in "Hamlet" and Anitra in "Peer Gynt". Her biggest successes included Adele in "Die Flaggermusen", Sally Adams in "Call me Madame", along with starring roles in "Annie Get Your Gun" and "The Merry Widow".

Norma Balean was the darling of Bergen, a prima donna, who in private life scarcly knew about the pretentious airs of the typical prima donna. Norma received the following testimonial from the mayor of Bergen: "She had the ability to identify with the characteristic Bergen temperament, pattern of speech and behaviour and represented the best of this city with energy and high spirits".

"Bergen at its best"

■ THE BERGEN CITY SONG

None of the authors of the Bergen city song actually comes from Bergen. One is not even Norwegian, but French. The song is entitled "Udsigter fra Ulriken" (The View from Ulriken) but is popularly called "Nystemten". The author of the lyrics was the poet and bishop Johan Nordahl ▶ Brun. The bishop's poetic tribute to Bergen was probably written for a festive occasion at the house of Johan F. Fosswinckel in Nygård in 1791 and came out in print for the first time the same year.

Created by 'foreigners'

Sofus Madsen's portrait relief of the poet of Bergen's city song adorns the memorial erected at Ulriken in 1970.

The melody is a French minuet, in all likelihood composed by Jean-Baptiste Lully, who was a composer at the court of the Sun King, Louis XIV. It was also used in Holberg's comedy, "Jean de France". Johan Halvorsen built his well-known Rococo variations on the same melody in 1921, and entitled the composition "Bergensiana".

The city song brought to pomp and circumstance by Halvorsen has been the annual overture to the Bergen International Festival. From 1977 the audience has also been allowed to join in. When the Icelandic director of the Festival in 1998 allowed this tradition to be broken for the first time, there were strong reactions.

The lyrics for the city song of Bergen were written to the melody composed by the French court composer Jean-Baptiste Lully.

The people of Bergen looked upon the decision as a sacrilege. The Festival audience, however, decided to have their say, so to speak. As soon as members of the royal family were led out of Grieghallen, the audience, true to tradition, stood up to sing the first verse of "Nystemten":

The first two bars of "Nystemten" form a musical fence outside the restaurant at Fløien – here seen in the foreground of a fog covered city with Løvstakken in the background. ▶

Bergensiana
Johan Halvorsen composed his "Rococo variations on an old Bergen melody" in honour of Bergen actor Gustav Emil Thomassen when his 40th acting anniversary was celebrated at the National Theatre. The composition was dedicated to the Copenhagen Philharmonic Orchestra, which Halvorsen conducted shortly after the anniversary celebration. According to the composer, we follow, through the variations, a Bergen man on his travels throughout the world. The finale depicts his homecoming to Vågen.

Song to Bergen

I took my newly tuned cither in hand
Sorrow left my heart on Ulriken's peak
Thoughts of beacons if their fire would burn
to call the men to fight their foes;
felt the peace, my spirits uplifted
and clasped my cither with a playful hand

■ BERGEN DOMKANTORI

**Elite choir
with a long
merit list**

Hardly a single piece of church music of any importance, be it classical or modern, has been kept from the public in Bergen during the last two to three decades. This is due, for the most part, to the high level of musical activity under the leadership of Bergen ▶ Domkirke's cantor, Magnar Mangersnes. His most important vocal instrument is the Bergen Domkantori (The Bergen Cathedral Choir), an elite choir consisting of about 50 well-educated, male and female singers. Along with the Bergen Oratory

Choir, which he also conducts, the cathedral is able to cover a wide range of church music. In 1995 the cathedral started a boys' choir as well.

The Bergen Domkantori was established in 1971 and has during all that time sung under the inspirational baton of Mangersnes. The musical merit list of the choir includes a large number of recordings, concert tours to several countries, and many distinguished national as well as international awards. The Bergen Domkantori has performed new compositions by some 15 different composers.

Established in 1971

The choir has come as far as the finals of the prestigious BBC competition "Let the People Sing". They have won the Spellemannpris (the Norwegian national music award) and were selected as "Performer of the Year" by the Norwegian Composers' Association. Several composers have written musical scores especially for the Bergen Domkantori. The choir has naturally been a part of the Bergen International Festival and in the concerts given by Harmonien. Both international and national critiques have been overwhelmingly positive.

Many prices

In addition to their busy concert schedule, the choir is present at all regular church services. The choir can be found in Domkirken every Sunday with various choir leaders. During holiday seasons, the choir often has extra performances.

Cathedral cantor Magnar Mangersnes established Bergen Domkantori in 1971. The choir has under his inspiring leadership become one of the top choirs in Europe.

◀

■ BERGEN KATEDRALSKOLE

Famous students

Bergen Katedralskole (Bergen Cathedral school), also known as Bergens Latinskole, has turned out quite a star-studded team of students. This institution was once called the 'learned school' after a decree from 1809, and not without reason!

An honour plaque, hung in the vestibule of Katedralskolen, contains a list of names of distinguished students, among others Absalon Pederssøn Beyer, Petter Dass, Ludvig Holberg, Claus Fasting, Hans Strøm, Niels Hertzberg, Jens Zetlitz, Wilhelm F.K. Christie, Lyder Sagen, Edvard Hagerup, Nicolai Wergeland, Christian Lassen, Georg Prahl Harbitz, Michael and Ernst Sars, Frederik Stang, Johan Sebastian Welhaven, Peter Andreas Jensen, Ole Irgens, Jacob Worm-Müller, Armauer Hansen, Henrik Mohn, Christian Michelsen, Alf Torp, Gerhard Gran, Lauritz Stub Wiberg, Nordahl Grieg, Per Hysing-Dahl and Harald Sæverud.

Educated clergymen of different faith

The Bergen Katedralskole was originally a clerical school, founded near the end of the 10th century. Following the Reformation, the school came to play a key role during the transition to the new faith. In 1554 it was established as a school of Latin by Bergen's first Lutheran bishop, Gjeble Pederssøn, on the property which now bears the address Lille Øvre Street 38. The purpose of the school was to continue to educate clergymen, although now it was in order to qualify them to preach the teachings of the Protestant faith.

Since 1840 Bergen Katedralskole has been housed in this late Empire style building on Kong Oscar's Street 36, near Domkirken (seen in the background).

▶

B

The rare half-timbered building that stands on the site today is from 1706, and was built after fires laid the four previous schools in ashes. On the west wall is a memorial plaque in honour of Ludvig Holberg, who was a student from 1694 to 1702.

From 1840 Bergen Katedralskole was given status as a seat of high learning, and at the same time moved into its current, elegant, late Empire style building on Kong Oscar's Street 36. The old building was left to the poor relief system. Today it is occupied by the council offices for social services. Plans have now been made to turn the building into a school museum.

Bust of headmaster Jens Boalth (1725-44) in the vestibule of the school. Boalth was the founder of Harmonien and wrote music as well.

'Katten', as the school is nicknamed, is today an ordinary sixth form school. The students come from Bergen and the nearby districts.Early on the school placed a great deal of emphasis on drama, voice training and music. The idea of a school play, with an educational purpose, was introduced to this country by Bergen Katedralskole. The students set up the first play in Norway, "Adams Fald" (The Fall of Adam), directed by Absalon Pederssøn Beyer. (See ▶ Theatre in Bergen.)

In 1671 Katedralskolen hired its own cantor for the music department. Music was an important source of income at the time. The students of the clerical school were paid for their musical performances at weddings, funerals and private functions. They held concerts in the cathedral and performed oratorios. The student choir was called "Discanten" (The Descant). Instruction took place alternately in the school and in the church. The school day began with choir practice in the church as early as 5.30 a.m. On special occasions the head masters Jens Boalth and Jacob Steensen, both knowledgeable in the field of music, would compose the necessary music for the school. (See ▶ Music in Bergen.)

Katedralskolen has the oldest library in Bergen, dating back to 1774. The shelves contain such items as Claus ▶ Fasting's private book collection, with literature in the fields of philosophy, natural history and aesthetics.

Holberg about Katedralskole

"The school master was the sovereign ruler. Disciples lived under strict discipline. Their striped backs, their bulging foreheads and swollen cheeks revealed a spartan school. Parents inquired daily as to whether their children received their expected blows, which the zealous teachers vilely acknowledged and as proof exhibited the embroidered bodies of their disciples."

■ BERGEN MUSEUM

**The beginning
of the Univer-
sity of Bergen**

Fridtjof Nansen
*was curator of the
Bergen Museum for
six years. Bust by
Dagfin Werenskjold.*

Vilhelm Bjerknes –
*the father of modern
weather forecasting.*

Michael Sars –
*both theologian and
zoologist and mem-
ber of Bergen Mu-
seum's board of
directors.*

The Bergen Museum, founded by W.F.K.
▶ Christie in 1825, must be one of Norway's
most prolific cultural institutions. One such
'legitimate child' of the museum is that of the
University of Bergen. It began its operations
in 1948 as a direct continuation of the scientific work of the museum. The museum became
at the same time a part of the university.

Material from the Bergen Museum has also
formed the foundation for new museums such
as Bergen Billedgalleri (Bergen Art Gallery),
Vestlandske   Kunstindustrimuseum   (The
Western Norwegian Museum of Applied Arts),
Bergens Sjøfartsmuseum (Bergen's Shipping
Museum) and Norsk Fiskerimuseum (Nor-
wegian Museum of Fisheries).

The Bergen Museum moved into the first
specially designed museum building in Norway in 1840, near Lille Lungegårdsvann. The
building was taken over by Lungegården
school in 1866, but was torn down in 1971 to
make room for Bergen's new administration
building. The new museum building (architect
Johan Henrik Nebelong) on Nygårdshøyden,
was completed in 1866, although the two
wings (architect H.J. Sparre) were not completed before 1898. The natural history collection of the museum is contained here, including geology, zoology and botany exhibits. On
the grounds of the botanical gardens is the
greenhouse, where tropical plants can be seen
all year round. Especially attractive is also the
collection of minerals where magnificent spec-
imens from all over the world, together with
some fine local samples, are exhibited.

Several prominent researchers have been
associated with the museum of Bergen. Fridtjof Nansen was the museum's curator during
the years 1882–88.

Vilhelm Bjerknes (1862–1951) came to Bergen as a professor in 1917 and founded modern meteorology. His new and revolutionary
method of scientifically based weather forecasting was known as the "Bergen method"
and was soon practised all over the world.

Bergen theologian and zoologist Michael Sars (1805–69) was the founder of Norwegian marine-biology research. As a vicar in Kinn and Manger, he used the museum's microscope to study marine animal life. He was married to J. S. ▶ Welhaven's sister, Maren. Their son, zoologist Georg Ossian Sars, laid the foundation of modern fisheries research.

Det Geofysiske Institutt (The Geophysical Institute) was established in 1917, and has since 1928 been housed in a building in Florida. The Institute continues research carried out by the Bergen Museum in the fields of oceanography, meteorology, earth magnetism and astrophysics. The new building also houses the weather station for western Norway.

Den kulturhistoriske samling (The Cultural History Collection) in 1927 received its own building, Historisk Museum (The Museum of History), designed by architect Egill Reimers, on Haakon Shetelig's plass 10. Norway's most extensive exhibit of church and religious art is presented here in a space of about 700 square metres. Here are hundreds of objects associat-

▲

The exhibition of church art in the Historical Museum displays this magnificent altar cupboard from Austevoll in Midthordland, made in 1520.
In the center is St. Sunniva, patron saint of Bergen, flanked by the apostle Peter and Mary Magdalene.

Religious art

Pieces from the Stone and Viking Age

Haakon Shetelig. The square in front of the Historical Museum was named after him.

ed with the hope and faith of Norwegians throughout a period of 600 years.

The exhibit also includes pieces from the Stone Age and the Viking Age along with foreign cultures, clothing and textiles. There are separate collections presenting town and country culture, coins and medallions. Among the treasures in the music history section is the oldest known Hardanger fiddle, Jaastadfela, from Ullensvang in Hardanger from the year 1651.

One of Scandinavia's most prominent archaeologists, Professor Haakon Shetelig (1877–1955), was associated with the Museum of Bergen for more than 40 years. He arrived in Bergen in 1901 and became a professor in 1914. Shetelig was responsible for the excavations from the Stone Age hunting grounds at Ruskeneset in Fana.

Art historian Johan Bøgh (1848–1935) was the first to begin working with the scientific material from the cultural history department. He founded, in 1887, the Vestlandske Kunstindustrimuseum. (See ▶ Permanenten.)

■ THE BERGEN PUBLIC LIBRARY

Private book collection formed the basis

Both beer and hard liquor accompanied books when the Bergen Public Library (Bergen Offentlige Bibliotek) began its work to quench the mental thirst of the inhabitants of Bergen. The library was first housed in the home of brewer Møller on Øvre Torgallmenningen, and the purchase of books was financed primarily by the sale of liquor. The private book collection of 12,000 volumes belonging to university librarian Paul Botten-Hansen formed the literary basis for the public library. The collection was bought up from his estate in 1869.

In the fall of 1879 the Bergen Public Library moved into its new home on the attic floor of the Kjøttbasaren (the Meat Market), and stayed there until a new library building on Strøm Street 6 stood finished in 1917. Oslo ar-

chitect Olaf Nordhagen won the architectural contest with a beautiful and distinctive design of a building in a style typical of the times. In 1993 it was decided to preserve the building as a historical monument.

The stone portraits of Nordhagen and state archivist Just Bing, chiseled by Wilhelm Rasmussen in 1912, flank the main entrance of the library on Strømgaten. Inside the library are marble busts of patrons Christian Børs and Oluf Bjørneseth (sculpted by Ambrosia Tønnesen in 1903 and 1929).

The library has ten city branches and a library bus. Most of the credit for the development and modernisation of the Bergen Public Library must be given to Arne Kildal (1885–1972), the head of the library from 1909 to 1920. When he took the position as head of the library at the young age of 24, Kildal brought along a number of new ideas for the administration of the library that he had picked up from a stay in the United States.

In 1924 the Bergen Public Library opened a music department, known as Musikkbiblioteket (the Music Library). Since 1966, the department has been housed in Grieghallen. The oldest collection of music in Scandinavia is located here, in addition to the extensive Grieg collection.

The Bergen Public Library has its own special collections associated with Ludvig Hol-

▲
Bergen Public Library moved into its new building on Strømgaten in 1917. It became a historical landmark in 1993.

Stone portrait of state archivist Just Bing by the entrance of the Bergen Public Library. Sculpture by Wilhelm Rasmussen.

B

Library architect Olaf Nordhagen is portrayed in stone at the entrance. Sculpture by Wilhelm Rasmussen.

berg, Amalie Skram and "Old Bergen". The latter includes a nearly complete collection of Bergen prints. The oldest writings are from 1721, when the city's first printer, Peter Nørvig, established his business.

Since 1994, the computers in the Bergen Public Library have been connected to both the Uninet and the Internet. The library offers the use of these services free of charge.

A bigger and better 'house of knowledge' is expected to be completed by the year 2000. The total area of the library will be nearly doubled with its new addition, from the existing 2,400 square metres to a total of 4,400 square metres. The expansion will make room for a café, a section for cultural travel information and services for special groups, such as immigrants and refugees.

■ BERGEN'S COAT OF ARMS

Mountain, fortress, ship and sea – and dried fish

The city's coat of arms, in its present form, was drawn by Johan Chr. Koren Wiberg. The motif is a round shield with a red background, framed in gold, set with a three-towered fortress in silver over seven mountains in gold. The city flag and seal have the same design.

The coat of arms received its present day appearance after the State Antiquarian objected to a rough draft approved by the city council in 1924 and sanctioned by royal decree. This draft was designed by Finn Berner, the architect who also drew the plans for the city's centre square, Torgallmenningen.

The oldest emblem from the end of the 13th century carried the inscription: "Dant Bergis Dignum Mons Urbs Navis mare Signum". In English this means: "Mountain, fortress, ship and sea give Bergen a worthy emblem". If the coat of arms was to reflect accurately the livelihood of Bergen, it would have to include dried fish. This was pointed out by the former mayor of Bergen, Knut Tjønneland. Welhaven

*Bergen's coat
of arms*
as it appears today.
Johan Chr. Koren
Wiberg (1870–
1950), who was
responsible for its
final form, was the
curator of the Han-
seatic Museum and
founder of the Ber-
gen School of Deco-
rative Arts.

◀

must have felt the same when he wrote about
the city of his birth:

"Her Bryst og Hoved er et Regnebræt, / Her
gjælder fisk foroven og forneden." In English:
"Here chest and head is an abacus, / It is fish
that matters from top to bottom."

■ ROLF BERNTZEN

Being a prophet in one's own town can be difficult enough. But a prophet who receives his
own monument in his hometown while he is
still much alive and active, is a very rare thing
indeed. A private initiative made certain that
actor Rolf Berntzen (born 1918) would be the
exception. We meet him outside the SAS hotel,
well-dressed as always, although here cast in
bronze, his alert expression forever unchanging.

Nearby is the place in which Berntzen, in
1970, invested all his savings, the Bryggetea-
tret (The Wharf Theatre), but he had to give up
his project after only one season.

The range of Rolf Berntzen's acting talent
stretches from Shakespeare to Holberg and
from Duun to Garatun-Tjeldstø. His dialect

*Portrait bust of Rolf
Berntzen on Bryg-
gen was sculpted by
Per Ung and un-
veiled in 1993.*

"Holbergenser"
Rolf Berntzen,
drawn by Audun
Hetland.

"Holbergenser" Rolf Berntzen, drawn by Audun Hetland.

sounds authentic whether he portrays the rural peasant from the district, the street urchin from the inner city or the fine gentleman from Kalfaret.

Prized for Holberg interpretation

The image of this cheerful actor is likely to be engraved in the mind of anyone who has had a place in a theatre audience in Bergen. Ludvig Holberg is Berntzen's idol, and he portrays the Holberg roles brilliantly. In fact, he has performed more Holberg roles than any other Norwegian. The Danes noticed his performances and rewarded him accordingly. Berntzen has also been the president of the Holberg club.

The only Holberg role in which he was anything but a success was in 1984, when Berntzen tried desperately, but in vain, to stop Holbergkjelleren from being torn down by placing himself in front of the bulldozer.

On the barricades for culture

Bergen patriot Rolf Berntzen has always been a front runner in campaigns to protect cultural landmarks. He struggled to protect Marken, fought against the narrowing of the

B

Fish Market and for the protection of the old wooden cottages along Skuteviken. These are the roles he has given himself, and he has never been afraid to perform offstage under his own direction.

Berntzen and his 'one-man theatre' sought out his audiences in workplaces, in nursing homes, and in meetings and assemblies. He has spread joy with his acting talents and has awakened public opinion on noble and important causes.

"Audience-seeking" theatre

■ KRISTIAN BING

The multi-faceted cultural personality Kristian Bing (1862–1935) was in 1938 commemorated with a memorial by Fredriksberg at Nordnes. Bing was a lawyer and practised as a solicitor in Bergen from 1891. His interests, however, included much more than just law.

Renewed the Olsok celebration

Bing was primarily known as a city historian, a collector of folklore and a mountain climber. He was involved in politics and in the New Norwegian linguistic movement. He was the first to lead the Boys' Drill Corps of Bergen into the world of literature through four publications for Dræggens Buekorps and Nordnæs Bataillon. He also rescued the Boys' Drill Corps when police chief Salicath prohibited noisy parades in the streets during the 1880s.

Bing made his most important discovery as a folklore collector in 1912 in Vingen, Nordfjord. Here he uncovered the first arctic rock carvings portraying hunting rituals in southern Norway. He is also responsible for the fact that the Olsok celebration in 1897 was revived as a yearly and non-political ceremony in memory of the death of Saint Olav at Stiklestad. This was the largest religious celebration in Norway during the Middle Ages.

The bust of Kristian Bing, by Sofus Madsen, was unveiled at Nordnes in 1938. Bing renewed the traditional Olsok (St. Olav's Day) celebration.

As a mountain climber Bing received a great deal of attention for his ascent of Hornelen in 1897, a feat only king Olav Trygvason was said to have previously accomplished. This familiar landmark for seafarers rises 915 metres, almost vertically from Frøysjøen in Bremanger.

To the top of Hornelen

Bing was the first to climb several peaks and glaciers between Finnmark and the Folgefonna Glacier. He also made a sport of climbing church steeples.

A burning 'YES' at Ulriken

Bing often went his own way. His highly unusual, but very effective methods were used in the struggle for Norwegian independence in 1905. The evening before the plebiscite vote on the dissolution of the union with Sweden, he built a series of campfires at Ulriken, so that together they formed a giant, flaming YES.

Secured recreational areas

Another important issue for Bing was the securing of a recreational area for children and city youth. He secured the acquisition of Nordnæsdalen, a 100-acre nature area, to be used as a gathering place for the Boys' Drill Corps.

Bing was the president of the Turistforeningen (an association for hikers and campers) in Bergen, and in 1894 he took the initiative to form the Bergen Historical Association.

■ BJØRNSTJERNE BJØRNSON

Became Norway's great leader in Bergen

The great poet Bjørnstjerne Bjørnson (1832 –1910) has been honoured by the city of Bergen with his own street in Solheimsviken and a statue outside Den Nationale Scene (The National Theatre of Bergen). The statue was created by Gustav Vigeland, and unveiled on May 17, 1917.

Bjørnson spent barely a year and a half – from the end of November 1857 to the summer of 1859 – in Bergen. For two months ▸ Wernersholm was his home. His stay will always be remembered because it was here that Norway's national anthem, "Ja, vi elsker dette landet", (Yes, We Love This Country), was written. Though his visit in Bergen was short, it would prove to be important in many ways, for Bjørnson himself as well.

Met Karoline

It was here he met his wife, the three-year younger Karoline Reimers (1835–1934). She

B

Detail from Gustav Vigeland's Bjørnson statue outside the National Theatre of Bergen. The monument was a gift from landowner Conrad Mohr.

◄

was an inspiration to him as an artist and a pillar of strength at home. Many of Bjørnson's most beautiful female characters have Karoline's characteristics. The two had a long and eventful marriage and were able to celebrate their golden wedding anniversary in 1908.

Bjørnson was asked to come to Bergen by Ole Bull, in order to take over the running of his new theatre, the first of its kind with Norwegian scripts. Henrik Ibsen had left Bergen just a short time before. When Bjørnsen arrived, the theatre was on the verge of collapse. He almost miraculously turned things around from ruin to positive development. Bjørnson staged a total of 25 plays in Bergen. His directing talents inspired the actors to give top performances, which brought the people of Bergen back to the theatre at Engen.

Inspired the actors

At the same time Bjørnson had the energy to take over the responsibility as editor-in-chief of Bergensposten, where he threw himself into the current political debates with great enthusiasm. From the editor's chair he drew up the national and democratic policy of the political party Venstre, before the dissolution of the union with Sweden in 1905.

Editor of "Bergensposten"

Karoline Reimers
from Bergen married
Bjørnstjerne Bjørn-
son in 1858. They
had five children.
Before her marriage
she worked as a
clerk in the family
bakery. She had a
few minor roles on
the stage as well.
The portrait is paint-
ed by Franz von
Lanbach.

With his rousing speech on May 17, 1859 Bjørnson achieved his breakthrough as a popular orator. For that very same May 17 celebration he wrote his first national song, "Der ligger et land" (There Lies a Land), which was followed a couple of months later by ... "Ja, vi elsker dette landet" (Yes, We Love This Country).

According to Professor Francis Bull one could say without hesitation that it was in Bergen that Bjørnson became Norway's leader, shining with genius. Bjørnstjerne Bjørnson wrote in all 16 novels and stories and 21 plays, in addition to a countless number of poems and articles. In 1903 he was awarded the Nobel Prize for literature.

A total of 800 music scores by 255 composers are based on Bjørnson's writings. The struggle he led for the rights of the smaller nations won attention all over the world. Bjørnson's strong personality, together with the range of his writing, his talent for rhetoric and social involvement made him an impressive spiritual leader.

To Bergen
against his
will – stayed
for 42 years

Johan Nordahl
Brun's tomb in the
Domkirke graveyard
was designed by
Lyder Sagen.

■ JOHAN NORDAHL BRUN

Johan Nordahl Brun (1745–1816), the poet-bishop from Trondheim who wrote ▶ Bergen's city song "Udsigter fra Ulrikken" (The View from Ulrikken), popularly known as "Nystemten", had already in 1881 a street named after him. It had to be a main street of course for this beloved and highly respected 'immigrant'.

The newly crowned Swedish-Norwegian king, Karl Johan, honoured the popular bishop with a beautiful monument in Bergen Domkirke (Bergen Cathedral). The monument by Hans Michelsen was unveiled in 1824. This work of art displays Brun's portrait in a medallion between two allegorical female figures, symbolising faith and strength.

Brun's gravestone in the churchyard of the cathedral was designed by Lyder Sagen. In honour of the poet it is shaped like a lyre.

Johan Nordahl Brun was ordered to come to

Royal Honour

Bishop Johan Nordahl Brun was honoured by King Karl Johan of Sweden with this magnificent monument in Domkirken. The two allegorical female figures most likely symbolise faith and strength. The inscription reads:

Hallowed and noble was his Spirit. His Northern Harp struck with a powerful Hand. Blissfully he spoke Words of Life. God's True Kingdom he promoted on Earth. For his Fatherland were shed the Tears of Truth. His King raised the Memorial on his Grave.

◀

Bergen in 1774 – apparently he was quite un-willing to do so – to take the position of vicar at Korskirken (The Church of the Cross). He stayed on for 42 years and became a bishop in 1804.

Brun's illustrious reputation reveals a masterful, impressive and colourful personality, a brilliant clergyman and a poet of considerable talent. He was an orthodox Christian, but also wrote drinking ballads. His warm Christian faith is evident in his many hymns, all of which are of high artistic quality. Many of the religious festival hymns, such as the Easter psalm "Jesus lever, graven brast" (Jesus lives,

Colourful personality

the grave has burst) and "Ånd over ånder" (Spirit of spirits) for Pentecost, are still frequently sung in churches today.

Brun wrote several plays for the city's newly established Dramatiske Selskap (Drama Group), and as a political writer and agitator also became a prominent figure in the struggle for national independence. On February 21, 1814 he preached to a full congregation in Bergen Cathedral, and gave the congregation the news that Prince Christian Fredrik of Denmark had decided to send troops to defend Norwegian sovereignty against the threat from Sweden.

The free-speaking bishop from Bergen once went too far, according to authorities in Copenhagen. Johan Nordahl Brun's strongly patriotic poem "For Norge, Kiempers Fødeland" (For Norway, the Birthplace of Giants) was prohibited by the police. There was a limit to freedom of speech in the Danish-Norwegian kingdom. The song appeared to unite Norwegians and became our first national anthem.

■ BRYGGEN

International cultural monument

A wooden sculpture of the mythical beast outside the "Enhjørningsgården" (Unicorn House).

UNESCO's World Heritage Monument list contains four 'heirlooms' from Norway. One of these is the group of 58 stone and wooden buildings dating from the Middle Ages at Bryggen (the Wharf) in Bergen. The oldest traces of a settlement are about as old as the city, or from approximately the year 1100.

A sense of history rests over Bryggen. Nearby stands Håkonshallen, Rosenkrantztårnet (Rosenkrantz Tower) and Mariakirken (St. Mary's Church). It was here at Bryggen that the cardinal came to King Håkon Håkonsson's wedding in 1247 and saw "such a number of ships... I have never before seen so many in one harbour". Moored in this very same harbour were also the ships of the Viking kings and vessels of the Hanseatic merchants. Over the centuries, eight fires have laid larger and smaller areas of Bryggen in ashes. All have been rebuilt, bigger and better for each recon-

struction. Moving the piers further out in the harbour made plenty of room for expansion. The city fire of 1702 razed the whole wharf. A third of the buildings that were rebuilt after this catastrophe were lost in the last great fire of 1955, when it was possible to save only six rows of houses.

Archaeological excavations that followed under Asbjørn Herteig's leadership were carried out more or less undisturbed for 20 years and gave remarkable results. About 400,000 artifacts found in the excavations are now part of the collection of Bryggen Museum. This unusually rich material has made it clear that the entire Brygge complex, both planning and building style, has remained unchanged since the early Middle Ages. Upon receiving a question from King Olav, Mayor Knut Tjønneland once jokingly answered that the age of the city was only relative to the amount of funding given. In other words, it depended on how long one could afford to continue excavations. Whether it was due to a weak financial situation in the municipality or to other causes, the date on which Olav Kyrre founded the city was never successfully determined. Many historians still believe that this occurred around the year 1070.

According to Herteig, Bryggen is the prime symbol of centuries of trade and shipping tra-

▲
Bryggen
has become one of the world's most important cultural-historical landmarks. The old buildings contain shops, restaurants and art studios.

A "Builder with Axe" decorates the building "Bugården".

"Bryggen's Madonna"
a game piece from the 1300s, was found during excavations.

ditions and the key to the city's distinctive character. It was here that the struggle for Norwegian independence took place and it was here a national merchant trading activity was developed.

The Hanseatic League (Hansaforbundet) had one of its four foreign stations, or offices, at Bryggen during the years 1360–1754. At its peak, the alliance numbered 1000 merchants. The office in Bergen was the largest. The Hanseatics later completely took over Bryggen, which became a separate city within a city, closed off to the rest of the citizens of Bergen. Until 1945 it was also called Tyskebryggen (the German Wharf). The Hanseatic League dominated trade in Europe for several hundred years. Bergen was one of its most important harbours, but never a member of the alliance.

A separate city within the city

The Hanseatic Museum (Det Hanseatiske Museum), which was established in 1872 in Finnegården at Bryggen, accurately depicts the German merchant's life and work in Bergen throughout several cultural epochs. The museum also administrates the Hanseatic dining and meeting rooms, the four so-called 'skjøtstuer' (public rooms) near the Mariakirken, (Øvregaten 50). It is still popular to hold parties in these historical surroundings.

New life and a new status

Culturally hostile politicians have on several occasions nearly succeeded in tearing down "the old pile of junk" in favour of new buildings and commercial interests. But public opinion has changed. Bryggen is today protected by law, insured against fire, and on its way to total rehabilitation. In addition to the business and commercial activity which still goes on in the historical buildings, several art studios and restaurants continue to give Bryggen new life and a new status. The empty space after the great fire of 1955 has been reverently "plugged up" by Bryggen Museum and Radisson SAS Hotel. The hotel is architecturally designed to harmonize with the characteristic, pointed gables of the Bryggen buildings.

▲
Tourists flock to Bryggen

Bryggens Museum (Bryggen Museum, Archaeological Museum) was opened in 1975, financed through donations from shipper Erling Dekke Næss. The architect was Øivind Maurseth. The museum has an art gallery and lecture hall, and supplements its permanent collection with frequent travelling exhibitions on different themes.

■ BUEKORPS

People of Bergen – stand at attention!
Wishful thinking for a sergeant at a military camp. A Bergen tyke is able to carry out military exercises long before he dons the obligatory army uniform.

　　Not only is he able to march in step, he is often competent in the most advanced of military drills. He has learned this and more in the

The Boys' Drill Corps

A proud moment for the boys of the drill corps – the admiral himself arrives for inspection. ▶

Nordnæstamburen on Tollbodalmenning was unveiled in honour of the 75th anniversary of the Nordnes battalions, in 1933. The sculpture was created by goldsmith Thorvald Olsen and donated as a gift by ship owner Harald Eide.

"Dræggegutten" was erected at Dreggsallmenning in 1956. Sofus Madsen modelled the sculpture.

Buekorps, or Boys' Drill Corps – a kind of military 'pre-school' and a longstanding tradition in Bergen. The corps are unique not only because of their military shape, but also in that the boys acquire their skills from each other and run the corps themselves, without the aid of adults.

The Buekorps Museum, which opened in 1972 in ▶ Muren, and the four Buekorps monuments will give the visitor an idea of how highly the people of Bergen value their corps. Two of the monuments, Dræggegutten (the Drægge Boy) and Nygaardsgutten (the Nygaard Boy) are memorials to fallen corps members during World War II. The third statue, Nornestamburen (the Drummer of Nordnæs), was erected as a symbol of joy and gratitude for what the corps has meant to all of those involved in it.

A boy in the drill corps is usually between the ages of 10 and 20. But before he is ready to join the ranks of the corps he has probably spent some time as a 'rævedilter', a boy who runs behind the corps as they march along the city streets. The boys appoint their own leaders through a democratic election. Any interference from an adult is forbidden, although financial contributions are gratefully accept-ed. However, there are always plenty of festive occasions which will allow 'gamlekarene' (the old boys – including fathers) and the 'damegar-

B

den" (the ladies' guard – including moth-ers) to rally around the corps, as they did when they themselves were children.

Until 1991 the drill corps permitted only boys to join. Girls have gradually won the right to form their own corps, though not with-out a fight. The Vågen Battalion was the first female drill corps.

At the end of the 1800s the precise marches and resounding drum rolls from over 100 corps signalled a noisy but sure sign of spring. In 1998 there were 14 corps marching under the corps' banners, among them, two girls' corps. Drill corps' season begins in March and lasts until May. Some corps meet on Satur-days, others on Sundays. The oldest drill corps still active was formed in Skuteviken and Dræggen in the 1850s.

The idea of a drill corps probably has its roots in the old citizens' militia. Each corps in-cludes 50 to 100 youths and is usually divided into 20 companies. Each company has two pla-toons, in addition to the flag bearers, drum-mers, a commander and an assistant. Some of the corps carry bows, while the corps carrying rifles are known as battalions. Scottish caps, jackets with a mark of rank and long striped trousers are all part of the basic uniform. Each corps, however, has its own colours and flag, and often even its own special marches.

"Nygaardsgutten" (The Nygaard boy), created by Sofus Madsen, has been standing at attention in Nygård Park since 1947.

Johan Ludwig Mowinckel jr. com-posed this march in 1931 for Fjeldets battalion. Here shown in the com-poser's own hand-writing. Sandviken Youth Corps, led by Tom Brevik, has recorded the entire collection of drill corps marches.

◀

B

The drill corps has successfully completed several group tours, and has travelled together throughout Norway, as well as abroad, including the United States. The drill corps continues to remain a tradition unique to Bergen. Involvement in the corps offers an opportunity for good and loyal friendships, and is also considered valuable in promoting good breeding and a strong character.

Tradition unique to Bergen

■ OLE BULL

Violin virtuoso and fairy tale figure

Ole Bornemann Bull (1810–80) was a violin virtuoso, adventurer and national hero from Bergen – an artistic personality verging on genius, who without the help of television had the musical world, both the old and the new, at his feet. Bull failed to create a new Norway in America, but succeeded in establishing the country's first theatre with Norwegian scripts in his hometown.

The young Ole Bull

Since 1901 this Peer Gynt-like, copper-rust green figure has towered at the top of a rocky slope at Ole Bulls plass, with its magical violin held high, but alas, silent. He was placed in the inspirational company of the mythical figure of Fossegrimen, playing the violin, by sculptor Stephan Sinding.

Powerful charm

Still we can sense the powerful magnetism and personality of this musical legend, which not only women fell for, but also led kings and queens to shower him with expensive gifts, and made audiences wild in the concert halls. Without any concrete evidence of his greatness other than the few but relatively unimportant compositions he left behind, it may be difficult to grasp his enormous popularity and fame. The self-taught violinist from Bergen was judged at his time to be one of the all-time great artists in the same category as Paganini.

There was one thing Ole Bull had in common with two of his equally famous townsmen, Ludvig Holberg and Edvard Grieg. They were all born on Strandgaten. Ole Bull's grandfather and later his father, Johan Storm Bull, ran a chemist dispensary, Svaneapote-

Ole Bull and Fosse-grimen on Ole Bulls plass. The monument was made by Stephan Sinding and was unveiled on May 17, 1901.

◀

An honour for our country

Edvard Grieg delivered this speech at the funeral of Ole Bull:

"Because you became an honour for our country as no one else could, because you elevated our people up toward art's bright heights as no one else could, because you broke the barriers for our young national music, faithful, warm-hearted and conquered all hearts as no one else could – because you have planted a seed that will sprout in the future and that later generations will bless you for – with thousands upon thousands of thanks for all of this, I place in the name of Norwegian musical arts this laurel wreath upon your casket. May you rest in peace."

B

ket. An ample amount of spiritual nourish-
ment in the form of both music and theatre
was the mixture prescribed by the chemist for
his son. Chamber music was cultivated in the
home with weekly quartet evenings. At the
age of five, Ole had his first violin thrust in his
hands and learned how to read music at the
same time as he learned to read words. The
child prodigy soon impressed those around
him by playing various kinds of melodies by
ear, including fiddle pieces he heard performed by country musicians at his family's summer home at Osterøy.

Ole Bull was finally 'discovered' at the age of
eight. The orchestra leader of Harmonien and
star musician of the chemist-quartet happened to be indisposed one evening and unable
to attend the session. Little Ole, to everyone's
surprise, proved himself to be a fully capable
understudy. This performance quickly led to
an audition and a position with the Harmoni-
en quartet. A year later he gave the first of
many solo performances of a violin concerto by
Ignaz Pleyel. Bergen soon became too small an
arena for the cosmopolitan Ole Bull. A contin-
uous series of triumphant tours took him to
countries all over the world. Two important
events in his marvellous life were, however,
very much connected with Bergen. In 1858 he
helped 15-year-old Edvard ▶ Grieg on his way
to a bright musical future. The 'fairytale god'
as Grieg called him, instilled a genuine Norwegian ear for music in the young musician.
In 1873 the two champions performed together for the first and only time in the Norwegian music world at a public concert in "Ek-
serserhuset" at Engen.

Long before this, however, Ole Bull created
theatre history by establishing the first Norwegian theatre in Bergen. On January 2, 1850
the curtain went up for the debut performance, "Den Vægelsindede" (The Fickle Woman)
by Holberg. Bull's theatre later became an important centre for both Ibsen and Bjørnson,
along with many others. (See ▶ Theatre in
Bergen.)

The best way to learn more about Ole Bull

Photo: Harry G. Henriksen

Ole Bull's villa on Lysøen was completed in 1873. It was as unique as the master himself, with a conglomerate of building styles. Lysøen became the last stop of Ole Bull's lifelong and worldwide concert tour.

◀

today is to visit two islands near Bergen, Lysøen and Osterøy.

After a brilliant career, the elderly Bull longed to return to his homeland. In Lysefjorden in Os, just south of Bergen, he found the place that would fulfill all his dreams:

"I have never seen anything so spellbinding. So magnificent and yet so sweet, so sad and yet so full of joy."

This declaration of love for Lysøen was written by Bull in 1872. That same year he bought the entire island. Lysøen became Bull's last stop on a lifelong and world-wide concert tour. The palace of a house built on the island, clearly visible from the fjord, was unlike any other. Bull's home was an architectural conglomerate, every bit as complex as his own artistic character.

Lysøen was a summer home for Ole Bull's

Bull home on two islands

Last stop

B

Getting there:
Lysøen: Lysefjord route from the bus station, platform 19 or 20, to Buene quay. About 50 minutes.
Valestrand: Bus from platform 15 to Breistein ferry quay. About 45 minutes. Ferry – 10 minutes.

American family from his second marriage to Sara Thorp, the daughter of a U.S. senator. A new chapter in the history of the island was opened in 1973, when the violinist's granddaughter, Sylvia Bull Curtis, relinquished the house to the Bergen office of the Cultural Heritage Association. A year later Lysøen was opened as a museum and a concert hall, used for intimate concerts, for example, during the Bergen International Festival.

Ole Bull had six children by his first wife, Frenchwoman Félicite Villeminot. This family inherited the family farm at Valestrand on Osterøy. Here too one can find a great many things to remember the violinist by. Ole Bull had the old farmhouse replaced with a magnificent mansion. The property belongs to Ole Bull's great great grandchild, former head of the Opera House in Oslo, Knut Hendriksen, who has spent a great deal of time and money on the maintenance and restoration of "Bullahuset". But neither does he wish to keep everything for himself: "Anyone who is interested in Ole Bull can call me when I'm here and I will show them around the place with pleasure," says Hendriksen generously.

Ole Bull's famous "treasure chamber violin" is exhibited in ▶ Permanenten. One of his grand pianos can be found in ▶ Rasmus Meyers Samling. (See also ▶ Assistentkirkegården and ▶ Opera in Bergen.)

"Bullahuset"
(the Bull House)
on Valestrand. ▶

■ WILHELM F. K. CHRISTIE

Cultural pioneer in Bergen

He looks out over Christie's Street from Muséplass in front of the Bergen Museum, from a monumental bronze statue. Instead of an ordinary watchdog, a snarling granite lion keeps guard at the foot of the 3.65 metre high base. This impressive monument is a memorial to Wilhelm Frimann Koren Christie (1778–1849), the president of the Norwegian Parliament. Koren was primarily responsible for the constitutionally based union between Norway and Sweden in 1814.

The Christie monument was Norway's first portrait monument, unveiled on May 17, 1868. By pointing to the constitution held in his left hand, Christie symbolically takes the oath for all later generations of Norwegians. Christopher Borch created the bronze statue, while Wilhelm Rasmussen's lion was not added until 1926. The monument was originally placed in the city square, Torgallmenningen, but was in 1925 moved to the spot in front of the Bergen Museum, which Christie established in 1825 and administered the first 24 years. Since the museum later led to the foundation of the University of Bergen, one could say that Christie was also the founder of the University.

Christie's cultural involvement had just as great an importance for Bergen as his political wisdom had for the country. As administrator of the museum, he saw it as his job to collect and preserve objects of antiquity. He himself worked to collect and prepare the materials and created an extensive archive of antiquarian information. Christie also published "Urda", a Norwegian historic-antiquarian pe-

Wilhelm Frimann Koren Christie with the Great Cross of St. Olav's Order on his chest. Christie was the undisputed political leader of Norway at the time and a cultural pioneer in Bergen. He was born in Kristiansund, but came to Bergen at the age of 11. Before he turned 16 he had completed his education at Bergen Katedralskole. He received his Latin-law degree in Copenhagen at 21.

Photo: Bergen Museum

Norway's first portrait statue

The Christie statue on Muséplass is Norway's first portrait monument, sculpted by Christopher Borch and erected in 1868. Christie developed close ties with Bergen after his appointment as county court judge in Nordhordland in 1808. He represented the city at Eidsvoll in 1814. When he withdrew from politics in 1818 he returned to Bergen, first as a regional commissioner and later as a customs inspector. He received an offer to become Supreme Court judge and was encouraged by King Karl Johan to come to Stockholm and take the position of Prime Minister, but turned down both. The main reason for this was that Christie did not wish to leave Bergen and give up his strong cultural-historic and archaeological interests.

Farm owner

The farm Straume between Nordåsvannet and Sælenvannet was owned by Christie during the years 1842–59. President Christies vei is located here. He has also given his name to Christie Park (near Brann Stadium) which he contributed to the development of.

riodical, together with Lyder Sagen and Bishop Jacob Neumann.

Christie was also a language researcher, and made a record of sagas and fairytales. His collection of words and expressions from the rural dialects in "Dictionarium" was the most comprehensive volume before the arrival of Ivar Aasen's "Ordbog" (Dictionary). He was the first city man to display an interest in rural culture. W.F.K. Christie was the parliamentary president, prefect, judge, chief customs officer and museum administrator who led the way in all manner of cultural affairs for the good of the city.

Valued rural culture

■ CINEMAS

In 1999 Bergen Kino (the Bergen Cinema) showed films in 14 different theatres with a total capacity of 2,316 seats. With the exception of Forum Kino at Danmarksplass, all of the cinemas are located in the downtown area inside a large complex on Neumann's Street 3–7 named Konsertpaleet. The building also includes the former Engen Kino.

Large cinema centre to be even larger

A new cinema centre with five auditoriums is being built on the neighbouring lot on Magnus Barfot's Street 12. It is expected to be completed by the year 2000. This will make Konsertpaleet one of Europe's largest cinema centres. There is, in addition, the Cinemateket in Kulturhuset USF where less commercial 'art films' are shown. The number of seats in the auditoriums in the Cinema Centre today range from 48 to 495. The largest auditorium is Forum with 779 seats.

They have expanded a lot recent years

Cinema administration in Bergen has since 1919 been a monopoly of the municipality, on a resolution from the city council. The council pointed out the important purpose of films "in a city which otherwise cannot be described as especially 'fun'." The very first "moving pictures" were shown to the public in Bergen around the year 1900 in Logen and Eldorado. Without public regulation of any kind, film projection was open to anyone who had a locale approved by the police. For a time the city was almost overrun by private cinemas, so-called 'world theatres'.

The municipality rented at first five locales for use as cinemas: Konsertpaleet, Logen, Eldorado, Det gamle teater and Tivoli. In the

Konsertpaleet and Engen have converged to form a giant cinema centre with 13 auditoriums and one main entrance and foyer.

▲
Forum Kino
was opened to the
public in 1946. Ar-
chitect Ole Land-
mark has obviously
been inspired by
the aesthetics of
Hollywood.

*This is
5 minute walk
from us. Sadly,
closed today.*

same district were also two smaller locales,
Boulevard and Verdensspeilet. The theatre's
smaller stage, Ole Bull, was used as a cinema
from 1934 until 1981. At Minde just outside
the old city limits stood Fanahallen (closed
down in 1985). Laksevåg also had its own cinema from 1933 until 1955.

Engen Kino was built on the lot where an
old theatre building had once stood. Konsertpaleet (architect Egill Reimers) was built in
1918 and was also a concert house for Harmonien and a festival arena, in addition to being
a cinema until 1974. The building, which had
1,200 seats, was rebuilt in 1981 to hold four
auditoriums.

■ THE CITY HALLS

**Both a new
and old city
hall in use**

In 1971 the city's new city hall on Rådhusga-
ten 10 was completed, and since that time
Bergen has had two city halls – one new and
one very old. The new city hall is 14 stories
and 52 metres high, and a dominant vision in
the district on the east side of Lille Lungegårdsvann. The architect is Erling Viksjø.

The dimensions of the old city hall on Råd-
stuplass 1 are much more modest. All the
same, it is almost impossible to miss this ex-
ceptionally beautiful and striking building.

The city council still holds its meetings here. Construction was started at the end of the 1550s. The building has served the city since 1561. Before that time it was the private residence of feudal lord Christoffer Valkendorf. At one time criminals sat behind bars in this building. Among them was the legendary master thief Gjest Baardsen (1791–1849), the criminal who became a Robin Hood-like hero because of his habit of stealing from the rich and giving to the poor, and because of his ability to escape from his prison. The cells in the city hall cellars are a horrifying example of the prison conditions for thieves and the mentally ill.

Both private residence and prison

The new city hall is an office building for municipal administration and contains the offices of the city's mayor and the municipal information department. One exception is the city's spiritual pursuits – recreation, culture and religion – which are administered from a former factory building on Møllendalsveien 2–4. According to the architectural drafts the new city hall is just a torso. Another building was planned as an annex to the north but was never realised. A cafeteria wing, opened in 1991, connects the city hall with "Manufakturhuset" from the year 1710. "Manufakturhuset"

The new city hall a torso

The old city hall has served the city since 1561. The city council still holds its meetings here. The building was originally a private residence for feudal lord Christoffer Valkendorf.

◄

The new city hall was taken into use in 1971. It has 14 stories and stands 52 metres high. The mayor of Bergen has offices on the top floors.

My dad works here ▶

has its name from a bleak past when the making of army clothes, the spinning of linen and cheesecloth, tobacco rolling and the production of nails were all carried out in this building by the use of slave labour. The house has also been used as a reform school and jail.

Variety of uses   The old city hall has over the years undergone a number of changes partly as a result of four large fires. It has had a variety of uses. The main floor has been used as a courtroom, police office and the city archives office. The cellar served as a county jail and until 1762 as an asylum for the mentally ill. After its reconstruction in 1789, the coat of arms of the reigning monarch, King Christian VII was mounted on the northern gable. Not much remains of the original interior of the city hall, apart from the vaulted arched central hall made of granite in the cellar with the jail cells, and one of the old wrought iron gates.

The city council and the executive committee were given meeting rooms in the city hall when the committee laws were passed in 1837. The committee hall proved too small when the meetings were opened to the public in 1989. Since then the executive committee has held its meetings in the city hall cafeteria.

C

■ THE COASTAL CULTURE

Bergen's geographically central location on the west coast, along with its excellent harbours, have been important prerequisites for the city's development as a centre for trade and communications. The coastal culture and the city of Bergen have had a mutual influence on each other. This will now become more visible and will be presented as an important part of the cultural background of the Bergen people.

Cultural centre in old boathoses

Five old preserved boathouses in Sandviken will be the framework for the Bergen Kystkultursenter (the Bergen Coastal Cultural Centre) which is expected to open to the public by the year 2000. The boathouses have a central spot in a unique cultural heritage area between Bergenhus and Gamle Bergen, which consists of technical cultural landmarks, houses and harbour buildings, with ties to the sailing ship traffic from 1600 to 1900. The environment surrounding the Sandviken boathouses has been described by international experts as one of the world's finest examples of cultural landmarks in the field of harbour technology. Most of the houses date back to the 1700s, although some may be even older. In two of the houses are traces of 18th century landscape paintings.

Five of the old boathouses at Sandviken are scheduled to be restored for use as a coastal cultural centre.
▼

The collection of the Bergen Kystlag (the Bergen Coastal Association) will be the main

Photo: Siri Myrvoll

Dried fish

Both research and public services

Access to the Aquarium
Bus nr. 4 stops outside the Aquarium. A bus leaves from Fisketorget to Tollbodhopen at Nordnes, from May 1st to September 15th. Walking distance to the Aquarium is three min. It takes about 20 min to walk from Fisketorget to the Aquarium.

nerve of the centre. Included in the collection are a number of vessels and smaller boats of significant antiquarian value, as well as some artifacts, arts and crafts activities. The dock area with the boathouses is administered as a veteran boat harbour.

Dried fish has been of great importance for the merchant town of Bergen, and will now have its own museum at the Coastal Cultural Centre. The Centre will also include a wide range of activities that tell the story of this culture. The different roles of men and women on the coast, as well as the city's role as a link between coastal culture and international trade, will both be displayed at the Centre.

When completed the Coastal Cultural Centre will be able to utilise a total indoor area of 3,500 square metres and an outdoor area of about 1,500 square metres. Both research and public activities will be a part of the Centre, which will be in close co-operation with other related museums and institutions in the Bergen area. Among these are:

Bergen sjøfartmuseum (the Bergen Maritime Museum) on Haakon Shetelig plass 2 was established in 1921. The collections include models of ships dating back to 200 years BC, old sea maps and ship logs, and paintings and construction drawings of ships.

Norsk Fiskerimuseum (the Norwegian Museum of Fisheries) is located on Bontelabo 2, and has ties to Bergen Fiskeindustri (the Bergen Fishing Industry). The museum was founded in 1880 by the Company for the Promotion of Norwegian Fish, with its objective of displaying the biological and oceanographic conditions relating to Norwegian fisheries. The collection contains tools and boat models.

Akvariet (the Bergen Aquarium) lies in Nordnesparken and is a part of the Institute of Oceanography. Both buildings were built in 1960. The Aquarium is one of the best-equipped and most comprehensive in Europe with nine large and 42 smaller tanks, in addition to

On board the sailing ship "Statsraad Lehmkuhl" thousands of young Norwegians have got their first training as seamen. When not sailing the proud ship can be admired in the Bergen harbour.

◄

three outdoor tanks for seals, penguins and carp. Among the natives are also sea turtles.

In the Aquarium's latest building from 1995 are, among other things, a bird mountain, an enormous landscape aquarium and a filmtheatre where one of Ivo Caprino's spectacular nature films about sea life can be experienced on a panoramic screen with a 225 degree field of vision. The main goal of the Aquarium is to display a representative selection of Norwegian marine fauna, but it is also in use as a research and educational facility. (See also ▶ Hordamuseet and ▶ Gamle Bergen.)

Maritime cultural history is usually on display on Vågen in the form of the steel barque, "Statsraad Lehmkuhl". The proud sailing ship has carried several thousand young Norwegian seamen on their first expeditions on Norwegian and foreign waters. The ship was built as a German training ship in 1914, and was purchased on the initiative of cabinet minister Kristofer D. Lehmkuhl for the same purpose by the Norwegian Ship Owners' Association in 1923.

The ship is today owned by the Statsraad Lehmkuhl Foundation and is rented out for seminars and entertainment purposes. Bergen's training ship has finished victoriously in several international sailing ship regattas.

**Seiling ship
a school for
seamen**

C

Wisdom (Stinius Fredriksen) is characterized by a snake twisted around an old man's right arm and by a book held in his left hand.

Justice (Stinius Fredriksen) is presented as a young man with a large sword positioned by his right foot. In his left hand he holds a pair of scales.

■ THE COURTHOUSE

Court trials and cardinal virtues

Four large granite statues of muscular men guard the impressive entrance to Bergen's courthouse, Tinghuset, on Tårnplass 2. The statues represent the four cardinal virtues Wisdom, Justice, Moderation and Strength and were created by artists Nic. Schiøll and Stinius Fredriksen.

The monumental building in neo-classical style is one of the most prominent in downtown Bergen. It was designed by Egill Reimers Sr. who won the architectural competition.

The building was constructed in brick with a green copper roof for added effect. The statues stand against four tall pillars, embellished at the top with winged griffens in bronze.

C

Moderation (Nic. Schiøll) is illustrated by a young man with a wine jug and an amphora. The wine vats indicate the advisable amount of wine one should consume.

Strength (Nic. Schiøll) is represented by a young man powerfully pressing a smooth column to the breaking point against his body.

The first court trials were held in the new courthouse in 1933. Centrally placed in the interior is a large hall with ceiling lighting, a locale also used for cultural purposes. During the International Festival of 1958, Ibsen's "Fru Inger to Østraat" was performed in the courthouse. Every May 17th the Student Song Club holds a concert here.

Theatre and music in the hall

The courthouse has courtrooms for Gulating criminal court, offices of the Midthordland and Nordhordland stipendiary magistrate, Bergen municipal court, Bergen public registrar, the notary public, and public prosecutors for Bergen and Hordaland. The regional commissioner's office of Hordland has also had offices in the courthouse.

Gulating and city court

C

■ JOHAN CHRISTIAN DAHL

The father of Norwegian painting

A statue of J.C.Dahl, created by Per Palle Storm, was erected in St. Jacob's grave-yard in 1991. The painter's earthly remains were, in 1934, transferred to Bergen from Dres-den, where he was first buried. The sta-tue was a gift from "Det Nyttige Sel-skab". In the same graveyard lies also Parliament President W.F.K. Christie and Edvard Grieg's pa-rents, Gesine and Alexander Grieg.

From his high pedestal over the entrance to 'Permanenten', Johan Christian Clausen Dahl (1788–1857) still keeps a watchful eye on his hometown. The painter from Bergen has been called the father of Norwegian art.

Another statue was raised in St. Jacob's churchyard in 1991. A marble portrait of Dahl by the Danish master Bertel Thorvaldsen stands in ▶ Bergen Billedgalleri. The street, Professor Dahl's Street in Sandviken, bears his name. Both the Bergen Billedgalleri and ▶ Rasmus Meyers Samlinger contain several of Dahl's greatest works, such as "Fra Stedje i Sogn" (1836) and "Bjerk i storm" (Birch Trees in a Storm) (1849), in addition to a number of sketchings and other work from a period in Italy.

Dahl grew up in simple surroundings. His mother was the daughter of a craftsman from Bergen. His father was a farmer's son from Gulen in Sogn and supported his family by working as a fisherman, sailor and logger.

At the age of 15, Dahl became the student of master painter Johan Georg Müller. His friend and benefactor, Lyder ▶ Sagen, discovered the peasant boy's rare talent quite early, and in 1811 he organised a collection which made it possible for Dahl to study at the Art Academy in Copenhagen. His stay in Denmark became the start of a lifelong 'exile' which culminated with a professorship in Dresden. Here he married and settled down for good in 1818.

Dahl's speciality was landscape painting. Although he lived abroad, his canvases usual-ly depicted Norwegian nature, and Bergen re-

Painter J.C. Dahl looks out over his hometown from his place of honour over the entrance to Vestlandske Kunstindustrimuseum (the Western Norwegian Museum of Applied Arts) or 'Permanenten'. The sculpture was unveiled in 1902. It was created by Ambrosia Tønnesen, and was the largest monumental work by a female artist in Scandinavia when it was completed. She was awarded the honourable medallion "Pro literis et artibus" by King Oscar 2. Ambrosia Tønnesen considered this her greatest work.

◄

"You Bergen's pride, Norway's honour."
Lyder Sagen in a poem for J.C. Dahl

"God preserve Bergen, and let me be its worthy Son."
Johan C. Dahl

D

Bergen gamle rådhus (the old city hall). A watercolour by J.C.Dahl painted in 1811 when he was 23. ▶

Unique visual memory

mained close to his heart. Thanks to a unique visual memory, he was able to see the Norwegian landscapes in his mind's eye. These images from memory were supplemented by sketches from five extensive journeys throughout Norway.

Dahl found his motifs primarily in western Norway. He painted the coast of Bergen during storms and high seas, but also the peaceful and beautiful landscape around Lysekloster in Os. He tenderly captured the images from his birthplace through a series of paintings, especially Vågen, Fløyen and Ulriken.

Symbolic paintings

Dahl was particularly attracted to the natural beauty of the mountains. The monumental paintings from Stalheim and Stugunset in Sogn are among his greatest work. Many of Dahl's motifs had a strong symbolic effect and became images of both Norwegian human nature and the country itself. An example of this is the birch tree standing strong and unyielding on the cliff during a storm. This famous motif was found in Måbødalen.

Not only paintings

When J.C. Dahl was not at his easel, he was working hard to establish Norwegian art institutions for cultural preservation. He was one of the founders of Bergens Kunstforening (the Bergen Art Association), and took the initiative to establish an art gallery in Bergen. Dahl strongly promoted the restoration of Håkonshallen, Rosenkrantztårnet and Nidarosdomen. He also took the initiative to establish the National Gallery in Oslo.

D

■ DAMSGÅRD MANOR

This stately manor, one of the city's architectural gems, lies secluded from Laksevåg's busy maritime industry. Once a private palace for the aristocracy, it is today open to the public as a museum. The elegant wooden building, in Rococo style, is said to be the only one of its kind in Europe and is surrounded by the finest Rococo gardens in Norway.

The property, originally named Håstein, was in medieval times a part of Munkeliv Cloister. The manor building today has the appearance of a miniature European palace and dates back to the 1770s. The owner at that time was the general war commissioner Joachim Christian Geelmuyden, with the aristocratic name Gyldenkrantz (1730–95).

In 1796 Damsgård was bought at an auction by Herman Didrich Janson. He was a shipowner and court agent and was perhaps better known as Nina and Edvard Grieg's great grandfather. His heirs later lived on the property all year round. Many inhabitants of Bergen still refer to the place as Jansongården (the Janson manor).

This jewel of a manor was well kept up by Janson's heirs until 1982. The place was then purchased with state and municipal funds in order to preserve the manor as part of the Norwegian cultural heritage.

Both manor building and gardens were extensively restored and Damsgård was opened to the public as a museum in 1993.

The Gardens of the Master and the Madam

The former state antiquarian Stephan Tchudi-Madsen writes about the gardens at Damsgård:
"The entire magnificence of Bergen and joy of nature – as it mirrors the European pulse – was recessed in the gardens. This more formal garden was 'The Master's Garden' – Østhaven. Here there was also room for more practical needs such as carrots, cabbages and herbs. 'Madam's garden' – Vesthaven – was given a willow pond and a carp pond. But there was also an 'English garden' – a miniature nature park – behind the gardens, with bridges and winding paths."

Damsgård manor *brightens up the landscape. Many Bergen citizens know the building as Jansongården because of the family who lived there from 1796 to 1982. The last private owner was Constantin Janson.*

Getting there: *Bus 16, 17, 18, 19 – or follow road nr. 582.*

D

◼ **PETTER DASS**

Popular poet and mythological figure

Petter Dass
drawn by Olaf
Gulbransson.

The poet/clergyman Petter Dass (1647–1707) shares a gravestone just outside the cathedral with hymn writer Dorothe ▶ Engelbretsdatter. Both are portrayed in bronze reliefs, created by Ambrosia Tønnesen, on each side of the stone.

Petter Dass was born on Nord-Herøy in Alstahaug. He became a vicar in 1689 in one of the country's largest and richest parishes. He followed his calling until his death. His Scottish father, Peter Don Dass, came to Norway from Dundee, became a Norwegian citizen in 1636, and settled in Bergen. From here, he ran a merchant trade in northern Norway until he finally resettled in Nordland county.

In 1660, after his father's death, Petter Dass was sent to his great-aunt in Bergen in order to receive an education. For six years he was a student at Bergen Katedralskole, and later struggled to complete his studies in theology in Copenhagen.

Dass had very happy memories of his years in Bergen. He wrote three poems about Bergen after the catastrophic fire in 1702, where he praises the city as "a mother for myself and others". One of the poems, called "Klage-Viise" (Song of Complaint) with a total of 34 verses concerns the way in which he felt the city should be rebuilt. Later when Dass needed some time away from his exhausting work as a vicar at Alstahaug, he went to Bergen, seeking to renew his mental energy with, among others, his poet colleague Dorothe Engelbretsdatter.

Petter Dass was an unusually popular clergyman. He was given status as a hero, and became a legendary figure with a reputation for tackling the Devil himself.

In the 150 years following his death the northern Norwegian fishing vessels sailed with a piece of dark cloth sewn onto their sails as a symbol of mourning. His words carried an authority equalled only by the Bible. Most of what Dass wrote came out in print only after his death, though his work was widely read. In

Bergen the splendid lady

When the great fire of 1702 laid down-town Bergen in ashes, Petter Dass wrote "A mournful lament over the wretched and pitiful destruction of Bergen City". Here is one of in all 34 verses:

Among places
in the north there
was none like you
You who stood as
the most splendid
Lady
And should anyone
ever say differently
He should be
ashamed.
Every ship and
every harbour
praises your name
And the mountains
would say the
same.

D

Memorial by Domkirken

In the churchyard of Domkirken by Kong Oscars gate stands this bronze relief of the poet priest Petter Dass in his pulpit. The relief was done by Ambrosia Tønnesen from a painting in Melhus church. Over Petter Dass are smaller reliefs with two angel heads and a northern Norwegian fishing boat.

◄

a distinctive verse, characterised by a definite sense of humour, Dass gives a colourful and vivid picture of the nature and people of the north. He is also the first to have retold the Bible stories and the Catechism in the form of verse.

Retold the Bible in the form of verse

The powerful Dass hymn, "Herre gud, ditt dyre navn og ære" (Lord God, your precious name and honour) continues to be one of the hymns sung most often. His "Nordlands Trompet" (The Trumpet of Nordland) stands as one of the great national works of poetry.

D

■ DOMKIRKEN

**Cathedral
of Bergen
since 1537**

The year 1464: The Church of St. Olav in Vågsbunnen was in a blaze of flames.

The year 1537: The year after the Reformation had been established by law. The church,
still ravaged by fire, was given status as the
new cathedral of Bergen and the bishopric.

The decision was made by Gjeble Pederssøn,
newly installed as Norway's first Lutheran
bishop. He saw to the restoration of the
church. The city's original Catholic Cathedral,
Kristkirken (the Church of Christ), which lay
at Holmen, just north of Håkonshallen, was
torn down in 1531 for military reasons.

**Remains from
two earlier
churches**

Today's cathedral is composed of remains
from two earlier churches. The oldest part is
the brick wall from under the windows on the
north side. This part comes from the old parish
church referred to in King Sverre's Saga and
was consecrated by Saint Olav. The king's men
sought refuge in the church from the baglers
(a clerical party during the 13th century Norwegian civil wars). The first church must
therefore have been built around the year
1150. Scarcely one hundred years later Olavs-
kirken was taken over by Franciscan monks to

Cloister

be used as a cloister. The church burned down
in 1248, but with financial aid from King Magnus Lagabøter, a new and larger church was
quickly constructed. When the king died in
1280, he was buried in the chancel of the
church, according to his own wishes. His remains were never found, however. In 1301 the
new church was completed. A good part of the
nave and chancel of Domkirken were originally part of this medieval church.

**Medieval
atmosphere**

In spite of the fires and the many changes
and repairs, the cathedral has endured; its
sacred atmosphere within the beautiful Gothic
portals is still reminiscent of the Middle Ages.
The tower with its distinctive green dome and
Baroque spires was constructed during the
restoration after the great fire of 1702. Some of
the valuable inventory has been preserved,
such as the parish chalice from 1690 and many
of the chasubles from the 1700s. A portrait gal-

lery includes bishops and cathedral deans dating back to 1649. The altarpiece from 1726 is
decorated with two paintings by artist Johan
Georg Müller. Just inside the main entrance
from the foot of the south wall of the tower
stands a monument to Bishop Johan Nordahl
▶ Brun.

A somewhat unusual historical monument   ***War memory***
can be seen high up on the façade of the tower.
A cannonball is lodged in the tower wall, a

D

Bjørgvin Kirkemusikk AS was established in 1991 as an administrative organisation for Domkirken's concerts. Responsibilities include Bergen Domkantori, Bergen Oratoriekor and Domkirken's boys' choir.

Cathedral organists of the 20th century:

Ingolf ▶ Schjøtt (1878–1922)
Karsten Solheim (1922–36)
Lars Heggen (1936–46)
Trygve Præsttun (1946–70)
Magnar Mangersnes (1971–)

souvenir from a sea battle fought in 1665 in the harbour of Vågen, between the English and Dutch fleets.

Under the leadership of architects Christie and Blix, the Cathedral went through an extensive restoration between 1880 and 1883. Peter Helland-Hansen suggested additional repairs, which took place from 1963 to 1969.

In 1997 the cathedral organist Magnar Mangersnes was able to release the first musical strains from the cathedral's new organ, a 61-stop, top quality instrument worth 11 million kroner, from Rieger Orgelbau in Austria. The present-day organ replaced a German Hollenbach organ from 1891, and is the fifth in a series of organs over five centuries. The first instrument was brought in by Bishop Gjeble Pederssøn in 1549. Absalon Pederssøn Beyer replaced it with an organ from Bremen, "a beautiful positive". The first organist was Niels Moegensen from Shetland.

The new and impressive organ serves not only the congregation and Sunday Mass, but also plays an important part in church music in general. The complex electronics of the organ are hidden in the back of the cathedral's old organ façade in neo-Gothic style. This was an unconditional demand of the antiquarian authorities.

The Cathedral also has a smaller organ from 1956 and received another organ in 1972, which stands in the vestment house. (See also ▶ Bergen Domkantori.)

■ JOHANNE DYBWAD

The first lady of Nordic theatre

Johanne Juell Dybwad (1867–1950), the first lady of Norwegian and Nordic theatre throughout two generations, was born the same year that her two actor-parents, Mathias and Johanne Juell were employed at Christiania Theatre. When their marriage fell apart four years later, Johanne was sent to Bergen where she grew up at Nygård with her aunt and uncle, Fredrikke Mathea (maiden name Juell) and Knut Rosendahl.

Detail from Per Ung's sculpture of Johanne Dybwad. It stands at the restaurant of Den Nationale Scene.

◄

Johanne Dybwad made an enormously successful debut at Den Nationale Scene (the National Theatre of Bergen) in 1887, in the starring role of the English comedy "Gertrude" by A. Harris. A sculpture by Per Ung now stands in the theatre in her honour.

Music and dance were at first more appealing than the theatre to this young, talented woman. As luck would have it, musician August Fries from Slesvig-Holstein also lived at the Rosendahl house. Fries was a well-known violinist and had been the conductor of the Harmonien for eleven seasons. Even before little Johanne's hands could stretch across a whole octave, "Uncle August" taught her to play her first, simple piano pieces. Some of the melodies were specially composed by Fries for his talented student. In 1882, 15-year-old Johanne accompanied her teacher when the theatre staged a benefit performance in cele-

Music and dance before theatre

D

Johanne Dybwad just before her debut in Bergen

bration of her father's 25 years as an actor. Johanne had otherwise had little contact with her father after his return to Bergen.

She earned her first salary as a clerk in a glove shop, but soon found more lucrative and interesting work as a music teacher. There was no problem finding enough students. She asked for only 50 øre an hour and had a reputation of being extremely good at her work. After Knut Rosendahl's death, Johanne and her aunt moved to Engen, coincidentally into the same building as Fridtjof Nansen. She admitted to having had a crush on the polar explorer, though her contact with him was limited to a few admiring glances when passing on the stairs. Amalie Hansen, sister of the well-known doctors Armauer Hansen and Klaus Hanssen, was Johanne's teacher at the private school she ran on Skostrædet. Hansen soon had a hunch that her student's talents lay in the field of the dramatic arts. Writer Gunnar Heiberg, however, was convinced of this. Heiberg was the head of Den Nationale Scene for four years. He discovered Johanne's great talent while directing an amateur performance, in which she played a role. Halfway through the rehearsal he stopped the play and immediately offered her a job as a professional actress.

Portrayed 20 roles in Bergen

Audiences in Bergen were given the pleasure of Johanne Juell's performances in the theatre only for one season, however. During this period she had managed to portray 20 different roles and received brilliant reviews in the newspapers, especially for her role of Nora in Ibsen's "A Doll's House", before Bjørn Bjørnson asked her to come to the Christiania Theatre. Only on one occasion did Johanne Dybwad return to the stage of her debut. In 1894 she performed again the role of Nora at a guest performance with Den Nationale Scene. Her performance was the high point of the evening, and according to Hans Wiers-Jensen, "the most remarkable thing ever seen on a Bergen stage". Professor Francis Bull called Johanne Dybwad "the divine genius of the Norwegian theatre".

The high point

D

◼ HANS POULSEN EGEDE

One spring day in 1721, Hans Poulsen Egede (1686–1758) left Vågen for Greenland on a Christian mission. With him on the journey were 40 other missionaries, his wife Gjertrud Rask (1673–1735) and their children. The group set sail in three ships with the gospel as their cargo.

Christian conversion of Greenland started in Bergen

The group landed on the west coast of Greenland on the 3rd of July. There they stayed for 15 years. Because of his pioneering missionary efforts, Egede received the nickname of "Greenland's apostle". He made an important contribution to the understanding of the culture and language of the Eskimos and laid the foundation for the colonisation and development of the island community.

During the time of his efforts to gather financial support for the expedition from the merchants of Bergen, Egede was a member of Korskirken (Church of the Cross). In his memory, a bronze relief of the couple was placed on the western wall of the church tower in 1976. In Sandviken there is a street named after him.

"Greenland's apostle"
Hans Egede and his wife Gjertrud Rask were honoured by this memorial plaque, made by Johan B. Hygen, on the tower wall of Korskirken.

◀

Gunnar Torvund's 'sin' in the church

■ EIDSVÅG CHURCH

A controversial altarpiece made Eidsvåg Church famous well outside the city limits when it was consecrated in 1982. Artist Gunnar Torvund had formed a crucifix out of birch and pine to create an altarpiece. The 'mistake' he made was creating a figure of Christ which appeared to be of uncertain gender. This was at first unacceptable to the parish council.

The artist was forgiven his 'sin', and later created another two sculptures for the church. Three other artists, Halvdan Ljøsne, Sissel Fjelldal and Tove Brekke, have also contributed to the embellishment of the church.

■ ELDORADO

Grieg's first concert hall in Norway

The great hall of the Arbeiderforeningen (the Labour Association), on the intersection of Olav Kyrre's Street and Nygårdsgaten, was the location of the cinema "Eldorado". Here Edvard Grieg gave his first public concert performance in 1862. The cinema had 700 seats and really was an eldorado for fans of the old-fashioned Western films, especially the ones with a lot of wild action. The cinema was closed down in 1981.

Exotic

Today, Eldorado houses the city's most exotic group of people. The Bergen International Cultural Centre uses the hall as a meeting place for immigrants from all over the world, and from many different cultures.

■ ELSESRO

Cradle for the "Peer Gynt" music

Elsesro in Sandviken was named after ship builder Rasmus Rolfsen's wife, Elsebe. The word 'ro' in Norwegian means calm or peace and quiet. Peace and quiet is also what Edvard ► Grieg sought, when he stayed at Elsesro two summers in a row, in 1873 and 1874, using the garden pavilion as a composing studio. The pavilion was not the biggest and most luxurious of workplaces, but the peace and the beau-

tiful view of the city were undoubtedly inspiring.

Here Grieg wrote the music for Bjørnstjerne Bjørnson's operatic piece "Olav Trygvason" and part of the music for Henrik Ibsen's masterpiece "Peer Gynt". Artist J.C. Dahl also found some of the motifs for his Bergen landscape paintings at Elsesro.

The Chinese-style, octagon-shaped pavilion still exists today and is a part of the Gamle Bergen Museum (the Old Bergen Museum). Edvard Grieg rented at the time a house in Sandviksveien 48, just down the road from his parents' home in number 85, the so-called Repslagerhuset (The Ropemaker House). Grieg's parents moved to Sandviken in 1870, after leaving ▶ Landås Manor due to poor health and a troubled financial situation.

When Repslagerhuset had to be removed in 1952 to make way for a new road, the Gamle Bergen Museum was its salvation. One must assume that Edvard played the piano in this house as well. Music was also later given a central place in the house when the first floor was used as a concert hall for a period of time.

▲
In this octagon-shaped pavilion Grieg wrote the music to Bjørnson's opera libretto "Olav Trygvason" and parts of Ibsen's "Peer Gynt".

The house in Sandviksveien where Nina and Edvard Grieg lived when he composed the music for "Peer Gynt".

▲
Manor house
*at Elsesro was origi-
nally a home for
clergymen's widows.
Shipyard owner Ras-
mus Rolfsen had it
moved from Sogn
or Nordfjord.*

In the back of Repslagerhuset was Bergen's longest rope walk, measuring 175 metres.

The manor building at Elsesro was original-ly a home for clergymen's widows, which Ras-mus Rolfsen (1760–1808) had moved to Ber-gen from Sogn or Nordfjord. His son, Tønnes Rolfsen, laid out a park in the style of an Eng-lish garden, complete with a duck pond, ro-mantic pathways and miniature waterfalls. The manor building was also given a more ele-gant look by the addition of two wings. In the dining hall are several paintings by artist Jo-han Georg Müller, J.C. Dahl's first teacher. To-day the building also houses the restaurant "Gamle Bergen Tracteursted".

Brewery

In 1844, Rasmus Rolfsen III closed down his shipyard and established instead the first malt brewery in western Norway at Elsesro.

E

This gradually led to the start of the modern brewery business in Bergen. The enormous, two-story, granite building of the malt brewery is Elsesro's largest building, about 50 metres long and 13 metres wide. It is probably also the oldest industrial building still in existence today in Bergen. Today the building is used as a warehouse and workshop like the mast house next door. Rolfsen also built a carriage house, a stall and several smaller storage buildings.

Postal road to Trondheim

A pathway leads up to Helleveien near the entrance to Gamle Bergen from the south. It dates back to the 1700s and is part of the old postal road between Bergen and Trondheim. A creek runs along the path, just as it did in the Middle Ages. It was then called Gunnildarå and provided the nearby mill with water. At that time the force of the water was powerful enough to turn as many as nine waterwheels and keep three grain mills in operation. The mill in the middle is now undergoing reconstruction and will contain an historical exhibition.

Grain mills

City limits

The grooves left in the ground after Gunnildarå are important historical landmarks because the river, according to Magnus Lagabøter's city laws of 1276, marked the borders of Bergen toward the north.

(See also ▸ Gamle Bergen Museum.)

■ DOROTHE ENGELBRETSDATTER

The hymn writer Dorothe Engelbretsdatter (1634–1716) was born in Bergen, and the city honoured her with a memorial stone near Domkirken. A park by the Lepra Museum is named after Dorothe. Dorothe's house, which was built in Kong Oscar's Street 42 after the fire of 1702, has been reconstructed in the Gamle Bergen Museum. The house was renovated in 1912 but had to be removed in 1963 owing to road development.

Popular hymn poet

Dorothe shares the memorial stone with fel-

E

A portrait of Dorothe Engelbretsdatter on copperplate, done by an unknown artist of the time.

▶

*Jeg sidder slet for Verdens Flok,
Som paa mig Kaster Øjet,
Men pijnted og Stafferet nok,
Naar Gud Kun er fornøjet.*

Petter Dass her guest and pen-friend

low poet Petter ▶ Dass. The bronze reliefs are placed on each side of the stone. Petter Dass had also been a guest in Dorothe's home. At the age of 33, he became acquainted with the 13-year older poetess from Bergen. She was already well-known while Dass had not yet had his work printed. He paid homage to her through his poetry, and for a time they were pen-friends, until Dorothe, for some unknown reason, stopped writing.

Wrote Dass, "My pen has three times / To Dorothea written / But no letter or answer / to this day has come."

Dorothe's father was a parish clergyman at the cathedral. Dorothe was married at the age of 18 to her father's successor, Ambrosius Hardenbeck. Family happiness was short-lived. By the time her collection of hymns was published in 1678, Dorothe had lost seven of her nine children. Five years later she became a widow. She also survived her two remaining children.

Short-lived happiness

The tragedy seemed to have had a prolific effect on her writing, however. She found a means of expressing her grief through the poem (published later in 1778) with the long title: "Sacrifice for the Soul. Includes a few sacred hymns as well as morning and evening lamentations for each day of the week." In 1885 she followed up with "Offering of Tears by Repentant Souls" reproduced from the orig-inal German text.

Dorothe Engelbretsdatter's hymns and songs became very popular. They were primarily meant to be used for religious devotions in the home, often sung to modern melodies and provided with music. As the first poet since the Reformation, she used folk melodies. Her hymns were reprinted as many as 24 times, up until the year 1868. Four of them were giv-en a place in Landstad's book of church hymns.

"The greatest poetess of the Nordic kingdoms"

Dorothe left behind 50 letters in rhyme and everyday poems, which revealed another side to this pietistic hymn writer and devoted Jesus-worshipper. She was also a lively and open poet.

Dorothe Engelbretsdatter was a female pioneer. She was beloved and praised for her writing both in Norway and in Denmark. Although her excessively formal, Baroque style poetry would not rate very highly by today's standards, it was quite popular during her time.

Ludvig Holberg rated her "the greatest poetess the Nordic kingdoms have ever had". Words of praise also came from colleagues such as Thomas Kingo and Petter Dass, while the king himself granted her lifelong tax exemption – a form of poet's stipend.

Relief of Dorothe Engelbretsdatter on the memorial at Domkirken where she is reunited with her friend and poet colleague Petter Dass. The relief was made by Ambrosia Tønnesen.

D

■ **FANTOFT STAVE CHURCH**

Rebuilt after intentional fire

In August 1997, the first stave church to be built in Bergen and the latest to be built in Norway was consecrated by Bishop Ole D. Hagesæther. The new church is a true copy of the 800-year-old Fantoft stave church that was completely destroyed by arson on June 7, 1992.

The old church stood originally in Fortun in Inner Sogn where it was built around the year 1170, though reconstructed and enlarged during the 17th century. In 1883 the church was purchased by consul Fredrik G. Gade who had it moved to Bergen and rebuilt on his property of Fantoft.

An exact copy of the Fantoft stave church. This ambitious reconstruction after the fire was left to the architectural firm Irgens and Andersen. Ole Johan Minde and Halldor Skaatun were the craftsmen who carried out the job. 400-year-old building materials from Kaupanger in Sogn were used. The stone cross from the graveyard north of the church stood originally in the Tjora graveyard in Jæren.

▶

When consul Conrad Mohr became the property's new owner in 1903 he allowed it to be furnished and consecrated so that church services could be held there. The church was given status as a chapel in the parish of Birkeland. In 1915 the church was sold to shipowner Jacob Kjøde and is owned today by his heirs, shipowner Johan J. Horn, Henning Horn and Mrs. Elin Horn.

A gift of love

The owners have themselves paid for the very complicated task of reconstruction, and have employed highly qualified craftsmen, Ole Johan Minde and Halldor Skaathun. The bishop characterised the reconstruction of the church as "a declaration of love for the Church and for the city of Bergen". The new stave church will undoubtedly be enjoyed by Bergen natives and visitors alike, since the church has been and continues to be one of the city's most popular tourist attractions.

A place of worship

The owners are still primarily interested in the church being used as a place of worship and for religious rituals, such as weddings and baptisms. On the altar stands an old crucifix, the only object to have survived the fire.

Supervision of the church has since 1915 been left to "Fortidsminneforeningen" (The Association for the Protection of Cultural Landmarks).

■ CLAUS FASTING

Writer, musician and councilman

Claus Fasting (1746–91) was one of the most important figures in Bergen's history, a multi-talented artist and a capable cultural contractor. He was a theologian with a degree from Copenhagen, a writer, critic, journalist and newspaper publisher. Fasting was, in addition to all this, a competent pianist and the motivating force behind the musical company Harmonien, together with its founder, Jens Boalth. Fasting was even known as the soul of Harmonien. In his later years, Fasting also presided as a judge at the courthouse at city hall, and in 1787, four years before his death, he was given the position of deputy mayor.

Plaster bust of Claus Fasting in the Historical Museum

Claus Fasting
portrayed in bronze
by Ambrosia Tønne-
sen.

▶

**Lyder Sagen
about Fasting:**
"His early inspira-
tion and lovingly
developed spirit, his
open, warm heart,
his sensitive feelings,
his sharp eye for
beauty and good-
ness, his sure sense
of the proper and
humane, his deep
contempt for all that
was low and mean,
was dressed in silk
and velvet, was
partly a gift of na-
ture, partly a result
of a careful upbring-
ing, also his soul
and heart's legacy
from wonderful
parents, even from
his ancestors."

Favourite
"As a disciple (of
Jens Boalth) Fasting
became his favour-
ite, and later as a
man his confidant."

F

During the 1780s he laid out a park in the style of the times at Sydneshaugen. The gardens were called "Lille Sorgenfri på Berget" (Little carefree place on the hill). The main building, which today has the address Møhlenprisbakken 1 and belongs to the university, has been named "Fastings Minde".

Fasting has been honoured by a bust outside the Bergen Public Library. A street has also been named after him on Fjellsiden. Fasting's five-octave clavichord where he "spent the happiest hours of his life" stands today in the Historical Museum, along with a plaster bust. His large book collection has since 1992 been kept in the library of Bergen Katedralskole.

In Copenhagen, Fasting studied music and languages in addition to theology, and began on his first literary works. He already enjoyed a certain reputation from "Det Norske Selskab" – since he was very well read. According to Wessel, Fasting turned 'French' when he became inebriated. He returned home in 1768. A year later he received a round of applause when his grandiloquent poem "Verdners Liv og Aanders glæde" (Life of the World and Joy of the Spirits) was presented in Harmonien to a cither accompaniment. His poem received status as the official song at Harmonien for a very long time.

As a writer for the stage, he made his debut in Harmonien's drama club with the pastoral play, "Pan's Celebration". This was followed by the tragedy "Hermione". Later he contributed both cantatas and songs, but distinguished himself principally as an essayist and critic. He had a reputation for mastering the epigram better than anyone else in either Denmark or Norway, and was less ornate in his use of language than most authors at that time.

From 1778 to 1781 Fasting published the weekly magazine, "Provinzialblade". It was considered at that time to be one of the most important publications in Scandinavia. The goal of the magazine was to be useful, educational and pleasurable. Fasting's wish was to "combine what the educated know with what

Claus Fasting, the critic

In "Provinzialblade" Claus Fasting wrote, in 1781, this strong critique:

"The city music is abominable, without exception. The instruments and musicians are but machines, the later ones even worse than the first. Euphony, Order, Strength, Feeling, Beauty are all unknown terms to these people. These poor sinners are but craftsmen and not artists. I was recently invited to listen to the music of these wretches on the occasion of a friend's birthday. Would that this friend had never been born, for the misery he forced on me. Each instrument was tuned, or should I say mistuned... Each note was like the grunt of a pig and the howl of a wolf."

Inscription on the grave of Claus Fasting at Domkirken

Great ambitions

the uneducated want to know, make the useful less dull and the pleasant more useful". He had great ambitions for the magazine and wanted to open the eyes of the "Bergensians" to the rest of the big wide world, especially to the ideas of Voltaire and Rousseau, both of whom he was especially interested in.

The magazine never gained any widespread circulation. Distribution was such a difficult process that readers outside the city limits were only able to purchase an entire year's worth of copies. The material was also too highbrow for the average citizen, considering the level of education most people had. Fasting struggled financially and was forced to work as a private tutor and to take odd jobs in order to make a decent living. He found comfort in his music during these difficult times.

Very popular

Nevertheless, Fasting became enormously popular, and in 1791 he confidently began a new publication, "Provinzialsamlingen". He was unfortunately only able to publish one edition before his life came to an end on Christmas Eve. A large flock of admirers followed Fasting, one of the finest representatives of the Age of Enlightenment, to his final resting-place in the churchyard of Domkirken.

Claus Fasting's beautifully decorated clavichord belongs today to the Historical Museum.
▼

At the commemorative gathering held by Harmonien, Bishop Johan Nordahl Brun made a moving speech.

Foto: Svein Skare

F

■ FESTIVALS

The Bergen International Festival is the largest and most important international cultural festival in Norway. Several new festivals have sprung up in Bergen in recent years, giving it the well-deserved title "Festival City".

Bergen has also played host to several non-annual festivals, such as "Hansadagene" (Hanseatic Days) in 1996, and Cutty Sark's Sailing Regatta for large sailing ships in 1994. In 1993 Bergen celebrated the 150th anniversary of the birth of Edvard Grieg by arranging a music festival which lasted the entire year.

On June 1, 1953 King Haakon VII officially opened the first Bergen International Festival. Great music artists, such as Leopold Stokowski, Yehudi Menuhin and Kirsten Flagstad appeared on the stage during the first two weeks of the festival. Since then, Bergen has been the arena for the country's leading national and international cultural event every year from May to June.

However, the overture to the festival actually began 55 years earlier. In 1898 Bergen had played host to Norway's first music festival with international guests. On Edvard Grieg's initiative the music festival came together at the time of a large fishery and industry fair. Grieg's idea was to present the finest possible performance by a group of professional musicians. He made every effort therefore to secure the great Concertgebouw Orchestra from Amsterdam, with its 70 members and their conductor, Willem Mengelberg. The suggestion was strongly opposed, but Grieg had his way in the end.

The Music Festival lasted from June 26th to July 3rd and was a great success. Concerts were held in a temporary concert hall in Nygårdsparken with a full house of about 2000 people every evening. Grieg was content with the fact that he had achieved his purpose: "The people of Bergen are saying the same thing as the people of Kristiania: We *must* have a better orchestra!"

(See also Edvard ▶ Grieg.)

Bergen has become a "Festival city"

Sitar player on the top of Ulriken decorated the program of the first Bergen International Festival in 1953.

Festival ouverture 1898

The first music festival in Norway was arranged in Bergen in the summer of 1898 on Grieg's initiative on the occasion of the large fishing and industrial fair. This is a commemorative medallion from the event.

In honour of Edvard Grieg

Sir John Barbirolli brought his famous Hallé orchestra to Bergen in 1963. In a speech for the Festival lunch Barbirolli revealed that he had once found himself in a deep crisis, where he had felt exhausted – even when music was concerned. The turning point came when he by chance came to hear Grieg's violin sonatas performed by Fritz Kreisler and Sergeij Rachmaninoff. "I just had to cry – and return to my music," said Barbirolli.

Festival prices

Alto singer Fanny Elsta became the 'godmother' of the festival when the idea for an annual event came up in 1950. The idea was modelled on the highly recognised Salzburg festival which revolves around Mozart, the city's famous son. It was only natural for Bergen to hold its modern festival in honour of Edvard Grieg.

The goal of the International Festival is to present international art and music, along with the artists and musicians, to the Norwegian public and also to present the best of Norwegian creativity in the same fields. The festival's program has expanded considerably over the years. In addition to music, there is also theatre, art, ballet, folklore and literature during a two-week event with well over one hundred performances. The music of Grieg still has a central position. His piano concerto has always been an important part of the program's finale.

Grieghallen, Troldhaugen and Den Nationale Scene are the main arenas for the International Festival. Concerts are also held at Siljustøl and Lysøen, in Håkonshallen and Logen and in several churches. Performances have also been given in Danseteatret, Gimle and Kulturhuset. Artist exhibitions are presented in Bergens Kunstforening. Some of the events are held outdoors. All musical genres are represented, from operas and symphonies to smaller, more intimate chamber concerts, jazz, and entertainment for children. Apart from the official program, there are several free performances, such as street theatre, which all help to create a special festival atmosphere in the city.

Prominent Norwegian composers have, throughout the years, had the honour of being invited to be Festival Composer of the Year. This tradition was replaced in 1997 by Festival Musician of the Year, with pianist Leif Ove Andsnes as the first to fill the role. Prominent artists and writers have been honoured in the same manner, with their own prizes. The first Festival Prize was awarded in 1961 to composer Arne Nordheim. A new award cal-

led the 'Edvard' was given in 1998 to seven creative Norwegians, writers as well as composers.

The Festival has had a number of impressive, first-time performances, all of which have been commissioned by the committee. Works have included the opera "Jeppe" (1966) by Geirr Tveitt, the ballet "Toward the Sun" from 1969 by Alfred Janson, Allan Petterson's "13th Symphony" (1978), and the folklore play "Dance, Called the Fiddle" from 1957 by Barthold Halle and Edith Roger. The Bergen International Festival has, over the years, been able to gather together a large number of the most prominent artists, orchestras and ens-embles.

The International Festival is organised as a foundation. Financing of the Festival is based on private and public support, although the foundation covers over 40% of the costs. The king is the patron of the Festival and a faithful guest, usually accompanied by the queen.

From 1996, the director of the International

▲
Central Festival Participants drawn as the Beatles, by Audun Hetland in 1964. From left: Orchestra conductor Arvid Fladmoe, Harald Sæverud, Gunnar Arne Jensen and composer Sverre Jordan. Among the audience in the first row: King Olav and Mayor Harry Hansen. Behind the mayor is a glimpse of the first Festival Director, Frank Meidell Falch.

Festival has been Bergljót Jónsdóttir from Iceland.

International contemporary music

• *Music Factory* is an annual international festival for contemporary music at a professional level. It takes place at the same time as the Bergen International Festival. About 40% of the program is geared toward children and youth. Chamber music and electronic music are prioritised, but the program for the next few years, until 2005, will include rock, jazz, chamber operas, new compositions, as well as seminars for composers and musicians.

New music

• *Autunnal-festival* for contemporary music in Bergen has been arranged each year in October-November since 1993 by the National Association for New Music. The primary goal of the festival is to support and encourage local composers and musicians.

Products of a new organ

• *Kirkemusikkdager* (Church Music Days) and orgelfestuke (Organ Festival Week) are both arranged each fall by an administrative organization called Bjørgvin Kirkemusikk (Bjørgvin Church Music). These festivals came about after Domkirken received its new organ in 1997. The Church Music Days last for one week in November and involve all categories of newer and older church music, in the form of concerts and seminars.

Pop and Rock

• *Uken* is arranged by the students at Norges Handelhøyskole, NHH (Norway's Business College), in March every other year. The last presentation took place in 1998. The program consists of pop and rock music concerts, and entertainment in the form of skits, songs and dances.

Rain dances, flipper races, and an umbrella parade are part of the program of the Rain Festival, an event Bergen is especially well-suited for.

• *Torgdagen* (Market Day) has been an annual festival day since 1977, taking place sometime between the end of May and the beginning of June. The festival revives the history of Bergen's marketplace through folk dancing, old-fashioned costumes, vehicles and customs. The festival has become quite popular. It has con-

F

▲
"Stril" Dance on the Strand Quay on Market Day in 1998.

tributed to a greater understanding of history and has bridged the gap between city and country cultures.

• *Ole Blues Festival* (Bergen Blues and Roots Festival) was arranged for the first time in 1994 and was established as a separate foundation in 1996. The festival lasts for one week between April and May. In addition to concerts with international artists, there are seminars and musical workshops about blues music and related music forms.

Concerts, seminar, workshops

Jazz at Night (see ▶ Jazz in Bergen).
• *Maria Music Festival*. Annual series of concerts in August. (See ▶ Mariakirken.)
• *Folkedansgildet* (Folk Dance Festival) (See ▶ Folk Music.)
• *Bergensiaden*. Marching band festival held in June every other year. Held for the first time in 1998.
• *Bergen Spillfestival* (Bergen Games Festival). Outdoor tournaments in various games such as chess, bridge, ludo, backgammon and yatzy. Takes place each year in July.
• *Hat Festival*. Every year, some time between March and June.
• *Rain Festival* (formerly known as Umbrella Day) takes place each year in October.

F

■ FJØSANGER ESTATE

Estate and recreational area

Johan Caspar Lange with his house-keeper, Laura Wickmann. Lange ran a wholesale business, import and export, and other undertakings in Bredsgården on Bryggen. He owned five sailing ships and established a commercial trading centre in Iceland.

Venerable estate, model farm and recreational park. All of these descriptions would suit the Fjøsanger Estate (Fjøsanger Hovedgård), a place rich in tradition. Today the people of Bergen would probably think of Fjøsanger's gallery of modern art, nature trails and an impressive banquet hall.

The history of the estate dates back to the 16th century. The beautiful property known as Gamlehaugen, on the east side of Nordåsvannet, is also a part of this history. Gamlehaugen was the first tenant farmer cottage at Fjøsanger. Prime Minister Christian Michelsen later became owner of the farm and built his "castle", which today serves as a royal residence.

Fjøsanger Estate was renamed Langegården by the local people, since the Lange family were the owners of the estate for 91 years, from 1844 to 1935. Johan Caspar Lange was a childless bachelor and the last member of this German-Norwegian family when he died in 1935.

Lange had, however, already in 1919 designated his heirs. He had decided that when he was gone, the entire city would have access to Fjøsanger. This was formally settled by establishing a legacy, the purpose of which would be to "create a lovely refuge for the walking public". He later donated the manor house to the Johan Langes Minde Foundation so that it might provide a home for the elderly in Bergen. The statutes of the legacy presented some difficulties and had to be changed after Lange's death.

It was written, for example that "communists, socialists and people speaking rural dialects are not to be allowed on the premises". There was also a rule against improper reading material. Services for the elderly have now been moved to a newer building.

Before certain areas were fenced in as private farms and tenant cottages, Fjøsanger covered more than 1500 acres and was the largest farm near Nordås Lake. The owners were businessmen from Bergen and were not personally

▲
The manor building
on Fjøsanger Estate
was built in 1810. In
the background is
Gamlehaugen, a
former cotter's farm.
Prime Minister Chris-
tian Michelsen's
'palace' is today
a royal residence.

responsible for the operation of the farm. An exception was merchant Jon Mariager, who became the owner in 1762. He was a pioneer in many ways. Under his direction, Fjøsanger became a model farm and was the first to begin the drainage of swamplands. He also constructed the first driveable road in Fana, between Fjøsanger and Solheimsviken, "for fun and pleasure", and was among those who took the initiative to start "Det Nyttige Selskab" (The Useful Company) for "capable encouragement of the city of Bergen and its district".

In 1774 Mariager sold his property to his brother-in-law, Danckert Krohn. He was a businessman and owned large areas of land around the city. Krohn's plan was to make Fjøsanger one of the most prominent recreational areas in the Bergen area – a kind of "amusement park" for the financially well-endowed. With the help of a German, Krohn laid out a magnificent garden, and the old carriage road became an avenue lined with linden trees.

The main building, a large and elegant, Empire-style mansion with a Rococo façade, was built in 1810 by its owner, merchant Paul Meyer Smit. The architect was Valentin Vedel.

"Amusement park" for wealthy people

**Successful
renovation**

Since 1980 the house has undergone a successful renovation and stands today as one of the best preserved buildings of its time. Many of the earliest details are intact, and it has been possible to recreate the original floorplan and atmosphere of the house. A memorial room has been included with furniture and objects once belonging to Johan Caspar Lange.

**Art gallery
and a model
farm**

The first floor is today used by Langegården Gallery with its exhibitions of modern art. The top floor is rented out for parties. A tenant farmer runs the farm, which offers an educational program to visiting schools and nursery groups. Fjøsanger's reputation as a model farm is one that the foundation is keen to preserve. Some of the buildings on the farm have also been fixed up as studios for artists and craftsmen.

Nature trails

Several attempts to sell the property to private house builders have been prevented due to strong protests from the public. Today there are laws protecting the 30-acre property as an area of natural beauty and cultural-historical importance. Nature trails and walking paths wind their way through the woods of Langeskogen toward Løvstakken. As many as 59 different kinds of trees have been registered along the trails, most of which were planted during Lange's lifetime.

**Remains from
the ice age**

A remarkable discovery was made in 1968. Plant and animal remains from the last ice age about 120,000 years ago were found in the ground just south of the manor house. The area where they were found lies farther to the northwest than any other fossil site in Europe. The site is now under protection.

∎ FOLK MUSIC IN BERGEN

**Melting pot
of folk music
traditions**

Folk music expressed through dance, song and fiddle playing have strong traditions in Bergen and have been especially popular among the youth in the many "bygdeungdomslagene" (rural youth clubs) in the district. The two largest clubs, Bondeungdomslaget (the Farm Youth

Club) and Ervingen (Heirs), also own the most important arenas for folk music, Fensal and Gimle (Kong Oscar's Street 15 and 18). In Café Columbia (Øvregaten 17) the folk music club Columbi Egg meets every second Monday.

A one hour long folklore program is set up at Bryggen every Tuesday and Thursday during the tourist season. Fana Folklore invites the public to a farm wedding with a church procession, to religious folk songs inside the 800-year-old Fana church, in addition to rømmegraut (cream porridge), folk dancing and Hardanger fiddle music in Rambergstunet under Fanafjell. All this takes place four days a week, (Monday, Tuesday, Thursday and Friday).

The Hardanger fiddle, or "hardingfela", has been the supreme instrument in Bergen. The first Hardanger fiddle competition took place in Bergen in 1897. (See ▶ Vestmannalaget.) The eldest known instrument, Jaastadfela from 1651, is kept in the cultural-historical collection in the ▶ Bergen Museum. Today, in 1999, there are about 30 active fiddlers in Bergen. These are organised in two separate clubs: Fjellbekken (established in 1929) and Fana Spelemannslag (established in 1981).

Folk music professor Jan-Petter Blom – here in close contact with the master and namesake of the Grieg Academy.

Since its inhabitants come from many different parts of the country, Bergen has become a melting pot of different traditions and musical dialects. The city also has close ties to the rural culture in western Norway, which has played an important role in the development and expression of folk music. The ▶ Grieg Academy offers the study of folk music for music majors. The next goal is to promote the Hardanger fiddle as a major instrument in the performing arts, on the same level as voice and piano.

The Bergen International Folk Dance Festival (established in1976) has made Bergen an international meeting place for folk dancers. The goal is to strengthen the interest for traditional folk culture and promote understanding between youth of all nations. An annual festival takes place under the leadership of the Bergen International Festival.

The most famous fiddlers with ties to the

International fraternisation

Arne Bjørndal, drawn by Bernt Tunold in 1904. Bjørndal was also honoured with a bust in Grieghallen, made by Sofus Madsen. Bjørndal was appointed Knight of the Order of St. Olav.

▶

city of Bergen include Arne Bjørndal (1882 –1965), Lorentz Hop (1887–1954), Jon Rosenlid (1891–1974), Halvor Sørsdal (1899–1996), Oddmund Dale (born 1921) and Finn Vabø (born 1931).

Fiddler, singer, writer and composer

Arne Bjørndal stands in a class of his own. He dedicated his whole life to folk music and was highly regarded as a fiddler, folk singer, composer, judge, writer and lecturer. He was born in Hosanger on Osterøy, but came to Bergen already at the age of 17. His first collection of folk music was published by his own publish-

F

ing company in 1905, and he was praised for his work by Edvard Grieg himself. From 1911 Bjørndal received a modest yearly scholarship to cover travelling costs. In order to earn more money he functioned as master of ceremonies and musician at over 600 weddings. He toured the entire country with his fiddle and his songs. He gave solo performances on several occasions at Harmonien.

Gave Bergen large collection of folk music

Bjørndal made a significant contribution to music history as a researcher and collector of folk songs throughout 50 years. Thanks to Bjørndal's work, the university of Bergen now owns the largest collection of instrumental folk music and folk music traditions in the country, and also one of the largest collections of vocal folk music. In 1951 Bjørndal donated his folk music treasures to the university. His collection provides an important source of information for research run by the Grieg Academy. Bjørndal also left a fund consisting of 180,000 crowns to be used for the good of Norwegian folk music. In 1957 Bjørndal gave a lecture on folk music, the first of its kind in the country. During the years to come, many students will receive their Ph.D.s in the field of folk music based on the work of this self-educated man from Osterøy. Bjørndal himself had received only an elementary school education.

The folk dance, Fanaspringar is named after Fana, a section of Bergen since 1972. Here the dance is shown on a stamp from 1976.

Bjørndal wrote books about his teachers Ola Mosafinn and Ole Bull, and began the literary work, "Norwegian Folk Music". He also wrote music for several plays, including the popular reinlender dance music for "På Ulrikkens topp".

■ FRESCOHALLEN

"The first modern, architectural painting in the country. Establishment of modern fresco decoration in Norway. One of the greatest works of Nordic art..."

The Hall of Frescos

This is the description of the magnificent centrepiece for the headquarters of the Foun-

**Axel Revold
on his artwork**

In "Kunst og Kultur" (Art and Culture) from 1927, Alex wrote about his artwork in the Bergen Stock Exchange:

"It was to be a common point throughout all the paintings: beauty in the young, strong worker. It represents the unchanging human toil throughout all time. A swaying rhythm – a swell of the monotonous infinity in this century old toil. No matter how varied the work – always the same unfolding of exertion. It would be even better if I through the movement of the figures could express the kind of work he does. I wanted the whole thing to appear as an objective beauty. Like the mirror of life or a rhythmic poem about everyday life – of the significance of all this activity."

dation for Bergen as a European Cultural City in the year 2000. This very same building housed the Norwegian Stock Exchange from 1862. Axel Revold (1887–1962) carried out his monumental decoration during the years 1921–23. The 30-year-old student of Matisse from Narvik began one of the greatest tasks ever bestowed upon a Norwegian artist. His sketches were chosen in competition with such famous artists as Per Krohg and Henrik Sørensen.

The prominent, renaissance-inspired building in Vågsbunnen, which until 1967 housed the Bergen Stock Exchange, is today owned by Den norske Bank (the Norwegian Bank). The Hall of Frescos was named for Revold's decorations.

In 1997 the bank generously allowed the information and administration centre of the Cultural Foundation use of it. The bank had up until that time freshened up the paintings for nearly 10 million crowns. Bergen Travel Information had also moved into the building with its tourist information office. The goal was to establish a permanent information centre for culture and travel in Frescohallen, combined with a ticket and booking office for all cultural events in Bergen and the surrounding district.

The area of the Hall is 26 x 19 metres. When the architects (Schiertz and Solberg) had finished, the task of filling in ten bare walls from floor to ceiling with artwork remained. Revold covered the walls with people at work. Indirectly the wall decorations reflect the many different activities and areas of employment which make up the basis of Bergen's economic life.

Through a kind of advanced "comic book story" in giant format, we meet fishermen in the Lofoten Sea, seamen carrying their products, workers at the Wharf, factory workers, farmers tilling the earth, businessmen and those who sow and harvest the abundant wealth of nature in foreign climes. In a subtle cubist style, the paintings tell the saga of a merchant town and sing praises of the work-

F

ing people. Thematically the story has been divided into a northern Norwegian wall, a Bergen wall and a World wall – as befits a city tra-
ditionally facing both the north and outwardly
toward the rest of the world.

Revold added the final touches after the war.
He painted the ceiling arches that bind the
pictures together and repaired some of the minor damage done to the artwork during the occupation.

*Fishing boats gather-
ed in Vågen – one
of the ten fresco
paintings in the Ber-
gen Stock Exchange.
In the fresco techni-
que, wall paint is
used to allow the
colours to achieve a
permanent chemical
compound with the
wet plaster.*

F

■ GALLERIES

**First gallery
at Bergen
Museum**

*Parliament president
Wilhelm F. K. Chris-
tie played an impor-
tant role in the gath-
ering of the collec-
tion of paintings for
the Bergen Museum
and by the founding
of the Bergen Art
Association. This
picture shows a
detail from the
Christie monument
at Muséplass.*

About 20 exhibition halls for arts and crafts lie
within walking distance of the centre of Bergen. Another few galleries lie just outside the
city. Whether one prefers the old masters or is
curiously looking for new names and more modern work, Bergen has a great deal to offer.

• *Bergen Museum,* established in 1825, had
planned from the very beginning to build up a
collection of paintings. The museum became
the city's first art gallery. In addition to the
Museum's founder Wilhelm F.K. ▶Christie,
J.C. ▶Dahl was actively involved in the gallery
and contributed with gifts of several of his
own valuable paintings.

• *Bergen Kunstmuseum* (Bergen Art Museum)
is the collective name for a group of galleries
in the municipality. These galleries include
Bergen Billedgalleri, Stenersens Samling and
▶Rasmus Meyers Samlinger. The three galleries all lie along the west side of Lille Lungegårdsvann, in Rasmus Meyers Alleé 3 and 7.

The annual exhibition program displays both old and new art, in addition to international art. The museum also offers tours, catalogues and brochures about museum activities.

• *Bergen Billedgalleri* (Bergen Art Gallery) was established in 1878 when the Bergen municipality took over the Bergen Museum's collection of 244 paintings. The collection is one of the most important in Norway and contains about 7,500 works, including several Norwegian paintings. The works of J. C. Dahl are especially valuable. The gallery's task is to document Norwegian art history, in addition to being a distribution and research institution. Old masterpieces as well as newer works of international art brighten the gallery walls. The collection increases in size each year, thanks to donations and regular purchases through the municipal budget.

• *Stenersens samling* (the Stenersen Collection) contains about 250 works by Norwegian and internationally known artists. The collection was donated to Bergen in 1972 by financier Rolf Stenersen. In a new building also housing Bergen Billedgalleri, the collection opened for the public in 1978. The gallery stands on the same site as the first train station in Bergen once stood, with Bergen Kunstforen-ing as its closest neighbour. The building underwent reconstruction during the fall of 1998 whereby Stenersens Samling and Billedgalleriet were given a common main entrance, auditorium, café and bookshop.

Rolf Stenersen *painted by Edvard Munch. He was born in Oslo in 1899 and died in Bergen in 1978. He was a financier, writer and patron of the arts.*

The galleries line the west side of Lille Lungegårdsvann. From left: Bergen Lysverker soon to be a cultural institution, Rasmus Meyers Samlinger, Bergens Kunstforening, Billedgalleriet and Stenersens collection.
▼

Stenersens Samling contains northern Europe's largest collection of Paul Klee, ten paintings by Munch and several works by Picasso, Miró, Kandinsky, Léger, Weidemann, and new pieces are continually introduced. One of the younger artists included in the collection is Bård Breivik, from Bergen.

**Lyder Sagen
first chairman**

• *Bergens Kunstforening* (Bergen Art Society) was established in 1838 under the inspiring leadership of J.C. Dahl, with Lyder ▶ Sagen as its first chairman.

The objective of the society, apart from holding exhibitions, was to build up a gallery of modern art, together with the older art collection from Bergen Museum. On Sagen's initiative the Art Society also served as an art school. In 1846 J.C. Dahl donated his painting "Norwegian Landscape" to the gallery. The painting became the gallery's foremost work.

Painter Frantz Bøe (1820–91) won support for his idea that the collection should become a public gallery for the city of Bergen, and that the society should concentrate on setting up exhibitions and arranging the sale of artwork. The original collection was therefore transferred to Bergen Billedgalleri in 1881. The collection contained 38 paintings and 11 sculptures.

Bjørnstjerne ▶ Bjørnson was a member of the board of directors in 1859. The poet was the first to propose open doors to the world of art. On his initiative admission for all citicens was allowed to gallery exhibitions that had previously been closed to the public.

**Friends of
the Arts**
Billedgalleriets
Venner (Friends of
Bergen Billedgalle-
ri), founded in
1909, is an active
support group. The
group arranges
membership meet-
ings with art lec-
tures, tours and
travels in Norway
and abroad. Mem-
bership gives free
admission to all the
local art galleries.

Among the high points during the first years was Statens Høstutstilling (The State Fall Exhibition) which opened in Bergen for the first time in 1886. The first separate exhibition of importance took place in 1895 with the paintings of Edvard ▶ Munch.

As a western contrast to the Fall Exhibition of Oslo, the society organised a Spring Exhibition each year from 1903 to 1908. On the initiative of Axel Revold, this tradition was carried on from 1922 under the name Vestlandsutstillingen (Western Norwegian Exhibition) – a yearly assemblage of the finest art available

Sonja Henie and art critic Olav Simonnæs study Henie's and Niels Onstad's art collection in the Bergen Art Society in 1963. The exhibition marked the 125th anniversary of the society and was also the exhibition for the International Festival the same year. This was the first time the collection was displayed in Norway.
It is now housed at Høvikodden in Oslo.

◀

for exhibition in the western part of Norway.

Since 1953 Kunstforeningen has been responsible for the art exhibitions during the annual Bergen International Festival – an event which has achieved great national prestige.

Art Academy

Sagen's idea to establish a school of art was taken out and dusted off in 1953. The school of art became the Art Academy and was administered by the Kunstforeningen. The Academy was followed in 1970 by Studieatelieret, which in turn received status as Vestlandets Kunstakademi (The Western Norwegian Art Academy) in 1982 and received state funding.

Vestlandets Kunstakademi is today a department of Kunsthøgskolen in Bergen (Bergen Art College) and is located on C. Sundt's Street 53.

Kunstforeningen moved into its own building by Lille Lungegårdsvann in the fall of 1935. The building was designed by Ole Landmark. The society has today, in 1999, about 2000 members.

Shipowner Reksten's collection

• *Fjøsangersamlingene* (The Fjøsanger Collection) lies in Stamerbakken 7 and includes

This bust of ship-owner and art collector Hilmar Reksten (1897-1980) stands outside the Fjøsanger Collection. Sculptor: Hugo Wathne

Reksten was strongly engaged in the cultural life in his home town. He was the first president of the Bergen International Festival. In 1971 he donated 60 million crowns to establish Hilmar Reksten's public utility fund.

paintings, Persian rugs and silver collected by shipowner Hilmar Reksten. Unfortunately a large part of Reksten's considerable collection was scattered when his estate after his death ended in bankruptcy, and the entire affair had to be settled in court. The Supreme Court gave their verdict in 1988.

As a result, the city of Bergen lost the country's largest collection of Astrup paintings and one of Europe's largest collections of English silver. Gone were also other treasures such as the world famous paintings of el Greco, van Gogh and Munch, art treasures which Reksten had donated to the public in 1971. The rugs and some of the silver were purchased by the government and have been deposited in the Fjøsanger Collection, together with some of the paintings belonging to Hilmar Reksten's heirs.

"The Portrait Gallery" is a special department of the Fjøsanger Collection. The goal is to develop this department in order to create a national portrait gallery. This collection also includes works by Per Ung and the immensely popular Bergen artist Audun ▶ Hetland.

• *Hordaland Kunstsenter* (Hordaland Art Centre), at Klosteret 17, was established in 1974 and has since 1985 been located in a building which in 1739 was used as a school for the poor, run by the Nykirken congregation. The Centre is formally a foundation and is run in co-operation with the district art and handicraft associations. The Centre has about 300 members, among them, 200 artists.

As an artist-run gallery, a prioritised objective for the Art Centre is to look after the artists' freedom of expression independently of the taste and financial situation of the gallery. The Centre understands therefore the necessity of including the works of debutantes as well as of allowing experimental art a place in the gallery. The centre also invites artists from other countries to contribute with new works of art during some of the 20 exhibitions arranged each year. There are, in addition, two to four mobile exhibitions per year.

See the complete list of galleries at the back of this book.

G

Hordaland Kunstsenter has a budget of between five and ten million kroner to allocate to artists in Bergen and Hordaland for the adornment of public institutions. There are two exhibition halls at the Centre, Gallery 1 and Gallery NK, a guest studio and a café. Since 1998, a wide selection of art books has been available for purchase at the Centre.

• *Gallery Nygaten*, Nygaten 7, is a spectacular gallery concept with a liquor license and a sophisticated interior spanning three stories. Reidar Osen, proprietor. The art experience is accompanied by soft music and candlelight. Exhibitors are usually well-known artists. The gallery has its own membership club. Concerts with classical music or ballet performances are set up on Saturdays.

• *Format Arts and Crafts* moved in 1997 into the empty building left by the Norwegian Bank in Vågsallmenningen 12, an Empire-style building from 1842. The gallery is a forum for Norwegian craftsmen. All forms of craftsmanship are represented, including pottery, textiles, metal, glass and wood.

• *Hotel Neptun* on Valkendorf's Street 8 has been deservedly described as an 'art hotel', under the direction of Hans Inge Bruarøy. Over 600 paintings and prints are included in the hotel's permanent exhibition of Norwegian and international art.

▲
Hordaland Kunstsenter
is housed in a very old, historic building called Grønneskolen (Green School). Merchant Mads Forman donated the building in 1739 to the congregation of Nykirken, to be used as a school for the poor. The name of the school comes from the colour of the school sweaters. Between the years 1885 to 1921 the property was used by the Bergen archives office.

Art hotel

G

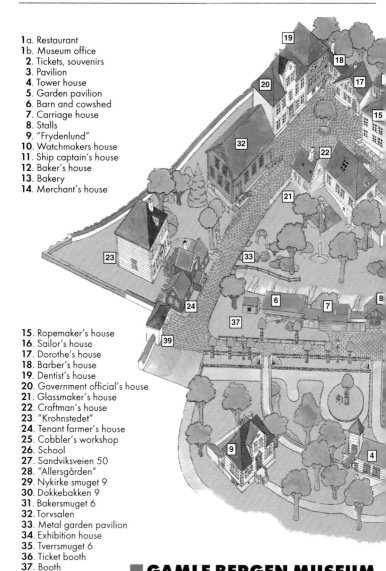

1a. Restaurant
1b. Museum office
2. Tickets, souvenirs
3. Pavilion
4. Tower house
5. Garden pavilion
6. Barn and cowshed
7. Carriage house
8. Stalls
9. "Frydenlund"
10. Watchmakers house
11. Ship captain's house
12. Baker's house
13. Bakery
14. Merchant's house

15. Ropemaker's house
16. Sailor's house
17. Dorothe's house
18. Barber's house
19. Dentist's house
20. Government official's house
21. Glassmaker's house
22. Craftman's house
23. "Krohnstedet"
24. Tenant farmer's house
25. Cobbler's workshop
26. School
27. Sandviksveien 50
28. "Allersgården"
29. Nykirke smuget 9
30. Dokkebakken 9
31. Bakersmuget 6
32. Torvsalen
33. Metal garden pavilion
34. Exhibition house
35. Tverrsmuget 6
36. Ticket booth
37. Booth
38. Open air stage
39. Main entrance
40. Mill

■ GAMLE BERGEN MUSEUM

A city within a city and many small museums within a greater museum. In short: Gamle Bergen (Old Bergen Museum) – also called a refuge for homeless houses. The Museum was

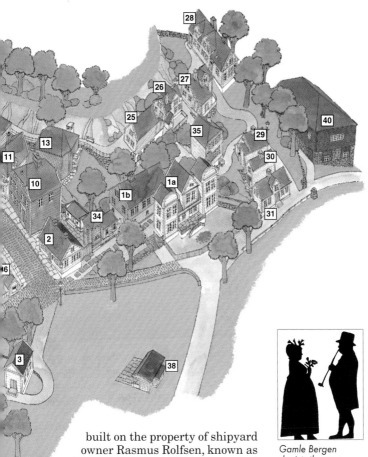

Gamle Bergen
depicts the way
in which our
ancestors lived.

**Access to
Gamle Bergen**

Bus from Bergen Bus
station to the stop by
Sandviken Hospital
in Helleveien.

The Museum is open
only in the summer.

built on the property of shipyard
owner Rasmus Rolfsen, known as
Elsesro, in Sandviken – an area
with historic ties to maritime industry, and a past as one of Bergen's
summer paradises.

Gamle Bergen has been described as
a living museum town comprised of historically interesting buildings, which throughout the years have been threatened by modern
urban development in a modern age with no
apparent appreciation of cultural heritage.
Gamle Bergen Museum became the salvation
for 35 preservation-worthy city houses, many

Two typical examples of wooden houses in Bergen.

of them with historical roots dating back to the 1700s. Several of these houses are architectural gems. To date, 26 houses have been completely rebuilt and restored.

Houses of varying size, originally erected in different parts of the town, have been brought together in Gamle Bergen to create a new sub-town. The Museum also contains ten buildings that originally stood on the grounds, along with horse stalls, pavilions and a park with an idyllic duck pond. Development has taken place gradually, keeping up with the rate of demolition which now appears to be at a standstill.

Ideally, it would be best to allow the old buildings to remain in their original environment. Several valuable houses have now been put into storage awaiting necessary funding for reconstruction. Many of these are boat-houses that in time will be used to portray the maritime history of the area when ships were built at Elsesro.

A very real and complete town

Today the mini-town resembles a very real and complete town. Visitors are given a living image of the exterior and interior architecture of earlier times, along with the way of life in the city between the seven mountains. Visitors to Gamle Bergen can gather in the market square, stroll along the main street, take a short cut through a back street or enjoy the view from the cloned "Fjellveien" (Mountain Road). A few lucky visitors might even chance upon Gamle Bergens's cheerful mayor, the forever young actor Rolf ▸ Berntzen, in official dress.

In the smaller "museums" one is given a living example of how traditional craftsmanship was carried out in the so-called good old days of our grandparents, great grandparents or great-great grandparents. Here are the cobbler, barber, captain, rope maker, printer, baker and of course an umbrella maker. Each craftsman or tradesman can be found in his own house or shop. The baker can even offer freshly baked cinnamon buns. Fine ladies, children with their dolls and toys, sailors and civil servants complete the picture of an histo-

Old house in an old setting.

▲
*Activity on the mar-
ketplace of Gamle
Bergen.*

ric town. There are also as many as three banquet and party halls which will give an idea of
what the society and festive life was like in
Bergen for the well-to-do around 200 years
ago. Schools and chapels are here as well. Solheimsviken chapel, reconstructed by the Bergen Missionary Society in 1881, emerged to
become the auditorium called Torvsalen. From
Torvsalen's stage, the visitor is presented with
Bergen entertainment in the form of music
and song, drama, literature, games and dance.

Gamle Bergen was opened to the public in
1949. The prelude took place in 1934, when
the Museum Association (open to the general
public) was established by a group of visionary
cultural historians led by architect Kristian
Bjerknes. He led the planning and administration of the museum until 1971.

**Opened to the
public in 1949**

Today the museum has become a popular
place to take the whole family. Food is served
in the restaurant, Tracteurstedet, and during
the summer season, especially on days with
activities in the old houses, there is regular
entertainment from the open-air theatres and
from other places in the old museum town.

See also ▶ Elsesro.

G

The logo of the Grieg Academy based on the Grieg monument by Gunnar Torvund.

■ THE GRIEG ACADEMY

At the University of Bergen, a separate institute of music known as the Grieg Academy was established in 1995. The institute, which came about through collaboration between the university and the college, offers a higher academic degree in the fields of music education, music studies and music performance.

The academy merged with the Bergen Music Conservatory (Lars Hilles gt. 3). Today this constitutes the Academy's department of voice and instrumental studies, and has been given two professorial positions. The Academy tries to build a bridge between music analysis and intuitive music performance.

The first professor to be appointed was Jan-Petter Blom, who had the study of folk music as his subject area. Close cooperation in this field has been established with the Ole Bull Academy at Voss.

Concerts

Concerts are an important and natural part of the Grieg Academy. Most concerts are held in the Academy's own hall, Gunnar Sævigs Sal, Grieghallen's nearest neighbour.

The earliest forerunner of the Grieg Academy was the music department at Harmonien's academy for the fine arts, established as early as 1775. This school was actually Norway's first music academy. In 1814 Bergen received a "singing school for both men and women between the ages of 10 and 20 years". During the 1850s F.W. Vogel's Organ School was established and given 600 kroner in annual state funding.

Borghild Holmsen *was Harald Sæverud's teacher of piano and theory of harmony at the Bergen Music Conservatory. Sæverud dedicated his opus 1, "Five capricci for piano", to her.*

Bergen's Music Association challenged Harmonien in 1898, by starting its own music school with room for 300 students. The school existed until 1905 when Harmonien's concertmaster, Torgrim Castberg, supported by Edvard Grieg, founded Bergen's Music Academy. Violinist Arve Arvesen took over the Academy in 1928 and changed its name to the Bergen Music Conservatory. The institution was run by Gunnar ▶ Sævig, Ernst Glaser, Rolf Davidsson and Kari Johnsen. Its administration was divided between a conservatory department which offered a professional music education, and a music school for children and amateurs. The administration of the music school for children was taken over by the municipality in 1974, while the conservatory became known as the Grieg Academy.

■ **EDVARD GRIEG**

Composer, conductor and pianist Edvard Hagerup Grieg (1843–1907) is probably the Norwegian the rest of the world is most familiar with.

The most famous Norwegian

Grieg's family on his mother's side came originally from Denmark. On his father's side, he had Scottish roots. His hometown has honoured him in a number of ways. As many as six monuments have been erected in Grieg's memory – among them, two at Troldhaugen. The others stand in Byparken, outside Johanneskirken (St. John's Church), by the entrance to Grieghallen, and outside the administrative

Ingebrigt Vik's Grieg statue in Byparken was erected in 1917 on the initiative of Conrad Mohr.

◀

Nina Grieg was also honoured by this Grieg monument made by Gunnar Torvund for the University of Bergen. Her profile stands out as a rhythmic relief pattern around the sculpted figure of her famous husband. The monument is placed north of Johanneskirken and was unveiled in 1995 on the 150th anniversary of her birth .

The bust of Edvard Grieg, made by Gunnar Torvund and unveiled in 1993, stands outside Kulturhuset USF.

building of cultural activities at Verftet. His name can be found on a street in Solheimsviken and on the square outside Grieghallen. The concert house and the music academy also bear his name. Bergen International Festival was established in Grieg's honour in 1953.

The composer's home, Troldhaugen, has been converted into a museum and contains its own concert hall. The composer's studio, where many an elegant melody made its way onto music sheets, stands down by the shore. The final resting-places of Edvard and Nina Grieg are also found at Troldhaugen, carved into the cliffs, as they themselves wished.

On Strandgaten 152 stands the boyhood home of Edvard Grieg. The house where he grew up and composed his first notes was unfortunately ruined in an explosion in 1944. A new house was constructed in its place in 1993, complete with a memorial plaque and a new number, 208.

In November 1906, ten months before his death, Edvard Grieg bequeathed his letters and music sheets to the Bergen Public Library. At the same time, he left all his money to the music company Harmonien by the establishment of a fund. One of the conditions of the fund was that "Harmonien must always endure". The proceeds from the Grieg fund have been large enough to pay the wages of as many as six musicians.

From the time Grieg was ten years old, his family spent their summers at Landås. Here Ole Bull discovered the 15-year-old's great musical talents during a visit in 1858. This became the start of Grieg's brilliant career. Following Bull's advice, Grieg began his studies that very same autumn at the conservatory in Leipzig. Four years later he passed his exams with flying colours.

Grieg made his debut in his hometown as a pianist and composer in 1862. As a mature and famous artist 18 years later, he took the position of conductor for the orchestra of the Music Association Harmonien for two seasons, from 1880 to 1882. An ambitious man, he embarked on major projects, such as Mendels-

sohn's oratorio "Elijah". Grieg demanded a great deal from his musicians, and his projects did not always proceed smoothly. It became a public scandal when some of the female choir singers preferred to attend a grand ball instead of the dress rehearsal for Händel's "Coronation Anthem". Grieg gave them their walking papers.

To his great indignation, Grieg had his request to complete his concert season with Mozart's "Requiem" in Nykirken in the spring of 1881 rejected. The reason given for the rejection was that the musical work was a Catholic Mass. The concert had to be held in a less suitable location, the Labour Party's meeting hall, later known as the cinema ▶ Eldorado.

On his 60th birthday, Grieg paid tribute to

▲
Conductor Dmitri Kitajenko is a great admirer of Edvard Grieg. Here is a warm meeting between the two at Troldhaugen, outside Troldsalen. The statue is a full-sized copy of Ingebrigt Vik's statue in Byparken. The monument was funded by Arild Haaland.

The first Music
Festival in Norway
was arranged in
Bergen in 1898 on
the initiative of Ed-
vard Grieg. There
was a great deal of
opposition when
Grieg invited the
Amsterdam Concert-
gebouw Orchestra
to play at the fest-
ival. The purpose
was to have Nor-
wegian music per-
formed by a fully
professional orches-
tra. This picture was
on the front of the
music festival's pro-
gram.

▶

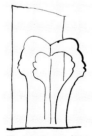

Gunnar Torvund's
sculptures give a
multi-faceted picture
of Grieg, and allow
the viewer a sense
of his music. Here
is a sketch for the
monument at Trold-
haugen.

the city of Bergen with the following speech:

"It is not just the art and science of Bergen I have been nourished with; it is not just Holberg, Welhaven, Ole Bull I have learned from. Not just Armauer Hansen, whose leprosy bacillus I have carefully studied. No, the entire environment of Bergen, which surrounds me, has been my material. The nature of Bergen, the people of Bergen, the deeds and initiative of the Bergen spirit have inspired me…The smell of the German Wharf delights me – yes, I firmly believe there is both cod and coalfish in my music."

In 1867 Grieg married his cousin, singer Nina Hagerup, who became the subject of many of his songs. After many years of rootless existence, the couple finally, in 1885, moved into their own home about 10 kilometres

G

south of downtown Bergen. From that point onward, Troldhaugen became Grieg's most important 'workshop'. Summers were spent there, but when autumn arrived the couple followed the migrating birds to warmer climes. Copenhagen and Leipzig became important bases during an extensive touring of the music metropolises of Europe.

Grieg had his international breakthrough as a composer in 1868 with his piano concerto in A-minor. His many lyrical pieces for the piano became classic favourites. With his music for "Peer Gynt" – composed in Bergen (1873 –74) – Grieg opened the door for the introduction of Ibsen's drama to the theatres of Europe. Grieg was one of the most celebrated composers of his time and a model for many colleagues.

With his roots in Norwegian folk music, Grieg formed and refined a genuine Norwegian musical language. His fellow Norwegians were given a musical identity, and Norway gained respect as a cultural nation. With compositions such as "Klokkeklang" (Bell Chimes), op. 56, nr. 6, Grieg became one of the first musical impressionists.

Grieg was an elegant writer as well. As a special correspondent for the newspaper "Bergensposten", in Bayreuth, he attended the first complete performance of Wagner's "Der Ring des Nibelungen" in 1876. Grieg wrote seven long articles describing the event.

See also, ▶ Troldhaugen, ▶ Landås Manor, ▶ Musikkbiblioteket and ▶ Elsesro.

"With his eyes closed and his mind open, ready to allow the notes to speak." This is how Edvard Grieg meets concert audiences outside the entrance to Grieghallen. Hopefully the audience will do the same when they enter the hall. The bust, entitled "The Listener", was sculpted by Asbjørn Høglund. His design won the competition for the Grieg anniversary in 1993.

■ "JOHN GRIEG"

The Siamese twin companies John Grieg Publishers and John Grieg Inc. celebrated their 275-year anniversary in 1996 respectively as Norway's oldest publishing company and the country's next oldest printing press. Despite changes in ownership and names, the combined business has been run without interruption since 1721.

Norway's oldest publishing company

Three Grieg generations

Georg Herman Grieg (1826-1910) started the Grieg family's tradition of printing and publishing in 1871. He also worked as a music teacher and was an eager advocate for the New Norwegian language.

John Grieg (1856-1905) bought the firm from his uncle in 1881 and gave it his name.

Alf Grieg (1885-1917) began the publication of the periodical "Art and Culture".

In 1989 publishing and production were split into two independent companies. The publishing house moved to a new building in Våkleiva, while the printing press still carries on in Vaskerelven 8, where they have been since the 1916 Bergen fire. Both companies have, however, retained the name of printer John Grieg (1856–1905).

The company was founded by the Danish typographer Peter Povelsen Nørvig. The enterprising Dane also became Norway's first newspaper publisher. One of the first products from the newly established press was the weekly paper "Ridende Mercurius" (Riding Mercury). After one year, the newspaper was stopped, accused of stealing material from the Copenhagen newspaper "Danske Relationer". The fact that the Danish newspaper 'stole' from the German papers did not change matters. Nor did the fact that Nørvig promised "to print, for the benefit of the inhabitants, information about all ships arriving and departing from Bergen, in addition to where they go and come from".

When the newspaper project had to be abandoned, Nørvig soon found other options. In 1723 he was granted a royal license to open the first bookstore in Bergen. The very same year he printed his first book, a folio of one hundred pages containing rather sombre subject matter: A "Ligpredigen" (Requiem). Among the first books were also "Katekismussangene" (Songs from the Catechism) by Petter Dass, and in 1741 came Ludvig Holberg's autobiography "Lifs og Lefnets Beskrivelse" (Description of my Life).

The company has been owned and run by three generations of the Grieg family. The first, Georg Herman Grieg, cousin of the composer's father, was both musician and writer, in addition to his work on the promotion of the New Norwegian language. He developed the old printing shop into a modern company. He was the first in Norway to procure a Linotype typesetting machine and could print illustrations on the company's own cliché plate. Among the company's publications were sev-

G

eral classic volumes, translated by Grieg into New Norwegian. Included were Luther's "Catechism" and John Bunyan's "Crusade".

In 1882 Georg Herman Grieg relinquished the company, including the city's leading newspaper, "Bergensposten", to his 22-year-old nephew, John Grieg.

Like his uncle, John Grieg was alert and interested in anything new, and was never afraid of experimentation. He bravely published the first works of poets like Vilhelm Krag and Sigbjørn Obstfelder. He also published quality magazines like "Naturen" (Nature) and "Samtiden" (Modern Times), in addition to a number of scholarly works, such as a piece on Dr. Armauer Hansen of Bergen.

His son, Alf Grieg, carried on the company's cultural traditions with the introduction of the periodical "Kunst og Kultur" (Art and Culture) with Harry Fett and Haakon Shetelig as editors. Most of the publications printed by Grieg were published by the company itself, such as the great standard work about Norwegian folk culture, "Det norske folks liv og historie gjennom tidene" (The Life and History of the Norwegian People throughout the Ages).

In addition to "Bergensposten", the company published newspapers like "Bergens Adressecontoirs Efterretning" and Claus ▶ Fasting's "Provinzialblade".

See also Hans Nielsen ▶ Hauge.

Here is the title page of the first book to be published in Bergen, a funeral sermon for Maria Elizabeth Tuchsen. She died in childbirth. The sermon was given by Povel Hansen Resen.

◼ NORDAHL GRIEG

The poet, dramatist and journalist Johan Nordahl Brun Grieg (1902 – 43) spent his childhood years at Møhlenpris. His family lived on Welhaven's Street 23 (today number 58), but moved to Hop in 1911, to the address now known as Nordahl Griegs veg 11. A memorial plaque marks each of his childhood homes. In 1957 a bronze statue of the poet, sculpted by Roar Bjorg, was erected near the entrance of Den Nationale Scene.

A national hero and a symbol

More than a portrait

The Nordahl Grieg statue in Teaterpar-ken was unveiled in 1957, and was created by Roar Bjorg. Professor Francis Bull wrote of the monument:
"The statue is not just a portrait but also an illustration of what he stands for in our literature and history: spirit and youth, enthusi-asm and sacrifice, idealism and activity."

▶

G

Nordahl Grieg became both national hero and symbol when he died in battle for his country. He was killed during a bombing raid on Berlin in 1943. On his first mission during the war, he assisted in the transport of gold from the Bank of Norway to England. His most important weapon, however, was his pen. His familiar and welcome voice with the distinctive Bergen dialect could be heard over the radio from London. As a reporter he followed the war at close hand, both at sea and in the air, and also in flights over Norway. Grieg showed the best of his poetic talent in many of his war poems.

Killed in bombing raid on Berlin

Nordahl Grieg displayed his journalistic talent in the newspapers "Tidens Tegn" (Sign of the Times) and "Oslo Aftenavis" (The Oslo Evening News). In his articles of high literary quality, he reported from unstable areas of the world, such as China, Russia and civil war torn Spain. Because of his political radicalism and communist sympathies, Grieg was excluded from the newspaper columns during the 1930s. He published instead his own periodical, "Veien Frem" (The Road Ahead). He warned early on against Nazism with a clarity of vision unfortunately lacking in most politicians. His analysis of Quisling would prove to be eerily prophetic.

Warned early on against Nazism

Strong action-filled, exciting plays with clear messages were the trademark of dramatist Nordahl Grieg. In several of the plays, he is the bold and fearless symbol of the working class struggle against cynical employers. The first performance in 1935 of "Vår ære og vår makt" (Our honour and our power) at Den Nationale Scene was dramatic both on and off stage. The play was set in Bergen and dealt with a shipowner's desire for profit at the cost of the crew's safety during World War 1. An attempt was made to stop the performance. Many of the members of the theatre's board of directors had ties to the shipping industry (among them were two shipowners) and conflict seemed unavoidable. Theatre director Hans Jacob Nilsen threatened to resign if the play could not be performed. The outcome was

Drama both on and off stage

determined, however, when Prime Minister Johan Ludvig Mowinckel became involved in the conflict. Although Mowinckel was himself a shipowner, he sided with Grieg, admitting ashamedly that the play's criticism of the shipping industry was entirely justified.

Great victory

The play was staged in Bergen in close collaboration between writer and theatre manager, resulting in a great victory for them both, with 60 full houses and a new record. "Vår ære og vår makt" was originally planned as a film project, but Nilsen talked Grieg into writing it for the stage instead. Most of the play was written at the Rosenkrantz Hotel near Bryggen. Grieg wanted to be living as close as possible to the scenes he worked on. When he was going to write the scenes about a hostel, he moved into a hostel owned by the Salvation Army in Bakkegaten.

"Romance of the century"

Grieg met actress Gerd Egede-Nissen for the first time in theatre-manager Hans Jacob Nilsen's house, on New Year's Day 1935. She was a guest at Den Nationale Scene in the roles of Hedda Gabler and Mary Stewart. The relationship between the poet and the actress grew more serious until it became known in Bergen as "the great romance of the century". The two married in 1940.

To Bergen for rest

Nordahl Grieg travelled almost continuously throughout his life. He usually came to Bergen only when he needed to rest. Attempts to tie him to the theatre with a permanent position were in vain. Throughout his life he stayed in close contact with his family through letters, particularly with his parents and his older brother, publisher Harald Grieg.

Cantata

Grieg wrote a cantata set to music by Sverre ▶ Jordan, for the great Bergen Exhibition in 1928. It finishes with the well-known poem "La Norge fylde vårt hjerte!" (Let Norway fill our hearts!).

Wanted to be a poet

Grieg displayed poetic talent during his school days at Bergen Cathedral school, where the school newspaper "Hugin" became his first literary forum. When the Norwegian teacher asked the students what they wanted to be, Nordahl answered right away: "Poet!"

G

Foto: TRYGVE SCHØNFELDER

■ GRIEGHALLEN

Grieghallen (the Grieg Hall) is Bergen's largest cultural auditorium. When it was finished in 1978, it replaced Konsertpaleet as Harmonien's concert house and main arena for the International Festival. Grieghallen has had an almost inexhaustible diversity of uses, including that of ice dancing. Everything from pigs to elephants has been able to move safely around on the large and flexible stage.

From March 1996 Grieghallen has also been utilised as a modern convention hall, with conference rooms spread out over 4,523 square metres.

Today Grieghallen has a capacity of 6000 people. There is also room for a music department – a branch of the Bergen Public Library – in addition to the Grieg Collection. (See ▶ Musikkbiblioteket – Music Library). This has been made possible through the reconstruction of the areas originally rented out for various business purposes.

Centre for culture and trade

Grieghallen's logo

G

▲

A marathon concert lasting for ten hours was part of the great event when Grieghallen was officially inaugurated during the Bergen festival in 1978. The first orchestra to make music in the new hall was Bønes School Orchestra, which is here seen entering the stage together with their conductor Hans Jacob Netland.

Important facts about Grieghallen:

The cultural
- Drawn by the Danish architect Knud Munk for an architectural competition in 1965.
- Administration wing in use from 1971
- Concert house opened in 1978 by H.R.H. King Olav
- Capacity: 1504 seats
- Maximum stage area: Approx. 1000 square metres
- Two large audience foyers, altogether 2,200 square metres
- Houses the administrations of the Harmonien Foundation and of Grieghallen
- 21 rehearsal rooms for the Bergen Philharmonic Orchestra
- Studio and control rooms for radio and television

Convention and conference
- Reconstruction starts 1994. Opens March 1996.
- Head architect: Grieg Architect Office
- Convention hall area: 4,523 square metres
- Peer Gynt Hall used as meeting rooms for approx. 900 people. Can, with the help of a mobile amphitheatre be converted into a concert hall with room for an audience of 750 people. An additional 12 smaller and larger meeting rooms.
- Grieghallen has a total capacity of 6000 people.

G

■ HARMONIEN

The history of the music company Harmonien dates back to 1765. The modest amateur ensemble established that year has grown over the years to a full size symphony orchestra with 97 permanently employed musicians. Harmonien stands proudly as one of the oldest orchestral companies still in operation in the world today. During the early days of Harmonien, the company had the opportunity to introduce Joseph Haydn to Bergen at their weekly concerts. This was at a time when the great master was still at his peak and Mozart had only reached the child prodigy stage.

National orchestra – one of the oldest in the world

The official name since 1987 is the Bergen Philharmonic Orchestra and Choir. From 1996 the Bergen Philharmonic has had national orchestra status with the Foundation Harmonien as its operating company, and the former musical society in a new role as a funding association. People in Bergen still refer to the orchestra as Harmonien.

The choir was formally established in 1857 with August Rohjan as its first director. The choir was given a renewed vitality when Ingolf ▶ Schjøtt took over as director in 1917. Well-known choir directors in later years include cantor Magnar Mangersnes and opera director Anne Randine Øverby.

Harald Heide
was the conductor of Harmonien for 40 years, from 1907 to 1947. He brought the orchestra up to a professional level.

The Bergen Philharmonic has since 1978 made its home in Grieghallen, where it holds one or two concerts each week, usually on Thursdays and Fridays, when in season. Both classical and modern music appear on the program. The Bergen Philharmonic has served as a foundation for the Bergen International

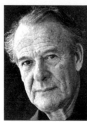

Karsten Andersen
was the artistic direc-
tor of Harmonien for
21 seasons, from
1964 to 1985. In
1995 he became
the orchestra's first
honorary conductor.

Great soloists
and conductors

Harmonien gives an
outdoor concert in
Nygårdsparken.
Soloist is the Bergen
tenor Bjarne Buntz.
Conductor: Øivind
Bergh.

Festival since the very beginning. For several years musicians have also given regular orchestra service at Den Nationale Scene. In addition to Harmonien's own concerts, its musicians contribute to the musical life of the city in many other ways, as performers, conductors, instructors and teachers.

The musical company Harmonien was established by the principal of the Bergen Cathedral School, Jens Boalth. His idea was for the company to become an academy for the fine arts with an orchestra, music school, art school and theatre, but as time passed, music took over as the main pursuit. The first orchestra leader was Samuel Lind. Niels Haslund, Edvard Grieg's great grandfather, took over the position in 1770. Haslund was the first to receive the Society's gold medallion of honour, when he left the position after 15 years.

The orchestra has later been directed by such noteworthy talents as Edvard Grieg, Iver Holter, Johan Halvorsen, Harald Heide, Olav Kielland, Carl von Garaguly, Arvid Fladmoe, Karsten Andersen, Aldo Ceccato and Dmitri Kitajenko. From autumn 1999 the orchestra will be headed by Simone Young. The list of guest conductors and soloists includes a number of distinguished international names – such as Arthur Rubinstein, Leopold Stokowski, Sir Thomas Beecham, Itzhak Perlman, Yehudi Menuhin and Wilhelm Kempff.

Two individuals have been of particularly great importance for the orchestra: Edvard Grieg, both as a conductor and especially by his generous testamentary gift to Harmonien, and Harald Heide, who was responsible for the development of a fully modern, profession-al symphony orchestra. The orchestra was not able to hire musicians for permanent positions until 1919. Heide made his debut as conductor for Harmonien at a memorial concert for Edvard Grieg in 1907. He became the authoritative artistic leader of the orchestra until 1947.

Karsten Andersen was appointed honorary conductor of the Bergen Philharmonic Orchestra after 21 seasons as the artistic leader.

H

The orchestra made its first international visit to Copenhagen in 1962. Arvid Fladmoe was conductor at the time. The Bergen Philharmonic can today look back on a long series of successful national and international tours. The orchestra has travelled through 20 different countries, including the USA, the Soviet Union and Japan.

The list of merits also includes recordings and first time performances, principally of works by Norwegian composers.

▲
Dmitri Kitajenko and orchestra leader Valdis Zarin take their bows following a concert in Valencia during the Spanish tour of 1995.

■ HANS NIELSEN HAUGE

The religious figure Hans Nielsen Haugen (1771–1824) from Rolfsøy in Tune is honoured by a street name in Sandviken and by a portrait relief on the western wall of ▶ Korskirken (Church of the Cross).

Most Norwegians know Hauge as the father of the layman movement, public educator and preacher, who broke the church's monopoly on Christian ministry and was forced to pay dearly for this with several long prison sentences. In Bergen, Hauge was also known for his work as a businessowner, merchant and shipowner. His closest assistants were cooper master Johan Loose and Samson Torbjørnsen

Evangelist and businessman

H

▲
Relief of Hans Nielsen Hauge placed on the western wall of Korskirken in 1971. The portrait was made by Sofus Madsen and donated by the Association of Church History (Kyrkjesogelaget).

Bishop Brun positive

Traae. They took care of the business while Hauge travelled around the country selling fish, grain and above all the Christian gospel.

In 1801 Hauge received citizenship papers as a merchant in Bergen. He saw this as God's will. He received the papers on the condition that he would be able to "secure a house and hearth". Loose took care of this by turning over his property in Klingesmuget above Øvregaten to Hauge. As a house owner, Hauge was given the right to a reserved place in Korskirken, under the pulpit of Johan Nordahl ▶ Brun.

Direct cooperation between the high clergy and the layman was unthinkable. However, the increasing "evil" of the times – rationalism and free thought – was their common enemy, and thanks to the positive attitude of the bishop, Hauge did not meet any hindrances to his religious work in Bergen. Brun even appealed to the chief of police to stop street kids from

H

disturbing Hauge's religious services or throwing stones at him on the street.

When Hauge first arrived in Bergen in 1798, his intention was to have his manuscripts printed and published. He was a productive writer, and for a while more widely read than anyone else. Hauge was able to have some of his work printed in Rasmus Dahl's publishing company (today known as John ▶ Grieg A/S).

Productive writer

In Klingensmuget he started his own bookbinding workshop. The bookbinding guild protested, however, since Hauge lacked the royal bookbinding certificate and his business was closed down.

Book binding

His other businesses succeeded far better. Hauge was able to purchase the large business property Valsengården at Nordnes in 1802. He moved to the property himself together with several of his assistants. The whole city was now talking about this remarkable man – a combination of apostle, charismatic speaker and businessman.

Good business

During the three years in which Hauge ran his affairs in Bergen, he completed two business trips to northern Norway. In 1804 he sailed with a fleet of four ships as far north as Målselv and Tromsø, carrying a cargo of grain. He suffered however, a painful financial loss in Bergen. He was tricked into buying a useless frigate while trying to secure a vessel in order to trade overseas. This mistake contributed to his departure from Bergen for good just a short time later.

Business trips

Composer Egil Hovland's opera "Fange og fri" (Prisoner and Free Man) is based on central episodes of Hans Nielsen Hauge's life. The opera premiered in Johanneskirken (St. John's Church) during the Bergen International Festival in 1995.

Hauge opera

◼ AUDUN HETLAND

He made it his life's work as an artist to make people laugh – even when the underlying message was a serious one. The smile was given a greater force than the verbal sledgehammer. He gave Bergen its identity

Gave Bergen its identity as a city of humour

I disse krisetider får vi være glad vi har juletre! Godt år - hilsen Kiss + (Audun)

Friends of Audun and Kirsten Hetland received this humorous Christmas card in 1988. Kirsten Hetland was an important inspiration to her husband, and she artistically stood on her own two feet – as a fashion designer, decorator and dazzlingly beautiful model. Kirsten Hetland is also known for her unique dollhouses.

as a happy city. Hence there were many people who mourned when illustrator Audun Hetland (1920–98) laid down his smiling pen for good in January 1998. It was the first time the wildly popular artist did not evoke tears of laughter, but of sorrow.

His memorial was not a modest one. "I can without a doubt say that Audun Hetland is one of the greatest Bergen artists of our century", said writer Gunnar Staalesen.

Hetland will live forever through the countless works of art he left behind, which hopefully will soon have their own museum. Several of his most significant pieces are housed in a separate wing of the Fjøsanger Collection. He is also represented in the National Gallery of Oslo and the Bergen Art Gallery.

Hetland made a name for himself early on

as a newspaper cartoonist. He was later very much in demand as a book illustrator. Jon Leirfall, Herbjørn Sørebø and Gunnar Staalesen were his inspiring collaborators. Hetland has also done decorative works both in and outside of Norway. His career had a difficult start. Hetland did not pass the entrance exams for Bergen Kunsthåndverksskole (Bergen Art School), but had to resign himself to short courses in free hand drawing and sketching. He was later able to gain a higher education through studies in other countries.

Hetland was first employed in 1936 at the Bergen Advertisement Bureau. He made his debut as a newspaper cartoonist in "Bergens Aftenblad" (Bergen Evening News) where he was employed from 1940 until the newspaper was stopped in 1942. After the war he was able to present himself to a larger audience. As a freelance artist, he worked for "Morgenavisen" (The Morning News), "Bergens Tidende" (The Bergen Times), "Aftenposten", "Bergensavisen" and "A-pressen". Incomparable commentary cartoons in "Bergens Tidende" contributed not least to his popularity and art-istic reputation in his hometown.

Both the top brass in Bergen and the town eccentrics were regular targets of Hetland's baroque sense of humour. Harald Sæverud was portrayed as a horse in the newspaper, actor Claes Gill appeared as a head on a Hardanger fiddle. His caricatures displayed a sharp eye for revealing details. His prolific lines could be daring, at times erotic, but never vicious.

One of his masterpieces is the Bergen poster for the city's 900-year anniversary. Here he collected almost every important figure from Bergen on one sheet of drawing paper. In his studio at Bryggen the folklorist Hetland dissected the life and soul of the typical Bergensian, and he did it with a smile. Altogether his life work composes a fantastic Bergen-mosaic where all the characteristics and many-faceted gallery of individuals of the city are joyously included. Hetland published seven books of drawings in all.

Harald Sæverud as a Norwegian pony – the best portrait I've ever done, said Audun Hetland. He feared an anathema but was instead invited to supper along with his wife.

Sharp eye for revealing details

The Danish polar researcher Peter Frøychen has arrived in Bergen by boat from America. Hetland greets him with his sketching pad.

◼ LUDVIG HOLBERG

Multi-talented Bergen man

Bergen's greatest Holberg treasure is this portrait medallion, according to former head librarian Hallvard S. Bakken. The medallion is kept in the Historical Museum. It was made by an unknown sculptor a few years before the poet's death.

Youngest of 12 children

Holbergsallmenningen and Holbergskaien at Nordnes are both named after the multi-talented Bergensian, Ludvig Holberg (1684 –1754) – comic writer, historian and philosopher. A bronze statue of Holberg, made by the Swede Johan Börjeson was unveiled at Vågsallmenning, near the Fish Market, in 1884. The theatre paid tribute to him with a sculpture, created by Matias Skeibrok. A memorial plaque with Holberg's portrait near the entrance to Mareminehullet at Rothaugen was unveiled in 1984. This was where Holberg's character, Niels Klim, supposedly started his underground journey to a utopic world where dreams could come true.

Holberg's birthplace in Strandgaten 190 was destroyed in a fire in 1686. The remains of the walls, the so-called Holbergkjelleren (Holberg cellar), were removed to make way for the Comfort Holberg Hotel in 1985. Two large memorial reliefs in bronze by Leon Roald were set up on the western wall of the hotel in 1995. The hotel also has a small portrait relief near the main entrance.

The writing of Ludvig Holberg is perhaps Norway's greatest literary legacy from the Danish era. He was also an important public educator. At the University of Copenhagen he became a professor in three different subjects – metaphysics, Latin and history. For a while he was Dean of the University and head of financial matters. In addition to this he enjoyed music, was a virtuoso on the flute, and played the violin and the viola.

Ludvig Holberg was the youngest of 12 children. His father, an officer and at one time a commander at Bergenhus, died when Ludvig was only one year old. When he was eleven, his mother died as well, and the family fell apart. Ludvig was first sent to his mother's cousin who was a vicar in Fron in Gudbrandsdalen. Here he stayed for two years, where-upon he returned to Bergen. His uncle, merchant Peder Lem, became Ludvig's foster parent. He made sure that his nephew received a good educati-

Holberg on the people of Bergen

"An inhabitant of Bergen is a horse where work is concerned, and a buffalo where manners are concerned. He feels like an accountant, marries like an adding machine and lives like an eight day clock. He is practical and logical, consults his general sense of balance before he takes a serious step."

"The people of Bergen are a cross of all kinds of nations; you can see in their ways of speaking, their habits and dress that they are different from other Norwegians."

Edvard Grieg had written a cantata for the occasion when Johan Börjeson's statue of Holberg – portrayed as a baron with a three-cornered hat – was unveiled in 1884 at Vågsallmenningen. The base of the statue was sculptured by Hans J. Johannesen from stone brought from Samnanger.

◀

H

Two memorial plaques by Leon Roald mark the birthplace of Ludvig Holberg on Strandgaten 190.

The opera entitled "Jeppe" was based on Holberg's comedy, with music by Geirr Tveitt. It had its premiere during the International Festival of Bergen in 1966. The composer is here sketched as a baron, by Sverre Bø from "Bergens Tidende".

on, first at a German school and then at the Bergen Cathedral School. When the school burned down during the fire of 1702, Holberg had to go to Copenhagen to complete his exams. In the autumn of the same year, he enrolled at the University of Copenhagen.

Around the time Ludvig turned 18, he was struck by another hard blow. His uncle, who was also his closest friend, died. Suddenly he was completely on his own. His ties to Bergen were now no longer as strong.

Holberg finished his university degree in theology and philosophy in record time. He then worked for a short time as a private tutor and clerical assistant to Dean Weinwich in Voss. The congregation enjoyed the young assistant's sermons, possibly because they were unusually short. The vicar's wife however did not approve of the tutor's strict teaching methods and fired him after only one year. This did not discourage Holberg. In Bergen he secured a position as a private tutor to Assistant Bishop Niels Smed, and was this time more successful at his work.

After a short stay in Kristiansand during the winter of 1705–06, Holberg left the country again, this time never to return to Norwegian soil. Traces of Holberg's experiences and impressions from Bergen can be found in his writing. Both Henrik and Pernille, characters from his books, are undoubtedly related to the urchins of Bergen. The hero of one of Holberg's novels, Niels Klim, is the parish clerk and a bookstore owner in Bergen.

With "Bergens Beskrivelse" (Description of Bergen) from 1737, Holberg has given the city where he was born, "my rightful fatherland", an historical monument that is both grand and enjoyable. Both here, in his first personal letters written in Latin and in many of his epistles, he describes several humorous memories from his childhood years in Bergen. His stories give an idea of how his apprecia-tion of comic situations arose already at a young age. "My innocent pen, it writes to laugh", declared Holberg. His sense of humour shone not only through his comedies, but also his other works. Those who were the target of the master of satire were probably not laugh-ing. Holberg's satire was especially aimed at all forms of arrogance and vanity, both in religious and social situations.

Holberg wrote more than 30 comedies. One of the most popular ones, "Jeppe paa Bierget" (Jeppe on the Hill), was made into an opera by Geirr Tveitt. It had its premier during the Bergen International Festival in 1966.

Holberg opera

Ludvig Holberg donated his fortune to the Sorø Academy. In return, the title of baron was bestowed upon him in 1744.

Baron

Mareminehullet
(the Marimine Hole) is a crack in the north mountainside of Rotthaugen, where Ludvig Holberg had Niels Klim start his underground journey. The crack leads through a narrow passageway into a cave. A memorial plaque, designed by Sofus Madsen and made by Tor Myklebust, was hung over the entrance to the cave in 1984. The pathway leads to the site from Ladegårdsterrassen.

◀

"Ludvig Holberg was a Bergensian by birth, but a citizen of the Spiritual Kingdom".

Johannes V. Jensen

Ambrosia Tønnesen

**Norway's first
female sculptor**
The home of Norway's first professional female sculptor, Ambrosia Tønnesen
(1859–1948) was moved to the Hordamuseet in 1992 from Fjøsangerveien 19, Runeplassen, because of a road expansion. Tønnesen was born in Ålesund, but lived and worked in Bergen most of her life. Both Edvard Grieg and Christian Michelsen sat for her. She also created the monuments of J.C. Dahl (over the entrance of Permanenten) and Ole Bull (DNS), and busts of Amalie Skram and Claus Fasting, in and outside the Bergen Public Library, respectively.

The "Ambrosia house" was built in the late 1800s, and was purchased by Ambrosia Tønnesen in 1911. After several changes throughout the years the house in the Hordamuseet is an elegant suburban

■ HORDAMUSEET

For those who are interested in how people in the past lived their lives in the rural areas around Bergen, the Hordamuseet at Stend will be able to provide some answers. The museum was originally known as Hordaland Agricultural Museum and displays a wide variety of cultures and everyday lives in the northern and middle districts of Hordaland. Mobile exhibitions also make room for art and art expression from our own time.

The history of Norwegian road development from 1880 to 1940 presented by the State Highways Office in Hordland has a separate exhibition wing. The plan is to move an old ferry dock to the museum area in Bjorvika at the head of the Fana fjord, making it possible to dock the showboat "Innvik". Connected to the road museum is also an outdoor traffic education area for children, with streets, roundabouts and electric cars.

The home of Hordaland Theatre is in the Hordamuseet. When the stage is available, the theatre is used for lectures, films and other cultural activities. See ▶ Theatre in Bergen.

The Hordamuseet is the only Norwegian museum, apart from Maihaugen in Lillehammer, with its own rural mountain village. The village includes ten mountain huts, originally used for dairy farming, located in a splendid area in the Fana Mountains, just a half-hour drive from downtown Bergen. A medieval church stands at the foot of the mountain on the way to the museum. From the highest hut it is possible to see all the way to Folgefonna

◄ *Tapestries*
*In addition to build-
ings and their con-
tents, boats and fish-
ing gear, handicrafts
and objects associ-
ated with agricultu-
re, the museum has
a unique collection
of tapestries, woven
by Ragna Breivik,
following the dra-
wings of Gerhard
Munthe.*

Glacier in Hardanger toward the east, while far out to the west is a glimpse of the ocean. In time the museum will hopefully be able to run an old-fashioned dairy farm in the village.

The historical-architectural department is laid out to resemble a western Norwegian landscape such as it looked during the years between 1850 and 1950. Up until now, 20 different buildings from various rural areas have been collected. They give an idea of the different building styles used in western Norway.

The Museum schoolhouse with its outhouse comes from Seim in Lindås. The property is composed of a set of seven buildings from different areas: two farm houses, a farmer's cottage, a sleeping attic, a stabbur (a shed standing on high pillars, used for food storage), a wood shed and a cooking house. The Museum also received a mill house from Samnanger. Near the water lies a general store and post office originating from Fusa, a fishing house with a history as a beach house by Paradisbukten near Hop, in addition to several boathouses and fishing gear. It is possible to meet a boat builder in the exhibition area of the museum building. A typical coastal farm is depicted with its coastal cottage, barn, stalls and forge.

Several historical landmarks have been excavated on museum property – a Stone Age settlement, the site of a longboat house (from approx. 70 BC) and two graves, one from the early Iron Age (400 AD) and a gravesite ring from the Age of the Migration (fourth to sixth centuries).

The Museum was founded in 1945 on the

*The first museum cur-
ator, Johannes Rev-
heim. He collected
objects for the mu-
seum during the
1930s. Revheim was
an agronomist and
had previously work-
ed as a policeman.*

The museum logo

H

Theatre

property of Stend Manor, with Johannes Revheim as its first director. The main building (by architect Einar Vaardal-Lunde) was built in 1977 and enlarged with the introduction of a theatre hall in 1998. The aim of the Museum is to collect, preserve and contribute to the knowledge of folklore, in addition to conducting research. The various buildings are furnished for public use, from baptism suppers to board meetings and exhibitions.

■ HÅKONSHALLEN

Norway ruled from Håkonshallen

During the 13th century, Bergen was Norway's largest and most important city. Håkonshallen (Håkon's Hall), the king's residence, was the very seat of power. It was from here the country was run.

King Magnus Lagabøter consecrated Håkonshallen with a wedding in 1261. This conventional portrait of the king stands in the chancel of Stavanger Domkirke.

When King Eirik Magnusson died in 1299, Bergen lost its status as the country's capital. His successor, his younger brother Håkon V Magnusson, had only just been hailed by the people of Bergen as the new king of Norway when he rode over the mountain to be crowned in Oslo, the new capital.

The solid stone walls of Håkonshallen have survived for centuries. Today it serves as a unique historical framework around the festivities and important cultural events in the district. Royal banquets continue to be held within its walls.

The architect and namesake of Håkonshallen was King Håkon IV Håkonsson (1217–63). The king had the castle built in a hurry, when his crowning in 1247 had to take place in a longship house by Holmen owing to the lack of a more suitable locality. It must have been embarrassing indeed for the king not to have a grander palace to offer his distinguished guests, including the papal representative, Cardinal Vilhelm of Sabina.

New royal stone castle

Fourteen years later, when everything was ready for the royal festivities in Bergen, the new royal stone castle was ready in all its splendour. It was called Breidastova and was

the largest secular building to be built in Norway. The castle was made of granite boulders and was three stories high, with certain details in soapstone. The banquet hall itself on the top floor measured 32.5 x 12.7 metres. The royal residence lay on the second floor, while the basement was used for supplies. The king's great building project included a smaller stone hall in addition to a surrounding wall and the strategically important ▶ Rosenkrantz Tower.

The inaugural celebration of Håkonshallen on September 11, 1261 was a grandiose event and included both a royal wedding and a crowning ceremony. The king's son, Magnus, who was later given the name Lagabøter, married the Danish princess Ingebjørg. At the same time, Magnus was crowned king and would rule together with his father.

Håkonshallen was the setting for yet another royal wedding 20 years later. In 1281 the Scottish princess Margareta married King Eirik Magnusson. For this occasion a congratulatory song was written in Latin, sung by monks and probably accompanied by dance during the party following the ceremony in Håkonshallen. This song is the oldest piece of secular music known in its entirety in Norway. Both the lyrics and the music have been preserved. See ▶ Music in Bergen.

When the royal residence was empty, both Bergen and Håkonshallen went through a

▲
Royal residence
Håkonshallen was built by king Håkon Håkonsson as a royal residence and banquet hall, and was completed in 1261. To the right the Rosenkrantz Tower.

Royal wedding and crowning

Early secular music

A loss for the city and for the country

There were negative repercussions for Bergen and for the country when the king moved to Oslo in 1299. The reputation of Bergen and Norway's position in Europe was subsequently weakened. When the king, his court and his men were gone, the road lay open for the German Hanseatics. They soon conquered the city, which by that time was also weakened by the Black Death. See ▶ Bryggen.

bleak period. During the next decennial the original function of the castle was all but forgotten. From 1683 it was basically used for the storage of grain. Decay became increasingly apparent.

The first person to rediscover the old royal estate was J.C. ▶ Dahl and Lyder ▶ Sagen. On their initiative, restoration work was carried about from 1880 to 1895 under the management of architects Christie, Blix and Fischer. The painter Gerhard Munthe put forth his idea to decorate the naked stone walls in the banquet hall with artwork, a task he achieved superbly during the years 1910 to 1916.

Håkonshallen was put to its most difficult test when it was damaged by the catastrophic explosion at Vågen in 1944. The entire restoration was ruined. Only the solid stone walls were left standing, though they too were partially destroyed.

The reconstruction after the war was left to Architect Johan Lindstrøm following an architectural competition. When he died, the work was carried on by his sons, Claus and Jon, together with another architect, Peter Helland-Hansen. They added a new reception hall in a converted stall building. The competition for the interior decoration and embellishment of the palace was won by Synnøve Anker Aurdal, Ludvik Eikaas and Sigrun Berg. The reopening took place in 1961.

Banquets and concerts

Håkonshallen is today used for public occasions. The banquet hall can seat 300 guests, while there are 500 seats available for concerts and other similar activities.

Gildesalen with the king's throne in the background.
▶

■ HENRIK IBSEN

The writer and dramatist Henrik Ibsen
(1828–1906) spent six years in Bergen (1851
–57) as a playwright and director for Ole Bulls
Norske Theatre (Ole Bull's Norwegian
Theatre), today known as Den Nationale Scene (The National Theatre of Bergen). During
Ibsen's six years in Bergen, he provided the
theatre with five new plays. His work has
been honoured by portrait busts inside the
theatre, over the main entrance, and by a
granite statue outside in the Theatre Park. He
was also the namesake of a street in Solheimsviken.

*Six years as
a playwright
at the theatre
in Bergen*

Henrik Ibsen has ties to Bergen also
through his family history. The Ibsen family,
originally from Denmark, grew new roots in
Norwegian soil. The first immigrant was the
writer's great-great-grandfather, skipper Peter Ibsen from Møn. Around the year 1720 he
landed in Bergen and became a Norwegian.
The widow of Peter Ibsen's son, also called
Henrik, remarried a vicar. He was transferred
from Bergen to Skien. There the writer was
born.

*Family roots
in Bergen*

On a recommendation from a writer colleague, Aasmund Olavsson ▶ Vinje, Ole Bull
found Ibsen a job with his newly established
theatre in Bergen in 1851. Ibsen was hired "to
assist the Theatre as a dramatic writer", and
was paid a monthly wage of 20 spesidaler
(about 160 crowns). After a short period he
was given responsibility for stage direction.
The board of directors gave him a grant to
study theatrical arts in Copenhagen and Dres-

*Erik Werenskiold's
painting of Henrik
Ibsen used on a
stamp from 1978.
This original portrait
is included in
Rasmus Meyer's
collection.*

**Bergen debut
a fiasco**

Sontum Hotel
*on the intersection
of Strandgaten and
Tollbodallmenning
was Ibsen's first
home in Bergen.*

First success

First residence

First great love

den. When hired, Ibsen's contract stipulated that he was to deliver a new play each year on January 2, the founding date of the theatre. The first play, the fantasy-comedy "Sancthans-natten" (Midsummer Eve), had its open-ing night on January 2, 1853. Ibsen began the play during his four month long study trip, but completed it in Bergen. The debut was a fias-co. The audience booed, and after only two per-formances the play was taken off the bill.

A new and improved version of "Kjæmpe-høien" (The Giant) was set up on January 2, 1854. During the summer of that same year he wrote the historical play "Fru Inger til Øster-aad" (Lady Inger of Østeraad). The play was named after the old farming estate near Trondheims fjord. Ibsen had just caught a glimpse of the place from a boat when the theatre company from Bergen was making a guest performance in Trondheim during the same year.

The next play, "Gildet paa Solhaug" (The Feast at Solhaug) from 1856 secured Ibsen his first success in Bergen. Several other success-ful plays were to follow, such as "Olaf Lilje-krans" (Olaf Lily Wreath) from 1857, and "Hærmændene på Helgeland" (The Vikings of Helgeland) from 1858 which was partly writ-ten in Bergen. Ibsen left Bergen in September 1857 to become a theatre manager in Kristia-nia.

Sontum's Hotel on the corner of Tollbodall-menning and Strandgaten was Ibsen's first residence in Bergen. He later bought his own apartment, a couple of rooms in the side wing of an old theatre that was destroyed during the bombings of 1944. One of the hotel owner's sons, a real sea dog, attracted Ibsen's attenti-on. In "Fruen fra havet" (The Lady from the Sea) from 1888, he apparently used this youthful figure as a model for "Den fremmede" (The Stranger).

In the house next door to Sontum, lived Rik-ke Holst, described by Ibsen as "a nature child and sixteen summers old". She became Henrik Ibsen's first great love. In June 1853 he pro-posed to her with a poem, and she accepted. In

I

Detail from the Ibsen statue unveiled in Teaterparken outside the National Theatre of Bergen in 1981. The statue was created by Nils Aas.

◀

the same way Ellida and her sailor in "Fruen fra Havet" were wedded by the ocean, they had planned to tie their rings together and throw them into the fjord.

Her father reacted with rage. To have a poor writer and man of the theatre for a son-in-law was absolutely unthinkable. One dark evening the two turtledoves were surprised by the young girl's fierce patriarch. He stormed out of the bushes on Nygårdsalléen toward the couple, with his hand clenched in anger. The scene must have been just as intense as the most exciting Ibsen drama, until it became clear that in this play there was no role for a hero. Terrified, the enamoured writer jumped to his feet and ran away, never daring to see his beloved again. "Face to face I was never a brave man", admitted Ibsen.

Henrik Ibsen fell for two Bergen women. Suzannah Thoresen, here pictured in 1873, became his wife.

I

Henrik Ibsen's watchful gaze over the entrance to Den Nationale Scene meets theatre audiences in Bergen.

The episode was immortalised in the poem "En fuglevise" (A Bird song) for which Edvard Grieg considerably composed a melody.

Ibsen got over his broken heart when shortly afterwards he met Suzannah Thoresen. She was the stepdaughter of the Danish born author Magdalena Thoresen (1819–1903). Her father was the Norwegian clergyman H. K. Thoresen. During Ibsen's time at the theatre, three plays by Magdalena Thoresen were staged, though the author remained anonym-ous.

Henrik Ibsen's six years in Bergen are described as a healthy educational period. The high points of his life there took place in 1856 with the success of "Gildet på Solhaug" and his engagement to Suzannah Thoresen. The wedding was in 1858 and was celebrated in Thoresen's home on Kong Oscar's Street 24.

KRISTOFER JANSON

The writer, teacher and clergyman Kristofer Nagel Janson (1841–1917) was born into a wealthy merchant family on Småstrandgaten, frequented by Ole ▶ Bull and earlier, by Johan Nordahl ▶ Brun. As a true "Bergensian" Janson surprised and angered many by being one of the most eager advocates of the New Norwegian cause. But in reality he was only following in the footsteps of his ancestors. His grandfather, Bishop Jakob Neumann, was the man who helped Ivar ▶ Aasen to print his first book on New Norwegian grammar. A street in Landås is named after Janson.

Kristofer Janson is perhaps best remembered for several familiar and beloved songs. His poem, "Vesle gut" (Little Boy), was the first poem in New Norwegian to be put to music by Grieg. A later poem, "Millom rosor" (Among the Roses) was also given a moving melody by Grieg.

The Edvard Giertsen publishing company published Janson's first book, "Fraa Bygdom" (From the Country) in 1865. It was a great success and was printed in several editions. According to the author himself, it was the melody and power of the language, in addition to the city people's condescending attitude toward the rural folk, that caused him to become a zealous advocate of the New Norwegian language. His Norwegian teacher at Katedralskolen was Johannes Steen, who later became the president of Stortinget (the Parliament) and Prime Minister.

Janson's versatile literary work spanned everything from poems and short stories, his-

"Bergensian" – but wrote in rural dialect

Kristofer Janson was a grand figure with great charm whether he delivered a sermon, a speech or instruction. Both Ibsen and Bjørnson used him as a model for their plays.

**Married
Drude Krogh**

Kristofer Janson married Drude Krog (1846–1934), a clergyman's daughter from Fana. Drude Janson published the novels "Mira" and "Helga Hvide". Like so many other talented women of her time, she sacrificed her career to care for her husband and children. Both Amalie Skram and Knut Hamsun had great expectations for her.

toric and religious literature to plays. He wrote the libretto to Gerhard Schjelderup's opera "Østenfor Sol og vestenfor Måne" (East of the Sun and West of the Moon) and published the periodical "Saamanden". He was honoured with a writing grant by the Parliament.

In his autobiography "Hvad jeg har oplevet" (What I have experienced), Janson paints a vivid picture of his hometown. He witnessed ▶ Bjørnson's great May 17 speech at Engen in 1859 when ecstatic Bergensians cheered the writer instead of the day itself. They later became neighbours and friends in Gausdal when Janson was hired by Christopher Bruun as a teacher at Vonheim folkehøgskole (Vonheim Folk High School).

Bjørnson used Janson as a model for the Reverend Sang in "Over ævne" (Beyond Means). Certain features of his personality are recognisable in the character of Hjalmar Ekdal in Ibsen's "The Wild Duck". As a student of theology, Janson delivered a sermon in Korskirken, but was scolded by a fellow student, the "spiritual police-chief" Lars Oftedal, for having committed "14 hidden heresies". Janson was the first clergyman to preach in the rural, New Norwegian language in a church.

In 1868 he married Drude Krog, the daughter of a vicar from Fana and a budding writer. The couple had six children. Their first home was an attic apartment in Nygård at the time Janson was teaching at several of the city's schools for girls. He was highly thought of, both as a teacher and as a lecturer. Many poems, Janson relates, were written on Saturdays during their engagement when he walked one and a half miles on foot to the Fana rectory. Unhappily the marriage did not last. The divorce, however, gave enough material for several books.

**Hamsun
his secretary**

Janson worked as a vicar for the Scandinavian Unitarian Ministry in Chicago for 12 years. At one time Knut Hamsun was his secretary. When he returned home from the United States in 1893, he set off on a lecture tour from Bergen and was given a warm welcome by a full house at a meeting in ▶ Logen.

J

◾ JAZZ IN BERGEN

Bergen has about 15 – 20 professional jazz musicians and almost 400 top-notch amateurs. Together they ensure daily jazz performances in Bergen – primarily in ▶ Kulturhuset USF at Verftet, but also in many of the city's clubs. As the number one jazz city in Norway, Bergen can offer the following:

Largest club. Bergen has three jazz clubs that together cover all the different jazz genres. Bergen Jazz Forum (started in 1971) is Norway's largest and most active club. It has about 800 members whose main interest is new and experimental music. Concerts are held every week in "Sardinen" in Verftet.

Greatest number of big bands. Bergen has no less than six big bands – more than in any other Norwegian city. The biggest is Bergen Big Band (started in 1976) and is lead by saxophone player Olav Dale.

Longest festival. Each year, 12 hectic nights in May transform Verftet in Bergen into a seething witches' cauldron of jazz. "Night Jazz" is Norway's largest jazz festival, if measured by duration and the number of artists. Among the 350 musicians who each spring have started things swinging during the last few years during Night Jazz, are stars like Miles Davis, James Brown and Chick Corea.

New model. Last but not least, the newly created "Vestnorsk Jazzsenter" (Western Norwegian Jazz Centre) has focused on Bergen as Norway's jazz centre. With 1.6 million crowns in initial capital from public funding, the centre introduced, in 1998, a new model for the organisation of jazz music.

Emphasis is put on distribution, educational activities and tours all over Western Norway. This occurs in cooperation with Bergen Jazz Forum. One of the objectives is to create an understanding of improvised music through education on all levels and for all ages, from music schools for preschool children to students of the Grieg Academy. This activity is directed from Kulturhuset USF at Verftet.

Norway's leading jazz city

Olav Dale
leader of Bergen
Big Band

Dag Arnesen
– talented pianist in
Bergen Big Band

Activities

Laila Dalseth
started her career
as a jazz vocalist in
her hometown in
1955. She was only
15 at the time. On
the photo she is a
little older.
▶

**Jazz in
Bergen since
the 1920s**

"Swingin' in the Rain" is a phrase jokingly
used to describe jazz in Bergen. And in truth,
Bergen has indeed been swinging to jazz
rhythms since the end of the 1920s. Musicians
who quite early made a name for themselves
include drummer Edgar Meyer Olsen, violinist
Arne Songnæs and pianist Carl A. Kroken.
The first jazz bands were named Frisco Band,
Bonzo Band, Big Band, and Charley Band or
the Rhythmic Six, as they later called themselves when the band expanded. Jazz could be
enjoyed in the restaurants of the Hotel Norge
and Hotel Rosenkrantz, in Stjernesalen on
Olav Kyrre's Street and in the Soria Moria
restaurant on Fløien.

J

The first big band of Bergen was formed in 1935 by unemployed members of the Bergen Music Association. Under the name, The Rhythmicans, they made their debut in Konsertpalæet, where the band had a permanent position for a couple of years playing jazz before the screening of the films. The ensemble was led by Lasse Dahl (trumpet) and Sverre Engebøe (drummer and conductor). At the piano sat the brilliant jazz soloist Arthur Wichstad.

First big band

Drummer Thorleif Larsen took the initiative in 1938 to form Bergen Rhythm Orchestra with Mikal Kolstad as its leader. Among the musicians were trumpet players Leif Slåtten and Egil Isachsen. Arthur Wichstad's quartet comprised a band within a band. Scala Dance Orchestra also experienced great success during the pre-war years. The music of the ensemble's rhythm section "Rolf Schade's Rhythm Quartet" was frequently played on the local Bergen radio station.

Bergen Rhythm Orchestra

The first jazz club in Bergen was the Bergen Rhythm Club, formed in 1940 and led by Omar Heide Midtsæter. The club did not survive for very long since all forms of jazz music were banned by the Germans during the war. It was not until the early 1950s that jazz fans found a new place to meet. Jørg Fr. Ellertsen took the initiative to start up and run the new Golden Club. Ellertsen was an impresario of sorts and published the periodical "Norwegian Jazz".

First jazz club

Several new big bands came onto the scene after the war. The first, in 1947, was led by Finn Nordal. Nordal was to influence the jazz culture in Bergen for more than a generation as an orchestra conductor, composer and tenor saxophone player.

There was a strong, growing interest in jazz in Bergen during the 1950s and a number of new talented artists emerged. Jazz singer Laila Dalseth (born 1940) began her career in 1955 in her hometown. She eventually became one of our most prominent vocalists and is especially known for her Billie Holiday-inspired swing style.

One of the many jazz houses in Bergen.

Star-studded events

Another talent from this period was clarinet player Tore Faye. He became the first Bergen jazz musician to record his music. In the years that followed, Neptune Hotel became the city's most important area for jazz, thanks to the hotel director and jazz fan, Gunnar Holm. He brought a number of international top soloists to Bergen and hired the Eivind Sannes Trio to be the house orchestra, with Leif Nygård on bass and Roald Wolf on drums. Many great jazz stars played in Bergen during the 60s, including Duke Ellington, Ella Fitzgerald, Oscar Peterson, Sarah Vaughan, Lionel Hampton and The Modern Jazz Quartet.

Jazz on radio

About ten years later, Arvid Genius introduced the public to jazz melodies from Bergen through the national radio station, NRK. Among today's eminent jazz musicians in Bergen are Olav Dale (saxophone), Dag Arnesen (piano), Per Jørgensen (trumpet/vocals) and guitarist Mats Eriksen. Skilled jazz pianist and composer Vigleik Storaas is also from Bergen, though he for many years has lived in Trondheim.

The manager of the Vestnorsk Jazz Centre is Bo Grønningsæter, while Jon Skjerdal manages Nattjazzen and Bergen Jazz Forum.

■ ROALD "KNIKSEN" JENSEN

Great football virtuoso

At breakneck speed toward the goal with the ball under full control. Unstoppable – by any rules of the game. The bronze statue of Roald Jensen (1943–87) on gratishaugen (the hill from where one can watch the game for free) above Brann Stadium brings back many happy football memories for many Norwegians. The popular football star from Bergen made the crowds go wild and soon received the very suitable nickname "Knicksen", a Norwegian football term for dribbling or doing tricks with the ball.

No one ever delivered a stronger argument

J

"Kniksen"
in a familiar pose.
The statue was crea-
ted by sculptor Per
Ung and was erect-
ed on the hill above
Brann Stadium in
1995.

◀

for the inclusion of sports as a cultural concept – a controversial matter at that time. Roald Jensen was a brilliant ball artist. His superb feints, his lightning-quick acceleration, his darting series of dribbles and flying kicks brought his ball-play, a thing of art and entertainment, to a high level. People flocked to the Stadium, not just out of interest for the game itself, but also to experience the phenomenal "Kniksen".

Jensen made his debut on the national team in 1960 at the tender age of 17, against Austria. Norway lost, but "Kniksen" played a great match. The same year games versus Finland and Sweden both ended victoriously, and with a breakthrough for the young man from Bergen. "17-year-old made the Swedish defence disappear", declared the Stockholm newspaper "Stockholmstidningen" in six columns. "Kniksen is today the one and only football wonder child in Scandinavia", stated the Swedish national coach a year later.

At the age of 20, Roald Jensen received a gold watch for having played 25 national football games. He was the youngest player ever to receive such an award. He managed to win

Youngest recipient of the gold watch

At home in his yard at Eidsvågneset, "Kniksen" spent many hours practising his football techniques.

two championships for Brann, to play on the Scandinavian team against Europe, and also to play in the professional Scottish top league for Hearts. Jensen had a rare, natural talent for ball play. One of the keys to his success was undoubtedly his long, self-imposed training practice at home in his yard at Eidsvågneset. It was here that the many unique skills, tricks and finesses were laboriously rehearsed.

Like any other artist, "Kniksen" had quite a temper. Sometimes he lost control of it, such as when his opponents realised that the only way to stop the irascible Bergensian was to kick him down.

"It was probably easier to let pressure out of the ball than out of the noggin when it was about to boil over," admits "Kniksen" in his autobiography "With Football in the Blood".

Tragically Roald Jensen also ended his days on the football field. During a practice game with the 'old boys' in 1987, he had a sudden heart attack, and died.

The Norwegian Football Association has honoured the memory of the eminent ball artist by the establishment of the Kniksen Prize, the association's highest award of honour.

■ SVERRE JORDAN

Pivotal force in the music world of Bergen

Composer and conductor Sverre Jordan (1889–1972) did not live long enough to wield his baton inside Grieghallen, but he can be found there just the same – recreated in bronze by sculptor Sofus Madsen.

Sverre Jordan committed his life to music in his hometown. He was conductor of the orchestra for Den Nationale Scene and at the same time a frequent guest conductor for Harmonien's orchestra. Altogether he conducted the orchestra for more than one hundred concerts. As orchestra conductor he will be remembered for his work on many operas.

Sverre Jordan left in all 85 opuses, including two piano concertos, a cello, violin and horn concerto, in addition to chamber music, piano pieces, choir pieces and romances. He received acclaim for his melodrama "Feberdikte" (Fever

J

Sverre Jordan
and his wife, actress
Nina Sandvik Kris-
tensen Jordan, ap-
plaud the orchestra
when his 50th anni-
versary as a compo-
ser was celebrated
in Harmonien.

◄

Poems) from 1921, and "Holberg-silhuetter" (Holberg Silhouettes) for orchestra from 1938.

He received his greatest recognition both nationally and internationally as a romance composer. He set music to about 200 poems in all. Many of the most prominent singers of the times had Jordan music in their repertoire, such as Cally Monrad, Kirsten Flagstad, Lauritz Melchior, Marian Anderson and Rita Streich. Jordan's musical style is described as neo-romantic with close ties to traditional Grieg.

Jordan was a pivotal figure in the modern music world of Bergen. He wrote a major work for the choir of Harmonien. He was also on the programme committee for the Bergen International Festival.

To show their appreciation, the music company Harmonien awarded Jordan an honorary membership, and in 1966 he received the company's gold medal and chain. For his enormous contribution to Norwegian music, he was also appointed Knight of the first degree of the St. Olav Order.

Sverre Jordan published a summary of the life and works of Edvard Grieg in 1954, and an autobiography in 1973 entitled "From the Long Life of an Artist".

Versatile composer with 85 opuses

Sverre Jordan
in bronze in Grieg-
hallen. The bust is
made by Sofus
Madsen.

J

■ KORSKIRKEN

Famous parish clerk

On at least one point Korskirken (Church of the Cross) distinguishes itself from the other places of worship in the city: Surely it's not likely that any other church has had a parish clerk who was just as important as the vicar. Ludvig ▶ Holberg made sure of this when he made the parish clerk Niels Klim (1620–90) the main character in the novel "Niels Klims underjordiske reise" (Niels Klims Underground Adventure). A lovely chalice and paten (a plate used for communion) which Klim and his wife donated to the church in 1673, still stands in the church today.

Celebrities

Quite a few celebrities have been on Korskirken's staff. Hans ▶ Egede was acting vicar there before his missionary voyage to Greenland. Johan Nordahl ▶ Brun was parish vicar at Korskirken from 1774 until he became bishop of Bergen in 1804. The lay preacher Hans Nielsen ▶ Hauge also had a regular seat in the church.

Royal chapel

Korskirken is mentioned for the first time in a saga from 1181. Originally it was a basilica with twin towers similar to ▶ Mariakirken and consecrated to the holy cross. Hence the name. Between 1615–32 the church was rebuilt with transepts so that it, in an architectural sense, became a church of the cross. Korskirken has been both royal chapel and palace church, and from the 17th century until after the Second World War, a garrison church.

Living study of styles

Through the years, the church has gone through many changes and restorations after having been destroyed by as many as seven

▲
Korskirken is central-ly located by Nedre Korskirkeallmenning and Kong Oscars gate.

large fires, the last occurring in 1702. The church has therefore become quite stylish with its Romanesque naves and fragments of late Gothic, Renaissance and Baroque. In 1928 a glass painting by Frøydis Haavardsholm was set in a window that once had been inserted in the east gable of the chancel. The richly styled portal in the north gable is considered one of the finest Renaissance portals in Norway. It bears Christian IV's monogram and the shield of nobleman Jens Juel and his wife Ida Gøye. In the churchyard, east of the church, a stone monument has been raised to commemorate four Norwegians and one Dane who fell at ▶Alvøen on May 16, 1808 in battle against the English frigate "Tartar".

Korskirken has 775 seats and status as a parish church for a congregation of about 3,500 people. The church's central location and open doors have made it an important meeting place for the whole city. In addition to church services, the church is often used for Festival concerts and by the Collegium Musicum. (See ▶Music in Bergen.)

Religious and musical meeting place

The church organ is German, built by Albert Hollenbacher in the 1890s, with 38 stops and a mechanical tracker action. The organ was later enlarged by three stops and was extensively restored in 1981.

K

■ KULTURHUSET USF

Norway's largest culture centre

At Georgernes Verft stands what was once Norway's largest sardine factory. This has been transformed into the country's most multi-faceted cultural centre – Kulturhuset USF (the Cultural House USF). USF is short for United Sardine Factories.

On a 10,000 square metre floor, art and culture is created, organised and expressed in various forms and genres. About 300 people spend their days working in Kulturhuset USF – painters, musicians, actors, writers, dancers, craftsmen, filmmakers, architects and advertising people. Here artists such as Karoline Krüger and Jan Eggum have their music-al base, and here yoga and meditation is practised. The Dixie Dive diving school is run from a location in the same building.

60 studios

Kulturhuset USF houses 60 studios and workshops in all, including a Nordic guest studio. For dancers and musicians there are rehearsal studios, and several cultural organisations and institutions have their offices here.

Meeting place

A popular meeting place for the many artists and workers employed in culture in the house is the Kippers Café. It is both a cafeteria and a restaurant, and it can offer an out-door

In 1983 artists and cultural workers moved into this large industrial building where there was once a lingerie factory and production of canned goods.

Inserted picture: A Company logo for United Sardine Factories still adorns Kulturhuset.

▶

dining area, with 500 seats during the summer season, along with a perfect view of all the boats and ferries sailing past on the Pudde Fjord.

The sardine factory was closed down in 1973. Twenty years later the old factory building was redecorated and transformed into a cultural centre offering an enormous variety of experiences and the most extensive artists' environment found under one Norwegian roof. The activities are organised as a foundation and are secured through a long-term contract with the house owners, Norwegian Preserving A/S.

From sardines to art in 1973

The Cultural House has five public areas, excluding the restaurant:

Five public areas

Cinemateket is a cinema with 93 seats. It functions as a valuable supplement to Bergen Kino, and instead of box office hits, it offers new, creative films and old classics. Films are usually shown every night except Mondays.

→ This was one of our viewing places

Sardinen is a club and concert hall with a maximum capacity of 500 seats. The repertoire extends from classical music to jazz and rock. The locale is also used for smaller cabarets and plays. Bergen Jazz Forum arranges

concerts there each week. The premises are also rented out for conferences and private parties.

Rock concerts

Røkeriet (The Smoke House) is the largest concert hall accomodating 700 people. There are usually very few seats available since the hall is mostly used for rock concerts. A number of national and international stars have performed there.

Theatre and ballet

Scene USF is a blackbox theatre with 144 seats in an amphitheatre setting. Here one can enjoy everything from children's theatre, dance and ballet for children to new dance, experimental theatre and performance. The location is rented out to professional theatre groups and dance schools.

Visningsrommet (The Show Room) is the exhibition hall for paintings, sculptures and crafts. Traditional exhibits are displayed here, as well as projects of a more experimental nature, by both Norwegian and international artists.

Industrial history

The oldest part of the USF complex was built in 1886 to house A/S Petersen & Dekke's textile factory, and was Norway's first lingerie factory. The 3000 square metre building has changed little during the century and now comprises one-third of the cultural centre.

United Sardine Factories Ltd. took over the building in 1910 and expanded the area to about 15,000 square metres in 1914–15. With the exception of two boathouses, which are now gone, the plant remained unchanged in its appearance. After the sardine factory closed down, packaging was manufactured there for a time.

Built wooden ship

The name Georgernes Verft comes from the wooden ship building business established by Georg Brunchorst and Georg Ferdinand Vedeler by Pudde Fjord below Fredriksberg in 1784. The shipyard was later called Dekkedokken and was in operation until the end of the 1800s.

K

■ LANDÅS MANOR

The venerable, white-painted Landås manor stands proudly at the foot of Ulriken mountain, in striking contrast to its rather warlike address: Kanonhaugen 39 (Cannon Hill). In a neighbourhood of small houses, row houses and apartment buildings, the beautiful, 300-year-old manor stands apart in a class of its own, with traditional ties to Norwegian cultural history. It was here that Edvard Grieg spent his childhood summers when the property was the Grieg family's summer home.

Landås was part of the king's estate at Årstad during the Middle Ages, and has changed owners many times during the following years. The property was owned by Consul Herman Didrich Janson (see ▶ Damsgård) and his wife, Christiane Benedicte Krohn. It was later inherited by their daughter Ingeborg Bene-

The Grieg family's summer cottage

King's estate

Landås manor is a sharp contrast to the modern church building below.
▼

Alexandra,
the only child of
Nina and Edvard
Grieg, died of me-
ningitis only 13
months old during a
summer holiday at
Landås in 1869.

**Great joy
and deep
sorrow**

**First music
studio**
At Landås Edvard
Grieg's parents built
the composer's first
workshop for their
son

dicte Janson and her husband, the prefect Edvard Hagerup, in the 1800s. They had eight children. One daughter, Gesine, later became the mother of composer Edvard Hagerup Grieg, and one son later became the father of Nina Hagerup Grieg. Nina and Edvard Grieg were in other words cousins.

Gesine inherited the Landås property from her parents. From the time Edvard Grieg was ten years old, the family spent their summers at Landås. The future composer had to walk six kilometres every day to get to Tank's School in town. Grieg's parents sold the property in 1870.

The manor building was known to the family as "The Fog Castle". This is how the house often appeared when dark and heavy rain clouds gathered around the Grieg manor in a mystical veil. Grieg wrote to his friend Frants Beyer in 1884 that he loved Landås with "all the power of his childhood memories".

Grieg experienced one of his greatest moments at Landås, but also perhaps his greatest sorrow. Here Ole Bull discovered the 15-year old's great musical talent and advised his parents to allow him to study at the conservatory in Leipzig. Eleven years later at Landås, in 1869, Nina and Edvard Grieg's only child, their daughter Alexandra, was stricken with meningitis and died, only 13 months old.

In despair over this tragic event, Grieg composed the music for the gripping New Norwegian poem "Millom rosor" (Among the Roses) by Kristofer ► Janson, a poem which describes a mother's grief upon the death of her child. The very popular piano composition "Brudefølget drar forbi" (The Wedding Party Passes) from "Folkelivsbilder, op. 19" was also composed at Landås.

On the hillside of Ulriken, Edvard Grieg's parents built him his first composing cottage. When the Grieg family moved from Landås, the cottage was made into a chicken house. The first cottage is now gone, replaced by a new cottage partly built from the original materials. Instead of music, sermons are now written here.

L

Nina and Edvard Grieg at Landås during the summer of 1869 together with Edvard's mother and sister, Benedicte.

◀

The municipality of Bergen took over the property in 1975, and the cottage has housed both vicars and curates in the parish of Landås. The house is a rare example of a church being overshadowed by the clergyman's cottage. Landås manor is today protected by law. The elegant manor house has been well cared for by its many owners throughout 300 years. The house contains one of Bergen's oldest and most beautiful portals from Baroque times. The ornamentation is part Rococo, part Louis XVI and part Empire style.

Home for vicars

On certain occasions over the years Grieg's rooms have been opened for public house concerts. Normally Landås Manor is not open to the public.

House concerts

■ THE LEPROSY MUSEUM

Norway's only medical museum

Science honoured for the first time by monument

The discoverer of the leprosy bacillus, Dr. Armauer Hansen, was honoured on his 60th birthday in 1901 with this bust in the Botanical Gardens in Bergen. This was the first time a scientific achievement in Norway had been honoured by a monument.

More than 20 countries have honoured Armauer Hansen by his picture on stamps, such as here in India. In many countries leprosy is called Hansen's disease.

The Leprosy Museum (Lepramuseet) is Norway's only medical museum. It forms a central part of Bergen's medical-historical collection. The museum is housed in the oldest existing hospital in Scandinavia, St. Jørgen's hospital on Kong Oscar's Street 59.

The history of the hospital dates back to 1411. The oldest part of the hospital building was constructed after the city fire of 1702. St. Jørgen's hospital church and Armauer Hansen's Memorial Room, which was opened in 1962 in the former Nursing Institute for Lepers on Kalfarveien 31, both belong to the museum as well. Here, in 1868, chief physician Gerhard Henrik Armauer Hansen (1841–1912) began his research, which resulted in the discovery of the leprosy bacillus. This important discovery made Hansen famous all over the world. In many countries leprosy has been known as "Hansen's disease".

The Nursing Institute from 1857 is one of the largest wooden buildings in Norway, with a floor area of 3,450 square metres. At one time it contained 40 hospital rooms and 250 beds. When the hospital closed down in 1957, the building was taken over by the Institute for Rehabilitation. Dr. Hansen's office in the Nursing Institute has been preserved as a memorial room. Near the entrance are busts of both Hansen and his colleague and father-in-law, Daniel Cornelius Danielsen (1815–94). Their efforts have also been honoured by a memorial plaque.

On his 60th birthday in 1901, Armauer Hansen was paid tribute to by a bust in the Botanical Gardens, modelled by Jo Visdal. This was the first time in Norway that a scientific achievement was honoured with a public memorial. This was also the first time in Bergen that a person who was still alive was honoured with an outdoor sculpture. When he died in 1912, the doctor's urn was placed under the base of the sculpture. There is also a street in Landås named after Armauer Hansen.

The Leprosy Museum was established in

1970 on the initiative of the medical faculty of the University of Bergen. The medical-historical collection (established as a foundation in 1972) was designated as a national centre for the documentation, research and medical history of leprosy by the Norwegian Cultural Council in 1992. St. Jørgen's hospital has preserved material on leprosy from the 17th century until the eradication of the disease. The hospital was probably built for lepers and for the terminally ill by the Antonius Brothers, an order of monks who took over the ▶ Nonneseter Convent in 1507. The last leprosy patient died in 1946. Armauer Hansen's microscopes and other instruments are on display in the operating room and laboratory, and the museum gives a grim impression of the gruesome fate of the victims of leprosy.

    The hospital church has existed as long as the hospital. Numerous religious songs written during periods in hospital bear testimony to the important role the church played in the lives of the patients. From 1749 to 1886 the church was also a parish church for the congregation of Årstad. The altarpiece from 1733 portrays Jesus and the ten lepers, and Jesus and the woman of Canaan. Today the church is used only for special and foreign language services. Every second and fourth Sunday of each month, services are held in English.

▲
The Leprosy
Museum *was set up in St. Jørgen's Hospital, which is also Scandinavia's oldest hospital. Both the hospital and hospital church on the picture have a history that dates back to 1411. Saint Jørgen is the patron saint of lepers.*

Sermons
in English

L

■ JONAS LIE

Student in Bergen

Jonas Lie
photographed just after he left Bergen.

Jonas Lie on his travels to Bergen

In 1893 Jonas writes:
"The eight miles over Hardanger Fjord and Bjørne Fjord to Bergen in the summer and winter I could still sail, because I remember it – every bay and every corner – in both calm weather and sea spray – during the day and with the monotonous stroke of oars at night within the black shadows of the mainland."

Author Jonas Lauritz Idemil Lie (1833–1908) has a street called after him in Solheimsviken. Lie's connection to Bergen relates to his student days at ► Bergen Katedralskole from 1847 to 1850. With Lyder ► Sagen as his schoolmaster, Lie laid an important foundation for his writing, which in time would secure him a place in the leading ranks of Norwegian writers of the "golden age".

In Bergen, Jonas Lie had the pleasure of asking Karoline Reimers to dance long before Bjørnstjerne ► Bjørnson became her lifelong partner. They did not meet at Bergen Katedralskole, since girls were not allowed to attend the school at the time. They met rather at a dance school. Perhaps also in "Jahns Conditori", a bakery on Kong Oscar's Street, where the glib Karoline worked as a clerk in the family business and sold everything from bread and cakes to the Bergen speciality "brøstsokker".

Hardanger Fjord became the school route to Bergen for northern Norwegian Jonas Lie when his father was appointed county court judge in Sunnhordland, with the Undarheim farm at Husnes as their home. Jonas was drawn to the sea in Bergen as well. "Every evening", he writes, "I hung over boats and sloops and journeyed with them, and knew each rope and each board."

Jonas Lie lived in a room on Lille Markevei in the house of a teacher, Herman Laading, who was also a director of Det Norske Teater. At school he received above average marks, at least up until the last winter when his attendance was cut short by a long-term illness. A fellow student, chief physician August Koren, wrote of Lie:

"Jonas Lie's range of intellect was broader and higher than most of the rest of us. His conversation was different from most, more creative, more disconnected."

Encouraged by Lyder Sagen, Jonas Lie wrote his first poetry in Bergen. He made his journalistic debut in the newspaper "Bergensposten" in 1854 in the form of a series of summer articles under the title "From Søndhordland".

Lie was well liked at Katedralskolen. His classmates were quite probably somewhat irritated when they were continually tricked into believing many of the strange 'experiences' Jonas Lie told of. His stories were usually revealed as pure fantasy – or perhaps the beginnings of an author's story.

Poems, articles and strange stories

■ LOGEN

Two concerts in Logen by the Amadeus quartet were one of the high points during the first Bergen International Festival in 1953. As many as 44 years would pass before the Festival could set up a concert in this cultural building. Meanwhile it was used – many would say misused – as a drapery goods and furniture shop. From 1997, the lovely hall in classic empire style has regained its position as a concert hall, banquet hall and cabaret stage. It has also been used as a cinema.

Music, theatre and banquets

Logen was built in 1883 by the society club "The Good Intention" as a substitute for an older, but no longer satisfactory, club premises from 1786. The good intention in this particular case was to give the city a much-needed elegant banquet hall. Here counts and heads of state would be received and celebrated. Club members and dancing school students could practise their steps at a yearly ball, and cultural events like the artist carnival could take place.

"The Good Intention"

The building is called Logen (The Lodge) because it was originally built by the city's first freemasons. Logen was used by Harmonien as a regular concert hall until Konsertpaleet was built in 1918.

Concert hall

Edvard Grieg gave four performances of his own compositions in Logen in 1884, and together with his wife Nina he was back on the stage in 1901. In 1903 Grieg's 60th birthday was celebrated with a grand gala concert in Logen. In the first row sat Karoline and Bjørnstjerne Bjørnson. A number of famous Nor-

Edvard Grieg celebration

Behind these windows both Edvard Grieg and Sergej Rakhmaninov gave performances. Logen is used today as a concert hall and theatre stage and is a ceremonial banquet hall. The building is owned by the society club "Den Gode Hensigt" and contains a popular bowling alley and the restaurant Wesselstuen.

▶

wegian and foreign artists have performed in Logen, including Sergej Rakhmaninov.

Bowling alley and library

Outside the banquet hall Logen has a club with a bowling alley, and the basement houses the restaurant Wesselstuen. But The Good Intention was not just a club for the sporting recreation of wealthy citizens. A library with 30,000 volumes was also at the disposition of the club members. The great book collection was unfortunately lost in a fire in 1980.

Logen more important than Parliament

It is said that when Christian Michelsen was director of Direksjonen from 1893 to 1899, membership in Logen was deemed more important than a seat in Parliament. The editor of "Bergen's Tidende", Olav Lofthus, was asked in the early days of the telephone if the newspaper might not have use for a telephone in its reporting duties. "Pretty unnecessary", answered the editor. "I go to Logen every day"!

L

◼ SOFUS MADSEN

In the studio of Sofus Madsen (1881–1977) at Landås, the prominent figures of the city once stood all in a row, and together with them three prominent foreign figures: Lenin, Grundtvig and Beethoven. Madsen created this gallery of fame in plaster and clay.

All 28 of Madsen's sculptures and memorial plaques adorn the parks, squares and buildings of the city today. No other artists have bequeathed more monuments to the city of Bergen. In return, a street was given his name near his home on Stormbakken at Landås. Both his home and studio were built in 1917 – designed by Madsen himself. The site was located in inspiring surroundings near Landås Manor, the Grieg family's summer residence. Address: Kanonhaugen 20.

The studio will be opened as a museum in 1999, dedicated to both Sofus Madsen and his wife, weaver Grethe Corneliussen Madsen. The art collection contains over 180 sculptures, medallions, sketchings and wall hangings. Some of them were created from the drawings of her husband.

Madsen was born in Kristiania, but came to Bergen at the age of three along with his parents, Sofie and Theodor Madsen. His father was a teacher and a writer. Three of his plays were performed at Den Nationale Scene. His childhood home stood on Kalmargaten just near the theatre. Sculptor Hans E. Johannessen had his studio in the same neighbourhood. The young Sofus was often an eager spectator and soon began to dream of an artist's career of his own. It started with three years of ap-

Sofus Madsen's sculptures in Bergen

Fountain boy
Nygård school 1922
Daybreak
Nygårdsparken 1918
Nygaards boy
Nygårdsparken 1947
Gabriel Tischendorf
Grieghallen 1930
Sverre Jordan
Grieghallen 1955
Arne Bjørndal
Grieghallen 1972
Crying boy
Byparken 1948
Spraying boy
Byparken 1927
Conrad Mohr
Byparken 1938
Merkur
Sundt Torgallmenning 1937

Sofus Madsen in his studio *together with portraits of Ludvig Holberg and Ole Bull.*

▶

Sofus Madsen's Bergen sculptures *Se also the preceding page.*

Young girl
Sentralbadet 1938
Henrik Ibsen
The Theatre 1928
Johannes Brun
The Theatre 1940
Christian Sandal
The Theatre 1957
Kristian Bing
Nordnesparken
1938
Memorial plaque
Bergen Post office
1946
Relief
Minnebøssen
Torget 1920
Drægge boy
Dreggsallmenning
1956
**Hans Nielsen
Hauge**
Korskirken 1971
Johan L. Blydt
Skansemyren 1928
**Johan Nordahl
Brun**
Ulriken 1970
The Sprinter
Brann Stadium
1925
Einar Olsen
Bergen's Gymnastic
Association 1968
O. Kavli
Kavli Inc. at Midtun
1942
Awakening youth
Laksevåg 1960
Hendrik J. Fasmer
Alvøen 1954
Hans B. Fasmer
Loddefjord 1955
Jacob Sæthre
Eikelund 1920

prenticeship with the Grieg statue master, Ingebrigt Vik, who ran a woodcarving workshop in Bergen. From Vik, Madsen went on to the Art Academy in Copenhagen in 1902 and continued his studies in Berlin and Paris. In 1914 Madsen held his first separate exhibition in Copenhagen. That same year he returned to Bergen and stayed there for the rest of his life.

Sofus Madsen is especially known for his many lifelike sculptures of children and for his striking portraits. His art form was naturalistic, but several sculptures, such as "The Sprinter" outside Brann stadium, also display a hint of expressionism.

M

◼ MARIAKIRKEN

Nearly 100 years after the founding of Bergen, members of the congregation could, toward the middle of the 12th century, gather for High Mass in Mariakirken (St. Mary's Church). With its two tall towers the church must have dominated the city skyline. Mariakirken is today the oldest preserved building in Bergen and is one of the city's most significant historical monuments. It has 330 seats.

Oldest building in Bergen

Although Mariakirken has always been a parish church, the grandiose style in the form of a basilica suggests it also held status as the city's major church. During the years between 1408 and the first part of the 1600s, when the Hansas dominated Bergen, it served as a church for German merchants. Until the last mid-war period, sermons were given in the church in German. It was therefore popularly called the German Church.

Mariakirken was supposedly completed around 1150, about 80–90 years after the founding of Bergen by Olav Kyrre.

Two city fires have damaged Mariakirken – in 1198 and 1248 – but the damage was not too extensive. It was possible, for example, to repair the two west towers. Since then, the church has been spared any further destruction. It escaped the fire catastrophe of 1702 and the explosion of 1944, when its nearest neighbours, Bryggen and Håkonshallen were considerably damaged. Uninterrupted use over so many years has resulted in an unusually well-preserved church.

Because of its connection with the Hansas, Mariakirken is more richly equipped and adorned than any of the other city churches. The magnificent interior with its artwork created through seven centuries makes the church an important tourist attraction. A richly decorated German altarpiece from the end of the 15th century can be admired in the chancel. This is the church's oldest piece of inventory and the only object from the Catholic period.

Richly equipped

The triptych has three sections with folding doors. The middle piece depicts Mary with child, surrounded by saints, including St. Olav. The doors show all the disciples except for Ju-

St. Olav

**Apostle
statues**

das. On the walls around the altar are 15 life-sized statues of the 12 disciples together with Moses, John the Baptist and Paul. The statues were made by Søffren Oelssen in 1634. Two Rubens copies were painted about the year 1650 by Elias Fiigenschoug. The oldest of several epitaphs (memorial paintings) date back to 1585.

Unique pulpit

The magnificent pulpit in Mariakirken is the finishing touch to the church's baroque interior, but at the same time an art-historic mystery. There is nothing like it in any other Norwegian place of worship. It was given to the church in 1676, though its origin is unknown. Over the pulpit is a canopy headed with a figure of Christ. Underneath, the canopy has been richly decorated with pictures of the zodiac. A sphere hanging by a thread probably symbolises the earth. The pulpit contains panels of the eight Christian virtues portrayed as women with various attributes.

**Christian
virtues**

There is no certain information about exactly who built Mariakirken, but the style is predominantly Romanesque, with an element of High Gothic character in the chancel. The four portals of the church distinguish themselves by extraordinarily rich and varied carvings resembling those of the great cathedrals.

Mariakirken is moreover the first building in Norway with window panes. The glass was fitted in 1336 when a German glass painting was bequeathed to the church, and was installed in a small window in the northern chancel wall.

The German organ builder Paul Ott is the master of the instrument in Maria-kirken. It was taken into use in 1974. The drawing shows the front of the organ.

Musical activity has today become associated, by many, with Mariakirken. The Maria Music Festival is arranged every year in August. The church's regular choir, Maria Vocalis, has recorded a number of CDs under the direction of organist Dag Fluge. The choir has performed at Westminster Abbey and St. Paul's Cathedral in London. The congregation has also provided a chamber choir and two emsembles – chamber orchestra Musica Maria and Maria-kirken's Brass Ensemble.

Mariakirken received a new, first-class or-

M

The chancel of Mariakirken *has a magnificent triptych from the 1400s, made in Lübeck, and 15 full-sized statues of the disciples, Moses, John the Baptist and Paul. In the foreground is the church's unique pulpit from 1676*

Photo: Aune forlag

◀

Paul Ott organ a German gift

gan in 1974. It was built by Paul Ott and was a gift from the Evangelical-Lutheran Church in Germany. Organ music has been played in the church since 1575. The new organ brought about a significant number of concerts, some in connection with Bergen International Festival. Smaller organ recitals are given both spring and autumn, every Thursday at 12 noon.

◼ CHRISTIAN MICHELSEN

Generous Bergensian in high position

He was highly respected by his fellow Norwegians – the Prime Minister who directed the peaceful dissolution of the union with Sweden in 1905. Physically he was placed even higher, in his hometown, by sculptor Gustav Vigeland. From the asphalt to the top of his head, Chris-

(Close to were we live)

▲
Gamlehaugen, *Christian Michelsen's "castle" at Fjøsanger is today a royal residence. The architect was Jens Zetlitz Kielland, who also designed the furniture. It was carved in wood by Ingebrigt Vik. Gamlehaugen is open to the public when not used by the royal*

Portrait of Christian Michelsen by Sofus Madsen.

tian Peter Hersleb Kjerschow Michelsen (1857–1925) towers 21.39 metres. In his lifetime he was a leading figure. The artist has effectively emphasised this position symbolically. This conspicuous statue was unveiled in Byparken on May 17th 1938.

A couple of blocks to the north lies Christian Michelsen's Street. In Fjøsanger, about five kilometres south of downtown Bergen, stands the palace-like manor of this legendary statesman and shipowner. The manor, Gamlehaugen, is beautifully situated in a park at the end of Nordås Lake. Gamlehaugen has since 1925 been nationally owned and serves as the royal family's home in Bergen. The second and third floors with their 13 rooms are for the royal family's private use. Crown Prince Haakon Magnus had a 'small apartment' at the manor when he was a student at the Naval College of Bergen. The first floor is generally open to the public.

While the whole country benefited from Michelsen's political talents, it was the city of Bergen that inherited his great fortune – that which he himself had amassed as a successful shipowner. Michelsen was educated in the field of law and practised in Bergen as a lawyer for two years. He founded the shipping company in 1880 together with a partner. Two years later he became its sole owner. At the

M

turn of the century the shipping company was the biggest in Bergen, with a fleet of ten ships.

For two periods,1892–93 and 1895–98, Michelsen was the mayor of the city. As a national politician – Prime Minister, cabinet minister and member of Parliament (elected by Venstre and Samlingspartiet), he was an especially well-articulated spokesman on behalf of the interests of his hometown. Among other things, he was to a great extent responsible for the building of the Bergen railway. For many years he was a board member of Den Nationale Scene. In 1902 he founded "Morgenavisen" (The Morning News), published until 1984.

Most of his fortune of 5.5 million kroner was bequeathed to the Christian Michelsen Institute (CMI) for science and intellectual freedom. This amount today would correspond to about 85 million kroner. Michelsen wished the Institute to reward young and especially talented researchers. They were to be offered twice the salary of professors working for the state. Research was, according to his will, to concentrate on four areas: 1) Intellectual science, especially the philosophy of religion and psychology. 2) The natural sciences and mathematics, and also technology, emphasising industry and business in the West Country. 3) Medicine. 4) Cultural or scientific work toward the promotion of tolerance and friend-ship between nations and races – in a relig-ious, social, financial and political sense.

The CMI has offices in its own building on Fantoftvegen 38, and has today two departments – one for the natural sciences and technology, and one for the social sciences and development. The Institute's natural science and technology research department agreed to a partnership with the University of Bergen in 1992 under the name Christian Michelsen Research Inc.

At Gullstølen south of Løvstakken, Michelsen bought a parcel of seven acres, where he built a cottage. This cottage was given to the Scouts in 1923. The cottage was destroyed by the Germans during the war and rebuilt during the 1950s. Unfortunately it had to be torn

Gustav Vigeland's Michelsen statue in Byparken is 21.39 metres tall.

M

Winning personality with a sharp tongue

down in 1967 due to repeated vandalism. According to his biographer Bernt A. Nissen, Michelsen had a sharp tongue and was quick-witted. He spoke easily and elegantly – sometimes monumentally. He was popular on account of his natural and winning personality.

Gamlehaugen was during the 17th century a cotter's farm under ▶Fjøsanger Manor. Michelsen bought the estate in 1898. He laid out a park near the water, and in 1901 he had his brick manor house built to resemble a Scottish-English model. The architect was Jens Zetlitz Kielland, who also designed the furniture.

■ EDVARD MUNCH

Found motifs and friends in Bergen

Bergen has inspired painter Edvard Munch (1863–1944) in four of his highly acclaimed works of art. Three of them are harbour paintings.

There is little doubt as to the origin of the motif for the fourth Bergen painting. In the background Nykirken and Strandgaten, where people hurry by, are easily recognisable. The motif in the foreground is unmistakable as well: the serious man in deep thought with intense, staring eyes is the artist himself. With this somewhat inscrutable self-portrait, probably painted in 1916, Edvard Munch left behind something both valuable and unusual on his visits to Bergen. The city gave him worries but also friends and great joys.

Rasmus Meyer's Collection contains this self portrait of Edvard Munch, painted during his stay at a clinic in Copenhagen in 1909 (100 x 110 cm). The painting suggested a new style.

While the Strandgate painting now hangs in the Munch Museum in Oslo, Bergen has secured another highly qualified self-portrait of the painter. This was painted in Copenhagen in 1909. A 'new' Munch was displayed here for the first time. The portrait is part of the ▶ Rasmus Meyer's Collection. There it shares a wall with 136 other paintings by Edvard Munch. All are part of the art treasure left by collector Rasmus Meyer and donated to the city of Bergen by his heirs. An additional four paintings are exhibited in Bergen Billedgalleri, while ten belong to the Stenersen Collection. The Bergen municipality administers the

Large collection

Self portrait
of Edvard Munch,
painted by Nykir-
ken with Strandga-
ten in the back-
ground in 1907
(90 x 60 cm).

◀

largest collection of Munch paintings outside of Oslo.

In addition to the 44 oil paintings, the collection includes 51 etchings, 23 woodcuts, 29 lithographs and two pictures done in felt pen and water colours. Together they give a representative picture of the artist's development – from the young naturalist, via impressionist experimentation, to the ageing master of expressionism.

Several of the pictures in Bergen are considered to be among Munch's greatest works. First, his breakthrough in 1884 with "Morning", thereafter the frieze motifs of the 1890s up to the self-portrait from 1909. According to the experts, this marks a turning point in Munch's art toward a new form of expression.

Main works

M

Bergen debut a fiasco

Munch's paintings were shown for the first time in Bergen in the autumn of 1895. His debut was a gigantic public fiasco. The ignorance and conservative attitude of the Bergen public made them blind to the genius of the artist. Instead of praise, he provoked anger and was scorned and sneered at. Not a single painting was sold.

Sharp letter

In 1909 Munch was persuaded to exhibit his work in Bergen again. This came about with the help of his old friend from his student days, teacher Sigurd Høst. Munch himself came to the city this time and stayed for two weeks. Before this he had written a fairly sharp letter to the Art Society where he stated, among other things: "The honourable Art Association must realise that I cannot live by catcalls and verbal abuse alone, but that I also need a little pecuniary support– and yes, sooner or later Bergen will also trot alongside and understand that there may be more to life than theatre and herrings."

Salvaged both honour and financial situation

The person who ended up saving both Edvard Munch's financial situation and the city's honour was Rasmus Meyer. With his large investments in Munch's paintings, he soon came to overshadow the National Gallery. The press and the public received Munch's work in a much more positive light this time, although some name-calling still occurred. The success in Bergen boosted the artist's spirits immensely. In a letter of thanks to Sigurd Høst, Munch writes:

Lovely days in Bergen

"The days in Bergen were wonderful. I will surely return again soon – The entire trip and especially the visit to Bergen will be among my fondest Memories – You can understand that – I had never been there before – and had such lovely weather... Give my best regards to the insatiable Meyer –."

■ **MUREN**

Home for nobility and drill corps

Aristocratic parties, a farmer's market, a rural café, a liquor store, a churchwarden's office and a drill corps museum – in the course of 430 years Muren has been a very solid frame-

◀ **Murhvelvingen**
(the Wall Vault) is
one of the oldest se-
cular buildings in
Bergen, built by Erik
Rosenkrantz. On a
steatite plaque on
the north wall is the
builder's coat of
arms. Today the
Boys' Drill Corps
Museum is housed
in the building.

work around a decidedly varied number of activities. The address is Østre Murallmenning
23. The original stone building stands in the
middle of the street, but has a passageway
straight through. It was built by feudal overlord Erik ▶ Rosenkrantz after the city fire of
1561. Parts of the building are evidently over
800 years old since the steatite used in corners
and in the framework date back to the Munkeliv Cloister. The cloister was torn down at the
time of the Reformation. Fredrik II gave the
feudal overlord permission, in a royal letter
from 1562, to collect all the stones he needed
from the ruins of the cloister. The building was
long known as "The Rosenkrantz Wall". The
coat-of-arms of the building master can be
found in a steatite panel on the northern wall.

Stones from Munkeliv Monastery

Rosenkrantz used the elegant building for
official gatherings and banquets. Already during his time merchant trade was going on in
the cellar. After a time, and because of its fa-
vourable location near the harbour, Muren became a center for farm trade and a natural
meeting place for both inhabitants of the city
and for travellers. The ▶ "Stril people" docked
their boats nearby.

Banquets and farm trade

The merchants in the cellars of Muren had
several famous customers. Both Fridtjof Nansen and Roald Amundsen were said to have
purchased a good deal of equipment for their
expeditions there. Polar explorers Sverdrup
and Riiser-Larsen met at one time by one of
the inside counters to discuss the type and
quality of goods which today have become mu-

Nansen and Amundsen customer

M

seum objects. The sale and purchase of items in and around Muren still goes on today, with a wide selection of goods which, as in the old days, hang from hooks on the walls. The atmosphere around Muren still has the feel of the pulsating city life of earlier times.

Liquor sales

One of the state liquor shops was located in Muren from 1877 to 1922 when the State Liquor Monopoly took over. The churchwarden's office was located on the first floor from 1929 to 1977. Muren was then put to use as the Boys' Drill Corps Museum.

■ THE MUSIC LIBRARY

Oldest and largest in Scandinavia

The music department of the Bergen Public Library is the oldest and largest music department in any Scandinavian library. Already in 1913, the library could offer free loans of music from its location in the "Kjøttbasaren" (The Meat Market) by "Torget" (the Market Square). Since 1996 the music department, including the Grieg collection, has been located in modern surroundings in Grieghallen.

In addition to listening areas where visitors can listen to both LPs and CDs as well as borrow them, there are grand pianos in the rooms containing the Grieg collections for the performance of live music. The music library is placed at street level, and thus is visible to passers-by, giving the library plenty of publici-

Letters to Edvard Grieg from his mother. On the computer screen it is possible to see the original handwriting and the printed letters. The purpose of the computer project is to be able to present original documents in the Grieg collection to a wide audience, without exposing the documents to wear and tear. ▶

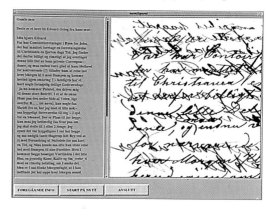

M

ty. The music library covers a total area of 555 square metres.

Musician Wilhelm Harloff, of German heritage, provided the basis for the music department, with his enormous collection of music from the library he ran in Bergen. The collection contained over 10,000 volumes and was bequeathed to the Bergen Public Library.

In 1924, the music department, headed by Clara Lampe, opened on the second floor of the new main library in Strømgaten 4. The collection grew rapidly thanks to many private gifts and donations. In 1959 Karen Falch Johannessen took over the responsibility for the department. At the same time the department had its own budget with an opportunity to make systematic purchases of music and sound equipment. NRK-Hordaland left its historic collection of 4,400 LPs to Bergen Public Library in 1998. Among these treasures is a recording of a 1948 campaign to save energy hosted by the popular radio personalities, Kallemann and Amandus. Another interesting piece is Albert Henrik Mohn's radio reports from China in 1949. Siren Steen has been head of the music department since 1992.

The Grieg Collection is an integral part of the Music Library and is based on Edvard Grieg's great testamentary gift to the Bergen Public Library. It consists of his private manuscripts, letters, music and other personal effects of a musical nature. The will was written in November 1906, ten months before Grieg's death. The conditions of the gift were that the material would "be maintained and made available to the general public of Bergen".

The Bergen Public Library owns today three quarters of all Grieg's musical items. Nina Grieg is also generously represented. In 1927 she handed over 28 sealed packages with letters for research purposes, but only after her death. The collection has later expanded by gifts and purchases, and today comprises about 25,000 pages of original documents.

The most valuable items include one hundred original scores of Grieg's compositions,

Began with a German sheet music collection

Wilhelm Harloff *(1828–1911), Norwegian musician of German heritage, was for many years a central figure in the music world of Bergen. Bergen Public Library's music department was originally based on his enormous collection of sheet music, about 10,000 volumes. In addition to playing the oboe in Den Nationale Scene's orchestra and the cello in Harmonien, Harloff ran a music shop and publishing company, a concert bureau and a music rental. He was also a capable flute player and occasionally sang in the Bergen Katedralskole choir.*

Photo: K. Nyblin, Photography collection, the University Library.

M

Nearly 6000 letters to and from Grieg

and his extensive correspondence with friends and colleagues both in Norway and in foreign countries. The collection contains more than 700 letters signed by Edvard Grieg, and in all 5000 letters addressed to him.

In 1986 the Bergen Public Library took over a large collection of music and letters from Grieg to his publishers, Max Abraham and Henri Hinrichsen in Peters Verlag, Leipzig. The material was offered to the Norwegian government for five million kroner by its owner at the time, Evelyn Hinrichsen of New York. The Norwegian Parliament decided to buy the collection, which was previously thought to have been lost during the war. First editions of Grieg's works were purchased from the Danish music dealer, Dan Fog, in 1962, increasing the value of the collection considerably.

Grieg on the computer

Computer technology is today opening new doors to the musical world of Edvard Grieg. On computer screens it will be possible to find music, lyrics and pictures, and at the same time listen to the music. The Bergen Public Library in co-operation with Vestlandsforskning and the Christian Michelsen Institute completed a project in 1990 showing that this is fully possible. Whether this will be accessible to the public in the future as a regular service, depends on the amount of financial support.

Bergen's last city musician, F. Schediwy (1804–77), drawn by his student, Edvard Grieg. Schediwy was cathedral cantor and the orchestra director of Harmonien. He wrote the music for Ibsen's play "The Banquet at Solhaug." (1856).

■ MUSIC IN BERGEN

Music in Bergen has a long history and many high points. The trio Edvard Grieg, Ole Bull and Harald Sæverud together with Harmonien and the Bergen International Festival has given Bergen an international reputation as a musical city. However, the full list of musical names is considerably longer, and this history begins many years earlier. Just the same, the musical life of the city has never bloomed more beautifully than now, at the threshold of the 21st century.

A faded score from 1261, today well preserved at the University Library in Uppsala, Sweden, is the first sign of secular music in Bergen

◄
Earliest secular Norwegian musical composition
The note sheet shows the beginning of a congratulatory song probably performed by monks at the wedding feast in Håkonshallen in 1281, for King Eirik Magnusson and the Scottish Princess Margareta. The song is the earliest piece of Norwegian secular music still preserved in its entirety.

– and indeed in Norway. This musical gem is a royal wedding song, which was probably performed by monks in Håkonshallen when King Erik Magnusson wedded the Scottish princess Margareta. The song is Norway's oldest complete and preserved secular piece of music. (See ► Håkonshallen.)

Church music has quite literally set the tone for the music of earlier times. The first church concert in this country took place in Bergen about 300 years ago. The headmaster of Katedralskolen, Søren Lintrup – Ludvig Holberg's learned teacher – had about 1,700 students perform a kind of oratorio in Domkirken.

First church concert

Already during the 1500s, organ music resounded from ► Domkirken (Bergen Cathedral) and ► Mariakirken. Bishop Gjeble Pederssøn provided Domkirken with instruments in 1549, and 400 years ago Absalon Pederssøn Beyer allowed a young man to travel abroad in order to study music. This was undoubtedly the first 'music scholarship' to have been granted in Norway.

First "music scholarship"

The position of chief musician, which existed for 257 years (1591–1848), and the establishment of a Kantor position at ► Bergen Katedralskole were both crucial to the development of music in Bergen.

The chief musicians were professional musicians with a licence, to play music professionally. The first chief musician was Lucas Jacobsen Nattheide and the last was Ferdinand Giovanni Schediwy, a Czech who was Edvard

The first music school

Harmonien's first logo.

Underground music in Fana

Gabriel Tischendorf – known for his melody to Bjørnson's poem "Jeg vil værge mit land" (I will protect my country). The bust was made by Sofus Madsen.

Many melody makers from Bergen

Grieg's singing master at Tank's School. Like his musician colleague Ole Pedersen Rødder, Schediwy was hired as the orchestral director for Harmonien. The first music school in Bergen was run by head musicians Paul Kroepelien and Rudolph Grip. Kroepelien came to Bergen from Altona in 1664.

Another head musician, Henrich Meyer, was involved in a strange occurrence in 1695 at Kyrkje-Byrkjeland in Fana where it was believed to be possible to hear 'fairy music' from underneath a boulder called Purkesteinen (The Sow Stone). The story became an international mystery and was finally solved by music researcher Arne Bjørndal, who provided a logical explanation. His hypothesis was that the tunes came from a fiddle played by a farm boy from Nå in Hardanger. The instrument was a Jåstad fiddle. The occurrence resulted in the very first notation of Norwegian folk music. The melody was an old version of the haymaking folk tune "Rotnheims-Knut".

The first precentor at Bergen Katedralskole was Peder Mogensøn Wandel, hired in 1671. His successor, Peder Stub, was appointed "director of all public music accomplishments in Bergen" in 1719.

The year 1765 was a memorable year for music, not just in Bergen, but in the entire country. This was the year the music company Harmonien was born. The first few notes from the little ensemble would later develop into the Bergen Philharmonic Orchestra and hold a pivotal position in the city's numerous musical activities. The Bergen Music Association, established in1894, made an attempt to compete with Harmonien for musicians and an audience. The feud ended with a fusion of the two groups. The new orchestra became the permanent theatre orchestra at Den Nationale Scene.

The rich musical soil of Bergen made possible the cultivation of musical creativity. Among the first composers to distinguish themselves from the rest were two headmasters from Katedralskolen, Jacob Steensen and Jens Boalth. Steensen wrote a song that was performed during King Christian VI's visit to Bergen in 1733. Boalth wrote several cantatas

One of the teachers from the school, H.B. Middelthon, composed a music-poetry piece in 1775 entitled "Hadding's Vision". This is considered to be Norway's first national choir piece. Harmonien's first concertmaster, Samuel Lind, who died in 1770, left behind two symphonies and a couple of 'concertos'. Other early composers included the organist from Korskirken, Christian Bohr (1773–1832). A symphony by Bohr was performed in Bergen in 1809.

Ketil Hvoslef
– one of the most prominent living composers in Bergen. Here in a portrait by his wife, Inger Bergitte Sæverud.

A vast number of composers have either had roots in Bergen or have worked here at some point in time. These include Ole ▸ Bull, Edvard ▸Grieg, Gabriel Tischendorf (1842–1932), Frants Beyer (1851–1918), Johan Ludvig Mowinckel jr. (1895–1940), Sverre ▸ Jorddan, Lars ▸ Søraas (both father and son), Alf Fasmer Dahl (1874–1933), Harald ▸ Sæverud, Sverre Bergh (1915–80), Lars Heggen (1877–1976), Sparre Olsen (1903–84), Finn Ludt (1918–92), Edvard Hagerup Bull (born 1922), Valter and Thorleif ▸Aamodt. One of the newer composers from Bergen is Sæverud's son, Ketil Hvoslef (born 1939).

Female composers have also contributed with brilliant works of music to the city of Bergen. Borghild Holmsen (1865–1938) was the first woman in the country to present an evening of her own compositions in the country's capital. The program contained a violin sonata, songs and a piano piece. She became Harald Sæverud's piano and harmony teacher at the Bergen Music Academy. Composer Signe Lund (1868–1950) was given very positive commendation by Edvard Grieg, while Anne-Marie Ørbeck (1911–96) who worked in Bergen most of her life, continues to be Norway's only female symphonic composer.

Anne-Marie Ørbeck
photographed when she was 85 years old. Her Symphony in D-major premiered in Bergen in 1954. This work is still the only symphony written by a female Norwegian composer.

The younger generation includes Ruth Bakke (born 1947) who has distinguished herself in the fields of church music, orchestral works and chamber music. Her bassoon concert, "Illumination", premiered in Bergen in 1995.

M

▲
BIT 20 has made two CD recordings of works by Edvard Hagerup Bull. The composer, here together with the conductor, Ingar Bergby, follow the recording. Hagerup Bull was born in Bergen and is related to both Edvard Grieg and Ole Bull.

Church music is presented each year in a series of concerts in ▶ Domkirken, ▶ Mariakirken, ▶ Korskirken and Johanneskirken.

Bjørgvin Kirkemusikk Inc. administers the extensive activities associated with Domkirken. The company organises about 80 concerts a year.

BIT 20 Ensemble is a permanent professional chamber ensemble for contemporary music, established in 1989. Most of the members are section leaders from the Bergen Philharmonic Orchestra.

The ensemble covers most of the Norwegian and international repertoire – from solos to sinfoniettas. Activities consist of concerts, educational projects, radio productions, CD recordings, tours in and outside the country and modern musical theatre productions.

Ingar Bergby has been the regular conductor for the ensemble since 1991.

Solo players in record long performance

Bergen Blåsekvintett (The Bergen Wind Quintet) is composed of solo wind players from the Bergen Philharmonic Orchestra, and has existed since 1946, an unusually long-lasting accomplishment for this kind of ensemble.

The quintet has completed a number of successful tours through the United States and in Europe, in addition to national concerts. Their CD with Carl Nielsen's music for wind instruments has been selected by the record company Gramophone to be a 'Best Buy'. In 1982 the quintet was awarded first prize at a chamber music festival in Colmar, France.

M

The Bergen Wind Quintet has constructed its own educational program, and the musicians have therefore been asked to serve as instructors for advanced students at American universities. Several composers, such as Harald Sæverud, have written music especially designed for the quintet.

Forsvarets Musikkorps Vestlandet (The Military Marching Bands of Western Norway) is the official name of the institution better known to the public as "Divisjonsmusikken". In the old days the name was "Brigademusikken".

The most important conquest of this group of musical soldiers has to be the Bergen audience. It is the only orchestra that often performs free of charge, and has done so for more than 200 years. For many years the band played each week in the music pavilion in Byparken. The soldiers also paraded to the resounding music of their band outside their headquarters at Bergenhus and were a popular public attraction. Unfortunately the band finally had to capitulate in the battle against traffic noise. Salvation arrived when they were allowed to play in the foyer of Grieghallen. The band performs here during the winter months, usually every Friday at 12 noon. During the summer, weekly concerts are held in Grieghallen or in Håkonshallen. The band also performs on official occasions, in addition to frequent performances at the Naval College and other schools. On formal occasions the band will contribute with dinner music at Håkonshallen.

The music soldiers have functioned as in-

Instructors

Conquered the public – lost to traffic

Bjørn N. Sagstad – conductor of the Military Band.

Bergen Wind Quintet has become internationally known. From left: Vidar Olsen, horn, Per Hannevold, bassoon, Gro Sandvik, flute, Steinar Hannevold, oboe and Lars Kristian Brynildsen, clarinet.

◀

Bergensiaden
– a national festival for marching bands was launched for the first time in June 1998. The event will be repeated every other year.

structors and conductors for many of the amateur marching bands in the Bergen district. This has probably been the military's best and most important weapon in 'charm attacks' aimed at the city's civilians.

The history of the Bergen Marching Band dates back to 1792, with the professional assistance of six musicians from Copenhagen. Today the band has 28 musicians, of whom three are music students serving their obligatory military term. Bjørn N. Sagstad began as band conductor in 1998.

Collegium Musicum (CM) is a chamber orchestra and choir with ties to Korskirken. The orchestra is composed of professional musicians, music students and talented amateurs.

Collegium Musicum functions as a bridge-builder between amateur musicians and the professional music world. It also serves as a rehearsal orchestra for the Grieg Academy. Their repertoire consists of Vienna-classical music and church music. The orchestra hires guest conductors from Norway and abroad.

Choir music has a rich and longstanding tradition in Bergen. The oldest choir belongs to Harmonien and is as old as the music company itself. The first assembly of singers from Bergen took place in 1856 when nine choirs met. The first four singing competitions were organised by Johan D. Behrens, from Bergen, the first of which was held in Asker in 1851.

In 1999 there are 45 choirs in Bergen, including 13 men's choirs and two women's choirs, all affiliated with the Hordaland Choir Association. There are in addition a number of church choirs, children's choirs and free choirs. Several of the choirs have done very well in competitions. Sandviken Congregational Choir (director Thorleif ▶ Aamodt) performed at the first Bergen Festival in 1953. Fana Men's Choir (director Sigmund Skage), ▶ Bergen Domkantori and Bergen College's Youth Choir "Voce Nobili" (director Maria Gamborg Helbekkmo) have all distinguished themselves both nationally and internationally.

Band music has always held a strong position in Bergen and Hordaland. The marching bands in Bergen had their own organisation long before the Norwegian Association of Marching Bands, now administered from Bergen, was formed in 1918. Arna Music Association is the oldest band in the West Country, founded in 1877.

65 marching bands

The Norwegian Association of Marching Bands in Bergen consists of 65 bands (1999), including 23 amateur bands and 42 school bands. The Association has altogether 2,500 members. There are in addition several free bands.

The city's elite marching bands include Sandvikens Ungdomskorps, Dragefjeldets Musikkorps, Krohnengen Brassband and Tertnes Brass. In the Bergen area there is also the Eikanger and Bjørsvik Brassband, which has twice won the European Championship for brass bands.

European Champions

Popular music has been written and performed by several talented artists from Bergen. The finest artists include: Duo performers Kurt Foss and Reidar Bøe, Arne Bendiksen (lyric writer, singer and record producer), Sissel Kyrkjebø, Karoline Krüger and Jan Eggum (who sings his own songs). Salhuskvintetten, led by Monrad Holm Johnsen from Bergen, became popular with their song "Gryta hennar mor" from 1963.

The popular Salhuskvintetten. Their leader Monrad Holm Johnsen on the left.

Sissel Kyrkjebø had her breakthrough as an international artist when the Eurovision Song Contest was televised from Grieghallen in 1986.

Bergen Kammermusikkforening (Bergen Chamber Music Association) was founded in 1935 and has as its objective the arranging of concerts of high artistic quality for its members. It holds as many as 12 concerts each year. Among these concerts is "De Unges Kammerkonsert" (Youth Chamber Concert), which is performed in Grieghallen. Harald Sæverud's first and third string quartet was written especially for the Chamber Music Association.

M

■ NEWSPAPERS

From six to three daily newspapers after 1945

In 1945, just after the end of the second World War, Bergen had as many as six daily news-papers: "Bergens Tidende" (The Bergen Times) supported by the left-wing party Venstre, "Bergens Arbeiderblad" (Bergen Labour News) supported by the Labour Party, the right-wing (Høyre) newspaper "Morgenavisen" (Morning News), the independent Christian paper, "Dagen" (Today), the communist newspaper, "Arbeidet" (Worker) and the New-Norwegian paper "Gula Tidend".

In 1999 only three of these newspapers still exist: "Bergens Tidende", "Dagen" and "Bergens Arbeiderblad" (which in 1991 was renamed "Bergensavisen", or BA for short). On the other hand, the newspaper market experienced a considerable growth in the number of smaller district newspapers. The oldest of these is "Bygdanytt" (Country News), distributed in Indre Arna since 1951. The largest of the local newspapers is "Fanaposten", which began publication in Nesttun in 1978. "Åsane Tidende" is the local paper for the northern district, while "Sydvesten" covers the districts of Fyllingsdalen and Bønes. In addition, "Annonse-Avisen" (printing primarily ads) has been distributed free of charge in Bergen and the surrounding area since 1984. The special-interest newspaper "Fiskaren" (the Fisherman) is also a regular publication in Bergen.

Oldest and largest

Bergens Tidende is the city's oldest and western Norway's largest newspaper, founded in 1868 by printer Johan Wilhelm Eide from

Stryn. In 1894 Bergens Tidende fused with Bergensposten. The paper was the main medium for the left-wing political party, Venstre, in western Norway until 1990, but is today a politically independent and non-socialist newspaper.

Circulation reached a high point in 1986–87 when more than 100,000 copies were printed. The newspaper considers Bergen, Hordaland municipality and Sogn and Fjordane municipality as its target areas, and it has come out seven days a week since 1996. The newspaper is edited in "bokmål", the main Norwegian language, although journalists have the freedom to use "nynorsk", or New Norwegian, if they so choose. As a result, Bergens Tidende has a greater number of articles in New Norwegian than any other paper. The editorial and production offices have been located on Nygårdsgaten 5–11 since 1919. A new printing office was established in Drotningsvik in Laksevåg in 1998. There are plans to move the rest of the staff from Nygårdsgaten to a new building in the Krinkelkrok quarter.

Both standard and New Norwegian language

Bergens Tidende has also had a hand in viewdata, radio, television, local newspapers and publishing.

Many media

Bergensavisen, BA, formerly Bergens Arbeiderblad, changed its name in 1991, at the same time as the newspaper declared itself editorially independent of Arbeiderpartiet (the Labour Party), though it continued to hold a social-democratic profile.

First Sunday paper in Bergen

The Norwegian Labour Party founded the newspaper in 1927 after the party's earlier newspaper, Arbeidet, was taken over by the Norwegian Communist Party. The first editor was Gunnar Ousland. The editorial office has been located in Christian Michelsen's Street 4 since 1935, and a new printing office at Fjøsanger has produced the paper since 1994.

Stopped by the Germans

The publication of Bergensavisen was stopped during the war and its offices were taken over by the German occupation authorities. From 1981 the paper came out in the morning instead of the afternoon, and was published in tableau format under the name BA. In 1990 it became the first newspaper in Bergen with a Sunday edition.

Mouthpiece for pietism

Dagen is a politically independent, daily Christian newspaper, founded in 1919 with Johs Lavik as its first editor. The newspaper advocates strict, pietistic Christian views. The board of directors stopped publication during the war to avoid a take-over by the Nazis. Since 1989 Dagen has been printed in tabloid format. Editorial offices are located in Sparebankgaten 4.

■ NONNESETER CONVENT

Monastery and convent – and estate

Nonneseter, the home of the order of Cistercian nuns, was Norway's only convent, founded in 1150. Certain things indicate that it could once have been a Benedictine cloister.

This drawing depicts Nonneseter Convent Church. The length of the church was about 50 metres. ▶

Only the western foot of the tower of the convent church and a small part of the chancel chapel have been preserved.

The foot of the tower – on the corner of Strømgaten and Kaigaten – belonged to the Maria church of the monastery, and contains a small vaulted room in Romanesque style. It was consecrated after World War II as a memorial to those inhabitants of Bergen who fell during the war. Hans Jacob Meyer's sculpture "Mother and Child" was unveiled in the hall in 1956.

On Kaigaten 3, a little farther south, stands the small chapel with room for up to 40 people. The chapel has a beautiful vault with Gothic arches marked with steatite stone. During the years from 1951 to 1989 the chapel was used as a church for the deaf. Today summer concerts are held there.

The saga tells of King Magnus Lagabøter who in 1262 left his newborn son Olav to be cared for by the nuns at Nonneseter. The king also bequeathed a large sum of money and a significant amount of worldly goods to the convent. In 1528 the property of Nonneseter was comprised of almost 300 farms between Nordfjord and Sunnhordland. The very wealthy and powerful convent owned several buildings

▲
Nonneseter's chancel chapel on the left, and the foot of the tower with the memorial to Bergen men fallen during World War II.

Summer concerts

The kings son left to the nuns

on Bryggen and half of Sydnes, now known as Nygård.

At the end of the 15th century the nuns were finished. They were accused of "immorality and poor conduct" and were chased away from Nonneseter. Things did not work out any better for the Antonius monks who took over in 1507. They did however attempt to do some good by running a shelter and caring for those afflicted by leprosy. The monks were not able to keep to the straight and narrow path. The result was that King Fredrik I in 1528 relinquished the convent and its property to State Council member Vincens Lunge. The convent was then in severe disrepair, and Lunge rebuilt it for use as a private residence. Nonneseter became the secular Lungegården (Lunge Estate).

Sinful nuns and monks

The history of the estate continued until 1891. A great fire led to an almost complete destruction of the buildings on the estate. The Historical Society was able to purchase and thus save the only remains, the tower and the chapel.

Ravaged by fire

■ NYE CARTE BLANCHE DANCE THEATRE

Modern dance theatre and ballet school

Nye Carte Blanche Dance Theatre AS was established in 1990 with Anne Borg as its first artistic director. The institution is a continuation of the dance theatre started by Carte Blanche in Oslo in Bergen the previous year, but that went bankrupt. Nye Carte Blanche is the only modern ballet ensemble in Norway that receives full government financial support. Instruction is offered in both classical ballet and advanced jazz ballet.

The company is housed in Danseteatret, the former gymnastics hall, an art nouveau building that was built in 1910. The theatre auditorium has 300 seats. In addition to the stage, foyer and offices, the theatre has two rehearsal halls.

Dansetheatret
(Dance Theatre), Si-
gurdsgate 6, has ta-
ken over the gym-
nastics hall which
was built in 1910
for the Bergen Gym-
nastics Association.
Architect: Egil
Reimers.

◀

The staff is comprised of thirteen dancers and nine employees who hold administrative and technical positions. Two or three main productions per season are given in Bergen, but the company also tours often both in this country and abroad. Karen Foss has been the company's artistic director since 1997.

■ NYKIRKEN

Nykirken at Nordnes represents not only earlier church history, but also a proud cultural history. Here Ludvig Holberg and Harald Sæverud were baptised, Edvard Grieg was confirmed and Amalie Skram married. It was here that the archbishop lived during his visits to Bergen. The building burned down in 1589, and today's church was raised over its remains.

Built over the ruins of The Archbishop's estate

During the Middle Ages the king and archbishop each dominated their own side of the seaward approach to Bergen. On the east side of Vågen towered the royal residency, Håkonshallen, while the archbishop's resplendent palace, no less imposing, challenged the throne on the west side. The Archbishop's estate was actually the larger of the two monumental stone buildings, with a length of almost 60 metres as opposed to Håkonshallen's 37 metres. A chapel devoted to St. Klements belonged to the building complex.

Larger than Håkonshallen

Following the Reformation part of Parliament was held in the Archbishop's estate be-

Nykirken
was built over the ruins of Erke- bispegården (The Archbishop's estate). ▶

Famous organist

The famous organ virtuoso, German- born Ferdinand W. Vogel (1807–92), was the organist of Nykirken from 1852 until his death. He also star- ted an organ school in Bergen. Among his students was Lars Søraas senior. According to Fr. Konow Lund, people came from far away just to lis- ten to the renowned organist playing his organ.

tween 1562 and 1577. It also served as a store- house for royal goods. King Christian IV al- lowed the northwestern part of the building to be used as a church in 1618. The first Nykir- ken could therefore be consecrated in 1622, but burned to the ground the following year. The building was quickly restored, only to be destroyed by fire again in 1660, 1756, 1800 and by the catastrophic explosion in 1944. During the reconstruction after World War II the church finally received its baroque tower dome and spires designed by architect Johan J. Reichborn for the reconstruction in 1756. This occurred after heated newspaper de- bates. The church has 750 seats.

Those who are especially interested may, with permission from the vicar's office, visit the historical ruins of the Archbishop's estate in the cellar under Nykirken. There is talk of opening the cellar as a museum.

N

▨ KING OLAV KYRRE

King Olav III Haraldson, with the nickname 'Kyrre' (the peace loving) (1050–93) founded the city of Bergen around the year 1070, or, as is told in the saga: "made a merchant town of Bjørgvin". He was 20 years old at the time.

Three years earlier Olav had been crowned king together with his brother Harald. At that time there were barely 200,000 Norwegians to rule in the entire country, less than the population of Bergen today. He became the country's sole ruler in 1069 when his brother died. His father, King Harald Hardråde, fell in bat-tle at Stanford Bridge in 1066. Olav followed his father to England, but did not fight in the battle.

With the enlightened, peaceable king as their protector, the prospective cultural town could scarcely have had a better start. Olav Kyrre was the first Norwegian king who was able to read and write. Symbolically, a monument has been raised in front of the Bergen Public Library in his honour. The monument, created by Knut Steen, shows the king riding on a horse of steel, and was unveiled in 1998 by the present day king of Norway, Harald V. Olav Kyrre's Street was named for the king in 1882.

During the reign of Olav Kyrre there was no war in the country. The king made peace with William the Conquerer and with Svend Estridssøn, who had earlier made a claim to Norway. The king took Svend's daughter Ingerid for his queen. He established a good relationship with the pope as well. He assisted the clergyman during services and set aside pro-

Peaceful king founded Bergen

King Olav Kyrre, as Nic. Schiøll imagined the founder of Bergen. Schiøll won the first competition to build the Kyrre monument in Bergen in 1928.

No war

Knut Steen is the master behind the Olav Kyrre monument erected outside the Bergen Public Library. Olav Kyrre was the first Norwegian king who learned to read. ▶

I LOVE this sculpture!

Constructed churches

perty for episcopal residences in Bergen and Oslo. He also began construction of Lille Kristkirke (Little Church of Christ) at Holmen (Bergenhus), and began the construction of a stone cathedral, Store Kristkirke (The Great Church of Christ) nearby. There are still some traces of the church's stone foundation.

Snorre Sturlasson gives this description of Olav Kyrre:

An elegant man

"Olav was a tall man and well built; people said that no one had ever seen a more handsome or elegant man. He had yellow hair like silk that suited him exceedingly well. He was fair, with remarkably beautiful eyes and fine limbs. He spoke few words and gave no speeches in Parliament, but was glad during drinking parties, and drank willingly, and then he was talkative and cheerful. There was peace as long as he ruled the kingdom."

Olav had no children by his queen. Magnus

Son by a mistress

III Barfot (1073–1103) was his son by a mistress.

In strong contrast to Olav Kyrre's peaceable reputation, the inhabitants of Bergen have fought a bitter battle about His Majesty's monument – its creation and location – all the way to the courtroom. From the first time the idea of a monument was brought up in 1893 until the founder of the city was finally honoured, 105 years had passed. Meanwhile, two sculpture competitions had been held, in 1928 and in 1968.

105 years from idea to result

■ OPERA IN BERGEN

A strongly acclaimed performance of Puccini's opera "La Bohème" was the debut of the Vest-Norges Opera in Grieghallen in March 1998. The operatic director Anne Randine Øverby wielded the conductor's baton herself for the occasion. This was also the debut for Norway's first regional music theatre, which had yet to become a regular financial item on the national budget.

Norway's first regional opera

In addition to Vest-Norges Opera, Opera Vest and the Bergen Chamber Opera have continued their activities as independent, private companies.

The foundation Vest-Norges Opera was established by the Hordaland county government and Bergen city council as a regional opera company of western Norway. The company receives financial support from privately owned businesses, but so far not from the state. Artistically the operations are based on co-operation with relevant cultural institutions in Bergen such as Den Nationale Scene and Nye Carte Blanche, with the Bergen Opera Choir and the Bergen Philharmonic Orchestra as their musical foundation.

The ambition of the company is to produce classical operas on a large scale, touring performances on a smaller scale, and a chamber opera – perhaps with smaller modern scores and performances for children. During the next few years, from 1999 to 2002, five different performances are scheduled per year. In addition the opera wishes to "remain culturally and politically correct, maintain and strengthen involvement by free artists and ensembles, and give talented Norwegian artists

Great ambitions

Anne Randine Øverby
– head of Vest-Norges Opera (West Norwegian Opera) and Bergen Opera Choir, and former leader of Opera Bergen.

▶

an opportunity to work in their home country".

The very active local performers on the opera stage are an addition to the yearly guest performances from Den Norske Opera, along with both national and international opera performances during the Bergen International Festival.

Stein Olav Henrichsen
– director of Opera Vest and BIT 20.

Opera Vest has its roots in the environment around BIT 20 and Music Factory (see ▶ Music in Bergen), and was in 1992 established as a foundation. Stein Olav Henrichsen has been the administrative leader for both Opera Vest and BIT 20 from the beginning, and has an office in Grieghallen. The musicians primarily come from BIT 20, while Opera Vest does not base its activities on any permanent choir.

In its choice of repertoire, emphasis is placed on new Norwegian and well as international musical drama. Classical works are also included now and then. Mozart's "The Magic Flute" has been a Christmas performance by the Danseteatret for many years. Opera Vest has also collaborated on certain performances with Den Nationale Scene. In 1994 Opera Vest contributed to the cultural program during the Olympic Games in Lillehammer.

Bergen Kammeropera (Bergen Chamber Opera) was established in 1982 as a free, professional group with Marit Karaskiewicz as its artistic director. The opera's repertoire ranges from Mozart to Menotti. The debut performance was Mozart's "Bastien and Bastienne", performed outdoors on the property of shipowner Hilmar Reksten, at Fjøsanger. The ensemble has toured in both Norway and Sweden, and has performed at the International Festival. The children's opera "Doctor Musikus" was, in collaboration with Den Nationale Scene, set up for more than 10,000 children throughout 70 performances.

Soprano singer Marit Karaskiewicz *is both the leader and an active singer in the Bergen Chamber Opera.*

Bergen has a rich traditional history as an opera city. Here are some milestones:

– 1831: The ballad opera "Mountain Adventure" by Waldemar Thrane is presented by Ole Bull. The first known opera performance in Bergen.

– 1888–89: Successful guest opera performance at Den Nationale Scene by Bjarne Lund's ensemble.

– 1899: Christian Danning becomes the theatre's musical director and presents two operas.

– 1907: Under the orchestral conductor Harald Heide, the opera becomes a permanent element at Den Nationale Scene for ten years until he steps down in 1927.

– 1932: Sverre Jordan becomes orchestral conductor at Den Nationale Scene on the condition that he is able to present opera. Thus a tradition has begun and continues until Harmonien's theatre services end in 1979.

Over 42,000 people in Bergen have seen the successful operettas "The Merry Widow" and "My Fair Lady".

– 1957: Bergen School of Opera is established by Frederica Anthonisen and Werner van Flandern. The school has 20 students and gives performances at Den Nationale Scene to-

**Opera School ▶
of Bergen**
could claim several
successes in the
1960s. This picture
is from one of the
rehearsals for the
Pergolesi opera "La
serva padrona".
Victor Rostin Svend-
sen was the conduc-
tor. The singers are
from left: Liv Dahle,
Norunn Illevold Gis-
ke, Kåre Pettersen,
Knut Gram Knud-
sen, Ferry Berg-Ol-
sen, Arne Grepstad
and Randi Lexau.

gether with professional singers. From 1960
their work is carried on by Victor Rostin
Svendsen, Ferry Berg-Olsen and Kjell Stormo-
en.

**Opera choir
and orchestra**

– 1975–81: Yngve Næss begins an opera production based on the music department at the
Bergen Teacher College. He formed the Bergen Opera Choir and the Bergen Opera Orchestra, and collaborated on performances at
Den Nationale Scene and in Grieghallen.

Opera Bergen

– 1982: Bergen Opera Choir withdraws from
the collaboration and starts Opera Bergen as
a free, idealistic organisation, led by Anne
Randine Øverby. Completed over 40 performances in Grieghallen, including several Norwegian premiers. Had great success with "Na-
bucco", "Aida" and "Otello" as outdoor summer
performances at Bergenhus. The operation of
Opera Bergen was carried on within the framework of Vest-Norges Opera from 1998. The
Bergen Chamber Opera is established.

Opera Piccola

– 1984: Anthonisen and van Flandern return to Bergen to run Opera Piccola for a period of ten years. Presents Emilio de Cavaliéri's
mystery drama "Play of the Soul and the
Body" in Domkirken in collaboration with
Domkantoriet.

– 1991: Opera Vest is established

– 1997: Vest-Norges Opera is established.
Opera Bergen closes down its operations.

▪ PERMANENTEN

The permanent exhibition building, popularly called 'Permanenten', and Vestlandske Kunstindustrimuseum (the Western Norwegian Museum of Applied Arts) have become synonymous terms. While other galleries such as the Fishery Museum, the Bergen Art Gallery and the Bergen Art Society have come and gone, Vestlandske Kunstindustrimuseum has literally become a permanent fixture in Permanenten since the house was finished in 1896.

The stylish, neo-Renaissance style building of Kristiania architect Henry Bucher is considered an architectural monument. It is also beautifully decorated. Twelve figure reliefs in gneiss by an unknown artist adorn the façades. The arches of the vestibules, embellished by four stucco reliefs, have been executed by sculptor Hans J. Johannsen. In a place of honour towers the city's most prominent painter, J. C. ▶ Dahl.

In 1993 Permanenten housed the great anniversary exhibition of Edvard Grieg. With all the other exhibitions out of the building, the Museum of Decorative Arts was, in 1994, able to present a wide range of unique examples of Chinese art and handicrafts, the largest of its kind of Europe. This exhibit is now partly held in a new annex. Most of the Chinese collection, in all about 2,500 objects of marble, porcelain, earthenware, bronze and jade, is a donation from General Johan Wilhelm Normann Munthe, a native of Bergen. Munthe lived in China from 1887 until his death in 1935. He served in the last Emperor's army and became Commander of the Guards in the first Chinese re-

*Home of
The Western
Museum of
Applied Art
since 1896*

*General Johan
J. N. Munthe
(1864–1935) is
responsible for the
unique China collection in the Vestlandske Kunstindustrimuseum. Here painted
by Hubardt Vos.*

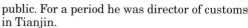

▲
The permanent exhibition building by Byparken was completed in 1896.

Art historian Johan Bøgh (1848-1935) *founded the Vestlandske Kunstindustrimuseum in 1887 and was its curator until 1931. He also started Den Nationale Scene.*
Photo: Joh. von der Fehr, Photographic colletion Bergen University Library.

public. For a period he was director of customs in Tianjin.

The museum accepted, upon its opening, a large number of gifts from merchant C. Sundt, and later also from the American artist couple Anne Brigh and William A. Singer. The Singer collection comprises 597 objects, including paintings, as well as European and oriental furniture. Several of the paintings come from Olden in Nordfjord, where the couple lived for many years. The museum's collection also includes artwork in silver, furniture from different periods, glass, porcelain and textiles such as tapestries. A large collection of Bergen silver makes up an especially interesting and valuable wing.

Locked inside a glass case is a musical gem of the grandest sort: Ole Bull's 'treasure chamber violin', built over 400 years ago by Gaspar da Salo and decorated by Benvenuto Cellini. The dream of one day hearing the world famous violin play music again was stopped by Bull's widow. She bequeathed the violin to the museum on the condition that it would never be played again, and that the glass case would never be opened, except in the presence of the city's mayor and the director of the museum. The violin received its name because it was supposedly kept in a treasure chamber at the castle of Ambras near Innsbruck for 200 years. When Bull succeeded in securing the violin, the event was celebrat-ed in Leipzig where he performed Beethoven's Kreutzer sonata together with Franz Liszt and Felix Mendelssohn.

P

RASMUS MEYER'S COLLECTION

Art collector and mill owner

A serious gentleman formally attired in a dark suit and bowler hat. This is how Rasmus Wold Meyer (1858–1916) appears in a large portrait in the museum bearing his name. The artist has, however, given the distinguished gentleman a tulip in his hand. An appropriate picture with lovely symbolism of the successful businessman who sacrificed all his spare time and profit on art.

The art-loving Bergensian left behind nearly one thousand paintings, 137 by Munch alone, in addition to furniture and other objects. According to Meyer's wishes, this extremely valuable collection was donated to the city of Bergen. In order to show its gratitude, the city gave the works of art a magnificent home in a separate gallery by Lille Lungegårdsvann – in Rasmus Meyers allé. The handsome building, drawn by architect Ole Landmark, stood completed in 1924. Before this time the collection had filled his home in Krybbebakken.

Meyer's father had founded Vaksdal Mill. This became the financial basis for Rasmus Meyer's art purchases. Under Meyer's leadership at the beginning of the 1900s, the company grew to become the largest milling industry in Scandinavia.

The core of the collection is Norwegian art, from J.C. Dahl to Edvard Munch. Several of the most prominent painters working during the period of 1880 to 1915 have been given a

Art collector Rasmus Meyer portrayed by Hjørdis Landmark. The painting was done on commission from Bergen municipality. It now hangs in the stairway of the art museum.
210 x 120 cm.

▲
This watercolour in Rasmus Meyer´s Collection was painted by Henrik Ibsen in 1842 – when he was 14 years old. The motif is from Follestad farm near Skien. Measurements: 16.5 x 43.5 cm.

wider representation in Rasmus Meyer's Collection than in any other art museum. The Munch collection in Bergen is considered especially valuable since each painting was chosen after deliberations between the artist and the collector. The objective was to display Munch's artistic development.

Many visitors will be surprised to discover pieces by Henrik Ibsen in the art museum. The dramatist appears not only as a motif on Erik Werenskiold's famous portrait, which later became a picture on a stamp from 1978, but also as an artist with his own painting. The painting was done in 1842, when the future writer was only 14 years old.

Great artists

Several of the great artists are thoroughly represented in the collection: Harriet Backer, Christian Krogh, Nicolai Astrup, Hans Fredrik Gude, Theodor Kittelsen, Thorvald Erichsen, Thomas Fearnley and Gerhard Munthe.

Interior decorations from Bergen have also been included. Mathias Blumenthal's colourful rococo paintings decorate both walls and ceiling. The decorations were made for the house of Consul Henrik Jansen Fasmer on Strandgaten after the fire of 1756. One of the most precious pieces in the museum is Ole Bull's grand piano, from the piano factory of Ands. Meyer & Sohn in Hamburg.

Ole Bull's grand piano

R

■ NORDAHL ROLFSEN

In 1892 the first edition of "Reader for the Primary School" by Bergensian Johan Nordahl Brun Rolfsen (1848–1928) appeared. The book was to become the most widely read book in Norway, second only to the Bible, and nearly eight million copies were to be published. The fifth and last edition of the five-volume series was printed in 1939, and it was used by pupils in many schools as late as the 1960s. By then one could say he had practically taught all the Norwegians how to read.

Wrote Norway's most widely read book

At Landås, where the teacher's training college is located, Rolfsen has long been honoured by a street in his name. A monument is soon to be erected at Klosteret near his childhood home in Holbergsallmenning 20 – an address which no longer exists.

Rolfsen inherited his Christian name from the bishop and poet Johan Nordahl ▶ Brun, his great-grandfather on both his mother's and father's side. Rolfsen passed on the creative talent to his son, painter Alf Rolfsen.

Nordahl Rolfsen studied literature in Kristiania, but never completed a degree. He was, however, able to gather some teaching experience at Hambros School in Bergen. In addition to being a literary consultant and stage director at The National Theatre of Bergen (Den Nationale Scene), Rolfsen was a prolific writer. He wrote, in rapid succession, two books of poetry, four short story anthologies, nine plays and a Bergen-based farce ("Nordlandstrompeten" – The Trumpet of the North).

Teacher and a prolific writer

His greatest theatre success, a fairy-tale comedy ("Svein Uredd" – Svein the Fearless) which includes the well-known "Solefaldssang" (The Sunset Song), was published in 1890. Ole Olsen composed the music to the play.

It was, however, as a pioneer in the field of children's literature and popular science that his unique skills yielded the best results. "World History for Children", "Light Upon the Land" and "Science for Everyone" were Rolfsen's main works during a period when child-

A pioneer

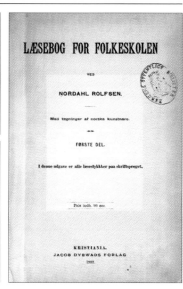

▲

This is the first page of Nordahl Rolfsen's reader from 1892, the first reader ever to be illustrated. Erik Werenskiold made this drawing for the theme "Saturday Night". Rolfsen applied for a 3000 kroner state grant for three years in order to complete the reading book project. The application was turned down by four votes in the Parliament. The foresighted publisher Jacob Dybwad then generously offered to give Rolfsen the grant himself, and he also offered to publish the book.

Photo: P. Christiansen, the University Library

ren's educational literature basically was virgin territory.

Rolfsen's magic formula for opening children's minds was to impart knowledge through a method of story-telling based on four main themes: sagas, fairy-tales, animal life and journeys to distant lands. He modernised education by introducing illustrations in school books, drawings that he commissioned some of the country's leading artists to make. Rolfsen first tested out his ideas in the "Illustrated Journal for Children" which he edited for nine years. He also hired some of the country's top writers, but reserved himself the right to make the material "edible" for children. Even Henrik Ibsen wrote a piece about his journey to Egypt where he attended the opening of the Suez Canal.

Edvard ▶ Grieg responded positively to Rolfsen's request to write music for songs in the reader; the result was "Childish Songs, op.61" (Barnlige Sange, op.61), which Grieg dedicated to Nordahl Rolfsen. The songs were considered the finest ever written for children in the 19th century, and several of them are still among children's favourite songs.

THE ROSENKRANTZ TOWER

Two Danish statesmen, Christoffer Valkendorf and Erik Ottesen Rosenkrantz have both had their names associated with the majestic Tower at Bergenhus. It is the latter who undoubtedly most deserves this honour, since it was he who ignored the royal command from Copenhagen to tear down the deteriorating castle. He decided instead, in 1562, to restore the old walls and have them rebuilt to form a significantly larger and taller tower. Today's Tower can rightfully be called the Rosenkrantz Tower. Sailing in toward Vågen, one can see the Tower looming tall, a venerable landmark, or perhaps even the eighth peak of Bergen.

Rosenkrantz were a feudal overlord at Bergenhus from 1559–68. But the foundation for the Rosenkrantz Tower was laid during the 1200s by King Magnus Lagabøter. The tower was the cornerstone of the enormous royal fortress he had built. In the north stood ▸ Håkonshallen surrounded by a wall, gate tower and fortifications. Rosenkrantz Tower is considered the oldest and most significant monument from the Renaissance in Norway, although it bears clear evidence of having had several builders.

The structure from the Middle Ages in the northern section constitutes a tower within the Tower. On the second floor are the remains of a chapel with Gothic windows, built by King Magnus in 1273. The king had his private chamber on the third floor. It was here, perhaps, that he worked on many of his law proposals.

The castle was left untouched throughout the Middle Ages, but was in bad disrepair and ruined by the fire of 1513 when the captain at Bergenshus, Jørgen Hanssøn Skriver, took over the responsibility for its reconstruction and fortification. The dimensions of the Tower were expanded by a few cubits when his successor, Eske Bille took over the project. Howe-

Ignored orders from the king – and saved the Tower

A simplified cross section of the Tower

Valuable symbol

"The proud, stately front of the Tower is rooted in our city skyline like no other building, and its fate reflects so closely the history of our city and our country in good times and bad, that the Tower has become a valuable symbol of that which was, is and shall be."
Professor Robert Kloster

Silhuett of King Magnus Lagabøter on the wall of the Rosenkrantz Tower.

▲
The Rosenkrantz Tower is the most significant Renaissance monument in Norway.

ver, some of the building material was taken from some of the city's most important ecclesiastical buildings, which Bille had thoughtlessly ordered destroyed. Kristkirken, Apostelkirken and Bispegården were all destroyed in 1531 by Bille, who maintained that they stood in the way of an effective defence.

The Tower was severely damaged again in the 1530s by an explosion in the gunpowder chamber. The damage was partly repaired by Valkendorf when his successor, Erik Rosenkrantz, received the fatal orders from Copenhagen, which fortunately were not followed.

Both castle and fortress

Rosenkrantz made the Tower into a monumental structure with a two-fold function as both a fortress and a castle. The interior of the top floors contains elegant halls with tiled floors and steatite hearths. The rooms were furnished as was fitting for the residence of a king and his deputy.

Most conspicuous from the Rosenkrantz' reconstruction is the wide façade with gun loops facing Bryggen. The object was most likely to frighten the Hanseatics who had dangerously increased their influence at the expense of the king's power. This certainly had an effect. One could say that the power of the Hanseatic League in Norway was broken by cannons that were never fired.

The battery of cannons in the Tower had their baptism of fire in 1665 when the Dutch East-India fleet of 50 ships was pursued by a British flotilla of 30 vessels all the way to Vågen. The fleet had a cargo valued at 600 barrels of gold. The attackers were forced to withdraw when the commander at Bergenhus took the side of the Dutch and fired a double round at the British. A cannonball from this dramatic battle is still lodged in the wall over the entrance to Domkirken.

The battle in the Bay of Bergen was an event that was spoken of all over Europe. It was also the first and last time cannons were fired from the fortress.

The years that followed were a period of decay. The Tower came to be used as an armament and gunpowder chamber. Near the end of the 1800s, on J.C. Dahl's initiative, work began on restoring the old fortress as a historical monument.

During the 1930s the Tower was opened to the public for the first time. The catastrophic explosion of 1944 caused what appeared to be irreparable damage to the Rosenkrantz Tower and Håkonshallen. Restoration began almost immediately and the Tower was completed in 1966. Heading the successful restoration work was Professor Robert Kloster and architects Gerhard Fischer and Fredrik Konow-Lund.

Since 1985 Leidangen (the organisation for voluntary military instruction) has been allocated a permanent exhibition in Rosenkrantz Tower's cannon loft.

Frightened the Hanseatic League

Erik Ottesen Rosenkrantz *(1519–75) – feudal overlord at Bergenhus 1560–68. He belongs to one of the most prominent noble families in Denmark. The family took the name of Rosenkrantz (Wreath of Roses) after an ancestor, who on a visit to Rome, received a wreath of roses as a gift from the Pope. Erik Rosenkrantz was born at Tørning. He became a very wealthy man with several pieces of property in Norway, Denmark, the Faeroe Islands and Shetland.*

R

S

■ LYDER SAGEN

Awakened the sense of the aesthetic in the people of Bergen

The bust of Lyder Sagen in Bergen Katedralskole.

Famous students

"I believe that one of Oehlenschläger's tragedies could now be a fitting task. You must begin rehearsing roles. Now then, those of you who have some talent for writing poetry may begin translating some of Homer's poetry into verse."

Faced with challenges like these, who knows how students of today would have tackled the situation. Lyder Sagen (1777–1859) utilised these unorthodox teaching methods at ▶Bergen Katedralskole. He was employed at the school from 1805 until his death – first as a teacher and later, from 1814, as a head teacher. He has been honoured both by his hometown and by the school, with a street named after him and with a portrait bust.

For more than a generation Sagen was the city's leading cultural personality. He was recognised both as a writer and a brilliant educator. His teaching of the Norwegian language was especially respected. Sagen was criticised by Bishop Claus Pavel for his classic ideals, which the bishop found sadly old-fashioned. Welhaven, however, tells that Sagen gave him a "sharpened sense of the chasteness and purity of the art of poetry".

Lyder Sagen awakened a sense of good speech, a respect for the classics and an aesthetic taste in several generations of Bergensians. His favourite students included ▶Welhaven and Christian Friele, the future legendary editor of "Morgenbladet" (The Morning News). He also steered J. C. ▶Dahl toward art when he discovered his great talent for painting.

Poetry

Sagen's own poetry consists for the most part of translations of Greek verse, in addition to a number of poems he wrote in his spare time. The best known of his poems is the drinking song "Diogenes Cross and Proud". He also collected "Unknown Remains of Past Poetry", some of which were found on a journey to Copenhagen where he was a member of The Norwegian Society.

Description of Bergen

Sagen published "Reading Book in the Mother Tongue", "Danish Reading and Recitation Practice Book" and "Description of Bergen" in collaboration with Herman Foss.

He was in addition a frequent contributor to the antiquarian-historical periodical "Urda" which was published in Bergen. He was one of the founders of the Bergen Museum and Bergen's Art Association, and took the initiative together with J.C. Dahl to begin the restoration of Håkonshallen and Rosenkrantz Tower.

Lyder Sagen
portrayed in 1843 by Wilhelm Gertner. The painting hangs in the Bergen billedgalleri.
◄

◼ INGOLF SCHJØTT

**Prominent
choir
conductor**

Ingolf Schjøtt
*immortalised in
bronze by Ambro-
sia Tønnesen – first
in Konsertpaleet
and today in Grieg-
hallen.*

Cathedral organist and cantor Ingolf Schjøtt (1851–1922) received a testimonial from Edvard Grieg as "Norway's foremost choir conductor". On Harmonien's premises in Grieghallen he is honoured with a portrait bust.

Schjøtt made a significant contribution to the musical life of his hometown as an organist, a singer and conductor. When Harmonien made the transition to a fully professional orchestra in 1919, Schjøtt's own mixed choir formed the foundation for the music company's choir, which he directed from 1917.

Ingolf Schjøtt appeared as a baritone soloist with Harmonien throughout 20 seasons. His last performance was in 1907 at a memorial concert following the death of Edvard Grieg. Grieg had accompanied Schjøtt on the piano in his first performance with Harmonien in 1871.

◼ SILJUSTØL

**Home of
composer
Harald
Sæverud**

**Largest
private
residence
in Western
Norway**

Siljustøl was the home of composer Harald Sæverud. The property was, in 1984, bequeathed to a foundation bearing the names of the composer and his wife, the painter Marie Hvoslef Sæverud. The aim of the foundation is to promote Norwegian music and art. In 1993 the Bergen municipality assumed responsibility for its administration.

On the 100th birthday of the composer, April 17, 1997, HRH King Harald opened Siljustøl as a museum for the public. The property is located in Rådalen in Fana, 14 kilometres south of downtown Bergen.

The main building was finished in 1939 and was the largest private residence in Western Norway, with a total area of 680 square metres. A 30-acre nature park originally belonged to the property and was later enlarged to 41 acres.

Visitors will not only be able to see one of the world's most original and magnificent artist homes but will also have a chance to wander

Siljustøl opened as a museum on April 17, 1997. Sveinung Sæverud, the eldest son of the composer, still has his private home at Siljustøl where he runs a music school.

Graphics: Bernt Kristiansen

down the six kilometres of footpaths and nature trails. There is a rich array of animal and bird life on the property as well. In the barn at Siljustøl there were once as many as 17 milking goats, rams and kids.

Siljustøl was a remarkably generous wedding gift to Harald Sæverud and his bride, Marie Hvoslef, when they married in 1934. The gift was given by the bride's Norwegian-American mother, Madsella Hvoslef. She had inherited a large fortune in the United States from her husband, the Norwegian born sea captain and shipping magnate, Fredrik Waldemar Hvoslef from Baltimore.

The gift included not only the magnificent property, but also money for the building of a house. The young architect from Haugesund, Ludolf Eide Parr prepared the drawings for the composer's home, in close collaboration with the builders. The architecture of the house with its granite stones and pinewood panelling blends with the untouched natural beauty of Fana.

The house is equipped with four balconies, a

Animals and birds

Hosts at Siljustøl. *Marie and Harald Sæverud received their home as a wedding present in 1934.*

S

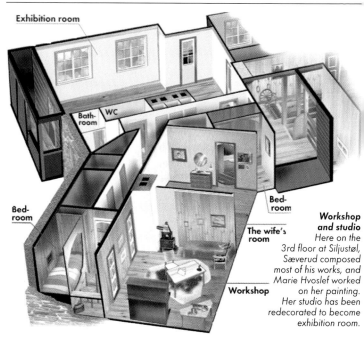

Exhibition room

Bath-
room

WC

Bed-
room

Bed-
room

The wife's
room

Workshop

*Workshop
and studio*
*Here on the
3rd floor at Siljustøl,
Sæverud composed
most of his works, and
Marie Hvoslef worked
on her painting.
Her studio has been
redecorated to become
exhibition room.*

**Drank sea
water**

terrace and eight exits. All of these lead direct-
ly onto the grounds. Harald Sæverud stepped
out barefoot every morning, in winter as well
as summer. His theory was that human beings
had to have direct contact with the earth, just
as birds did, in order to have access to important minerals. These, he believed were absor-
bed through the feet from the morning dew. He
also had a firm belief in seawater as a preven-
tive medicine. Every morning he drank a
small glass of salt-water, taken from Kors
Fjord at a depth of 20–40 metres.

63 rooms

It took three and a half years to build this
impressive castle, containing 63 rooms. Almost
everything inside was specially constructed,
such as the doors. Much of the furniture was
crafted by the composer himself, including several triangle-shaped tables – to save room.
Sæverud had an upside down cross carved
into the foot and head boards of the bed. This
was not because he was a satanist, but on the

contrary, to drive the Evil One quickly down into the ground again, should he show up. The composer's studio was placed on the top floor in a room with a westward view. Most of his compositions were written in this room. The name of the property was inspired by Christian Skredsvig's famous painting "Gutten med seljefløyten" (The Boy with the Willow Flute). Sæverud preferred the Telemark dialect of the word 'willow', which was 'silju'. He felt it promoted a stronger feeling of the willow sap rising in the branches during springtime.

The heating of the house is a chapter of its own. The composer's home at Siljustøl was the first house in Norway with electric heating in the ceiling, a method invented by Sæverud himself.

The final resting-place of the composer at Siljustøl was picked out ahead of time by Harald Sæverud himself. The gravestone comes from Osterøy.

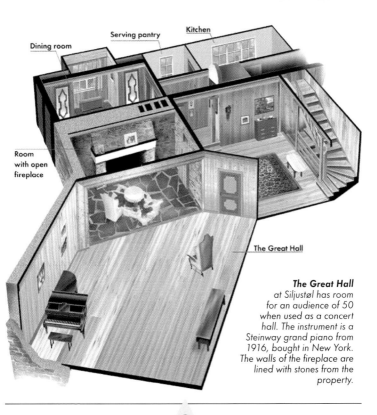

Dining room
Serving pantry
Kitchen
Room with open fireplace
The Great Hall

The Great Hall
at Siljustøl has room for an audience of 50 when used as a concert hall. The instrument is a Steinway grand piano from 1916, bought in New York. The walls of the fireplace are lined with stones from the property.

We have the current rights to both these authors

■ PER SIVLE

Per Sivle
drawn by Gustav
Lærum in the
1890s.

Writer and editor Per Sivle, from Voss (1857–1904), has had a street named after him in Solheimsviken. Sivle was married to Wenche Nilsen from Bergen; he was able to get some of his first poems published through the publishing company Andreas Lavik in Bergen.

Rousing national and political poetry is Sivle's most important distinguishing mark. In the rural dialect and his own Voss dialect, he pours verse from his verbal horn of plenty. Several of Sivle's poems have become folk songs, such as "Den fyrste song" (The First Song) and "Vesle lerka" (Little Lark), both put to music by Lars ▶ Søraas, also from Bergen. Politically, Sivle was one of the leaders of the fight for independence toward 1905.

■ AMALIE SKRAM

A beauty when alive, and also in bronze

The most beautiful woman in Bergen – such was the legend of Amalie Skram, born in Alver (1846–1905). Adorning her hometown, she stands at Klosterhaugen, sculpted in bronze by Maja Refsum. The statue was unveiled in 1949 displaying a woman glowing with inner strength. In Bergen Public Library there is a separate Amalie Skram room with a portrait bust of her in marble, modelled by Ambrosia Tønnesen.

The writer has also been honoured with a street name, Amalie Skram vei, located in Sandviken, which is where she picked up material for her main work, the chronicles of "Hellemyrsfolket". Amalie's childhood home was an old wooden house in Cort Piil alley at Nordnes. The house still stands and was marked by a memorial plaque in 1994.

Sharp and shrewd

It was not just Amalie Skram's beauty that attracted attention, but also her acuteness and intelligence. Her writing could be sharp and shrewd. It was said that her voice was like silver and her conversations as sharp as the edge of a sword. Nina Grieg told of her impression of her school friend: "Though she was two

S

Amalie Skram's beauty is clearly shown by Maja Refsum's statue at Klosterhaugen. It was unveiled in 1949.

◀

years younger, she governed us all. I looked up to her and always asked her for her opinion. Her judgement was decisive." Another good friend from Bergen was writer colleague Drude Krog Janson, the first wife of Kristofer Janson. She brought Amalie Skram in contact with Bjørnstjerne ▶ Bjørnson, who was to become of great importance to her.

It is said about Amalie Skram that she did not make up her stories, but only described her own experiences, including those most intimate. Her life was far from blissful, with two broken marriages and two admissions to an asylum. Her parents were divorced when she was 18. Her father, a farmer from Alversund in Nordhordland, ran different businesses on Strandgaten, but went bankrupt and ran off to America.

Described her own tragedies

The Skram Room
in the Bergen
Public Library is
the former Grieg
room. Here stands
this marble bust,
created by Ambro-
sia Tønnesen.

**Gives
information
about Bergen**

**"Hellemyrs-
folket" as
theatre**

Amalie accepted her first proposal from ship captain Berent U.A. Müller whom she accompanied on yearlong travels around the world. She later married the Danish writer Erik Skram. They were divorced in 1900.

Amalie Skram's own marital tragedy is intimately depicted in her first novel "Constance Ring" (1885). The book was an important contribution to the moral debate of the times. Skram was the first writer to dare to candidly write about the tabu subject of frigidity – a woman unable to make love. Her books accommodate an entire register of human pain. "I cry through all my books", she once wrote. She caused quite a sensation with her books "Professor Hieronius" and "At St. Jørgen's", in which she launched an attack on the treatment of the mentally ill, based on her own experiences. The debate led to the dismissal of the assistant physician from the psychiatric ward where Amalie Skram had been a patient.

With her four volume chronicles about the people of Hellemyr, "Hellemyrsfolket", she reached a high point not only in her own writing career, but also in the field of Norwegian naturalistic literature. The story of the Western Norwegian family from Hellemyren depicts the way in which a series of failed lives could depend on both inherited traits and on the environment. The books draw an accurate picture of both rural and city life. According to the critic of "Samtiden", volume 3 is "the best document one could read in order to learn about the city of Bergen".

Bitter over the reception her books received in Norway, Amalie Skram decided to call herself a Danish citizen, Danish subject and Danish writer. Still, it was the way of life in her hometown that more than anything else gave her the background material for her novels.

A dramatised version of "Hellemyrsfolket" was performed at Bergen International Festival in 1992 by Den Nationale Scene. The play was a great success, despite the fact that it lasted all of nine hours. The dramatisation was written by Gunnar Staalesen.

S

▪ STADSPORTEN

In the old days, as in modern times, people were required to pay to come into the city. Stadsporten (the City Gate) was actually a kind of 17th century 'tollbooth', though undeniably more elegant than the newer 'city gates' visitors have been forced to pass through after the toll laws were carried 1986.

"Toll booth" and defence building

In earlier times, toll charges were only levied on foods imported from the countryside, a so-called consumption tax or excise tax. Since the only road into Bergen from the south, Kalfarveien, was blocked off by the tollbooth until Nygård's bridge was completed in 1851, control must have been fairly simple. When the lord of the manor, Oluf Parsberg in 1628 laid the cornerstone, Stadsporten was considered an important defence structure. The building has, however, never been used for military purposes.

Only access to the city from the south

Stadsporten has gone through several changes, and received its present appearance after restoration work in 1792. The loft was first used for the Bergen diocese archives, and later for the City archives, until 1982. Its original function as a roadblock eventually caused great traffic problems, and there was once talk of tearing the building down. It became possible to steer both streetcar and automobile traffic around the other way, and in 1927 Stadsporten became protected by law. It is today the only ancient city gate left in Norway.

Archives in the loft

Stadsporten (the City Gates) – Bergen's oldest toll booth.
◀

Insult has
become
a term of
honour

**Troubadour
Ivar Medaas**
has contributed to
bettering the reputa-
tion of the stril
group. In Bergen he
learned to play the
Hardanger fiddle
with Arne Bjørndal,
and received an
education as a
farmer at the Stend
School of Agri-
culture.

A stril couple.

■ STRILER

'Stril' is a term used for an inhabitant living
along the northern and western coastal areas
of Bergen. The term was once derogatory, but
has now almost become an honourable desig-
nation. This is in some part due to popular
music artists like stril farmer Ivar Medaas
(born 1938) from Alversund, the ten year
younger Johannes Kleppevik from Sotra,
along with the eminent classical guitarist Njål
Vindenes from Fusa.

Ivar Medaas had all the odds against him
when he performed his own brand of stril pop
music with his Hardanger fiddle at Chat Noir
in Oslo. The blasé audience in the city capital
had never heard anything like it, but Medaas
became a success. The cross-eyed troubadour
joked and sang in his rural stril dialect and
went on to conquer an entire nation.

After the tragedy in Telavåg during World
War II, city people were no longer quite so ready to look down upon the rural stril people. As
a revenge for the shooting of two Gestapo offi-
cers, the Germans razed the entire fishing village and sent 71 men to the concentration
camp Sachsenhausen. Of these, 31 never returned home. 'Torgdagen' (Market Day), also
called 'Striledagen', a regular event since
1977, has clearly contributed to a better understanding between the stril people and the
citizens of Bergen. (See ▶ Festivals.)

The stril people have through the years
played an important financial role in Bergen.
They have particularly influenced the district
around Vågen and Torget (the Market Square). Strils came here on Wednesdays and
Thursdays to sell their products, fish and farm
articles, and to buy or trade city wares. Several of the stores in Bergen were based on this
kind of trade. Thursday later became the big
"Stril Day". It was the only day the stores stayed open until 7 p.m. Those who couldn't get a
ride on a fishing boat, hopped into a rowboat
at 5 a.m. and rowed into the city. After a hard
day of shopping and trading, a hearty and in-
expensive meal was called for. A "stril" then lo-

oked forward to a meal of potato dump-lings with salted mutton, yellow peas, mashed yellow turnip and crisp, fried bacon. On Thursdays many of the city's restaurants still offer potato dumplings, or raspeballer, on the menu. This is a culinary delicacy – a blessed mix of culture and passion.

No one knows exactly where the word "stril" comes from. According to local historian Nanna Ebbing, Stril Country stretches outwards from Bergen, across 70 kilometres. Geographically this would mean the coastal area from Fedje to the north and through Selbjørns Fjord to the south. It extends into Oster Fjord and Samnanger Fjord, but not up into the valleys.

A large part of Stril Country was a gray and barren kingdom, with 300 islands and 1000 holms and rocky islets. Today this kingdom is coveted by the oil industry, and has become a source of wealth for both the city and indeed the entire country. There were many different types of strils. Those from the islands were called "havstriler" (sea strils), while "overlandsstriler" (land strils) lived on the mainland. Along the fjords were "kipestriler", named for the woven baskets they bore on their backs, which contained everything from wares to dung. The genuine "stril", however, was the sea or fishing stril.

Writer Kåre Fasting has made the term stril

A world of its own

Johan S. Welhaven on Stril Country:

"As the long row of islands outside the mainland of Nordhordland, Stril Country forms a geographic world of its own; the inhabitants, the "strils", create a kingdom of their own, with their unique characteristics and way of life. Seen from above, their country would give a lasting impression of loneliness and melancholy. It is a barren country. Only rarely does one see a green bush, while moss and heather are in abundance."

A stril has gone on land at Torget (the Market Square).

▼

Quick-witted

widely known by his novels. He says that "a stril is a term for a daring and quick-witted man who knows how to turn around in a pinch, whether it be between the ladies at the Bergen marketplace or out in the little boat on the foamy waves near Marsteinen or Fedje".

In the city strils distinguished themselves both in dress and in dialect. Some of the "finer" people of Bergen approved of neither. The strils were exposed to a great deal of scorn and derision, also in literature. Holberg was among the most condescending. The tense relationship between Bergen and Stril Country culminated in the Stril Wars – the many bloody rebellions against taxes and harsh government officials in Bergen. Four of the rebels were sentenced to death in 1765.

Merchants of Bergen have looked toward Northern Norway, as it created an export market and a way of living from dried fish. The merchants became blind to the fact that their nearest neighbours, the strils, could become just as important through the export and delivery of dried and salted fish and herring.

Johan Chr. Juuhl is one of the few writers from Bergen who took the side of the strils. Through his poetry, he gives a vivid impression of life in Stril Country in the unique dialect of the people. A rough translation of one of his poems:

A sculpture of Sunniva, made by Stinius Fredriksen, was erected in 1970 at Bergenhus.

Way out on the western coast
between mountains and ocean blue
An island lies, which is so fine
We struggle there, we work and dig
and live on potato cakes, herring and gruel

■ ST. SUNNIVA

The patron saint of Bergen

The patron saint of Bergen, the holy St. Sunniva, has been honoured with a street name in Solheimsviken. A monument was erected by the entrance to the chapel of Florida Hospital, on the property of Store Kristkirke at Bergenhus, where the casket with St. Sunniva's

S

earthly remains was placed on the high altar in 1170. A statue of the saint, made by Wilhelm Rasmussen, stands on a ledge along the stairway to the National Archives on Årstadveien 22.

According to legend, Sunniva was an Irish princess who landed on the beach at Selje in Nordfjord when she fled from a heathen suitor and was caught in a storm at sea. When her company was attacked by the army of Håkon Jarl, they sought refuge in a cave. They prayed to God for help. Their prayers were answer-ed by a rockslide, which buried everyone inside the cave.

An Irish princess

When King Olav Tryggvason later saw a beam of light over Selje, he ordered the re-mains of the martyrs to be removed from the cave. Sunniva's body was found undamaged. Her body was first enshrined in the church at Selje, which during ▶ Olav Kyrre's reign be-came the first bishop's see in West Norway. In 1170 the bishop's see was moved to Bergen and the saint's shrine followed. Moving day on September 7th became a day of celebration in the churches of Bergen.

■ HARALD SÆVERUD

My uncle was "his" photogra-pher for many years...

When Harald Sæverud (1897–1992) died on March 27, 1992, he had long held the position of Norway's most distinguished musical per-sonality and the most prominent composer since Edvard Grieg. The composer's home ▶ Siljustøl is today a museum. He will soon be honoured with a monument in Byparken near his famous colleagues and fellow Bergen citi-zens, Edvard Grieg and Ole Bull.

Popular modernist

Harald Sæverud sculptured by Nils Aas. The bust stands in Grieghallen.

Sæverud was a modernist who became po-pular, "house-trained", and a living legend, writes his biographer Lorentz Reitan. He is responsible for a long list of musical master-pieces: "Kjempeviseslåtten", "Rondo amoroso", "Sinfonia Dolorosa", "Peer Gynt", "Minnesota Symfonien" and "Galdreslåtten". These are compositions that have long been a part of the standard repertoire of our institutions, and

S

Two pianists on Sæverud's music

Jan Henrik Kayser:
"It is always interesting to play his music. It demands not only a very developed technique, but also a very nuanced interpretation. Its expressions shifts continuously and bubbles with melodic springs, and it always has an undertone which moves me."

Einar Røttingen:
"The music is so clean, personal and free of any effect-making. It contains almost all the elements – on the one side, the lyrical, singing and many inspiring melodies, on the other side, a rhythmic drive which almost makes the music overflow... He had that rare gift of being able to depict the nature of western Norway with an imaginative melodic language."

have become a part of the heritage of Norwegian music.

Sæverud was born on April 17th on Nordnesbakken 9. The house where he came into the world stood on an old, discontinued churchyard for criminals and the destitute. This explained, he felt, why his music was so often written in a minor key. He was the fourth of eight sisters and brothers and belonged to a wealthy merchant family. But the abundance and harmony ended abruptly when the family business went bankrupt and his father went to prison, a man who had even been the president of the Home Mission! The future did not look bright for the young boy. But Sæverud dealt with the shame and transition to poverty – starved and suffered to follow his composer calling. At times he made a living as a music teacher and cinema musician, wrote critiques in "Bergens Tidende" and received help at times from friends and grants. But like the young hero in the fairy tales, he won both the princess and the musical kingdom. The princess was Marie Hvoslef, daughter of a Norwegian-American multi-millionaire. They married in 1934 and all his financial troubles were over.

Sæverud received no formal musical education before the age of 18, when he became a student of Borghild Holmsen at the Music Conservatory. During this period he wrote his opus 1: Five capricci for piano, dedicated to his teacher. At the same time he worked on the first of in all nine symphonies.

A symphony orchestra would become a treasured instrument for Sæverud. Most of his orchestral pieces were first performed by Harmonien, usually with himself as conductor. While his masters were Haydn and Mozart, Harmonien's orchestra served as his academy.

With such musical gems as "Rondo Amoroso" (1939) and "Kjempeviseslåtten" (1943), he eventually won recognition for his unusual, dissonant melodies, though they were at first considered rather difficult to listen to. In 1934 Sæverud wrote the stage music for Shakespeare-Obey's "Violence Against Lucretia", which was performed at Den Nationale Scene and directed by the head of the theatre Hans Jacob Nilsen. The two would later collaborate on the unromanticised version of "Peer Gynt",

Harald Sæverud was commemorated with a stamp in 1997 on the occasion of the 100th anniversary of his birth. He received a state artist's wages from 1955, and was in 1977 decorated as Commander of the Order of St. Olav.

Berlin debut with help from Bergen

While Sæverud studied at a college in Berlin in 1921, he was able to listen to a movement of his 2nd symphony performed by the Berlin Philharmonic Orchestra. This was arranged by another Bergen citizen, his good friend and fellow student, Johan Ludwig Mowinckel Jr. He rented the whole orchestra and conducted it himself.

to which Sæverud contributed a controversial, but highly praised, musical composition.

56 opuses

Sæverud did not have to travel far out into the world to find inspiration. A flower in his garden at Siljustøl could often be enough. Most of his 56 opuses were written in his hometown. Sæverud did not only leave behind his music. He was also strongly involved in the musical life of the city. He was the head of the board of directors for Harmonien for four years, was appointed an honorary member and awarded a gold medal. See ▶ Siljustøl.

■ GUNNAR SÆVIG

Music-educational pioneer

Gunnar Sævig
was deputy leader of Harmonien, but also often led the orchestra as its conductor.

Violinist, conductor and teacher Gunnar Sævig (1924–69) played first violin for many years in Harmonien. In honour of his all-around efforts, Grieg Academy's combined auditorium and concert hall in Nygård School (near Grieghallen) has been named Gunnar Sævigs Sal. Friends created the "Gunnar Sævig Memorial Foundation" where all profits go toward music scholarships.

From 1952 until his death, Sævig was the director of the Bergen Music Conservatory and laid the foundation for the establishment of a more advanced musical education in Bergen at the Grieg Academy. As a teacher at Bergen Teacher's College from 1958 to 1969 he worked to build up the school's music department – the first of its kind in the country.

Sævig will also be remembered for his performance of great church music. In 1952 he founded the Bergen Music Conservatory choir, which later was named the Bergen Oratory Choir.

■ LARS SØRAAS, SR. AND JR.

Folk song pioneers

The following three songs are among those most often sung in Norway: "Den fyrste song eg høyra fekk", "Og vesle lerka, ho hev det so" (Per ▶ Sivle), and the Christmas song "Det ly-ser i stille grender" (Jakob Sande). The master behind the melodies for these poems is Lars Søraas.

The melodies of the first two songs were written by Søraas senior and the last by his son with the same name. Lars Søraas Sr. (1862–1925) and Lars Søraas Jr. (1887–1976) have both made an impression on the musical world. Søraas Sr. has been called "the pioneer of folk songs" and his efforts for choirs and school songs were followed up by Søraas Jr. Their home in Søråsbygda in Fana stood within a kilometre of both Grieg's Troldhaugen and Sæverud's Siljustøl, and formed an important 'triplet' in the Norwegian music world.

For 40 years Søraas Sr. was an organist in Sandvikskirken. He started his own Søraas Choir, took the initiative to start Hordalandske Collective Choir and in 1904 became one of the founders of the Norwegian Organists' Association. For ten years (1914–24) he led this organisation, which was the predecessor of the Norwegian Cantor and Organists' Association.

Søraas Sr. achieved record-breaking sales with his very popular song collections for mixed choirs, "Religious Choir Songs" and "Light Youth Choirs", both published through Einar Kaland's Music Publishing House in Bergen. The collections were sold in hundreds of thousands of copies. Some of Søraas' own songs, such as "Vesle lerka" and "Den fyrste song" have become folk songs.

His colleague, Thorleif ▶ Aamodt, characterised Lars Søraas Jr. as "a herald of folk songs and church songs". From the 1920s Søraas Jr. was a gathering force in the secular as well as the Christian choir groups. As an educator, he followed up his father's school song works with new versions and gave several summer courses for choir conductors. He led the "Lærerstandens Kor", "Fasmer Dahls Lille Kor" "Søraas' Kor", and "Bergen Ynglingeforenings Sangforening". For his outstanding efforts Søraas Jr. received the King's gold medal along with several Norwegian and Scandinavian distinctions.

In a prologue to the song collection published by Lars Søraas Jr. in 1945, he wrote:
"May lyrics and melodies awaken a rush of Norwegian song all over the country. It will give strength and courage."

Lars Søraas, Sr.

Lars Søraas, Jr.

■ THEATRE IN BERGEN

Bergen first to stage a theatre performance

Adam and Eve acted by Arne Jacobsen and Astrid Bye on the National Theatre of Bergen in 1962, during the 400th anniversary of Norway's first theatre performance, "The Fall of Adam". The director of the mystery play, Absalon Pederssøn Beyer (1528–75), was a teacher at Bergen Katedralskole and a central person among the so-called Bergen humanists.

Adam and Eve were not only the first two people on earth, they were also the first two theatre characters to appear on the Norwegian stage. This historical theatrical event took place in front of Domkirken in Bergen in 1562 in the form of a mystery play "The Fall of Adam", directed by Absalon Pederssøn Beyer.

When the performance was repeated on Den Nationale Scene 400 years later, it proved to possess a message and a dramatic power strong enough to capture the modern public as well. Director Kjell Stormoen found he had to put certain limitations on the paradisaical conditions on stage. Even though the actors were in biblical character, none of them were dressed historically correct.

On the night of the Norwegian premiere, the roles were played by students of Katedralskolen. Local amateurs were also among the cast members when two plays by Johan Nordahl ▶Brun were performed in 1791, "Einer Tambeskielver" and "The Republic on the Island". Public interest in these performances led to the establishment of "Det Dramatiske Selskab" (The Dramatic Society) in 1794. In 1800 the company secured its own theatre, "The Comedy House" at Engen, with about 900 seats, which was the first theatre building in Norway. The members of the company belonged to the upper class and served as both performers and members of the audience. From the 1820s a Danish ensemble rented the building. The uncontested prima donna in the "Danish period" was Adeline Werligh, Nina Grieg's

mother. Her husband, Nina's father, was merchant Hermann Hagerup.

Theatre history was made in the Comedy
House when "Det Norske Theater" (The Norwegian Theatre) was opened by Ole ▶ Bull on
January 2, 1850. This day was considered to be
the founding date of the Norwegian stage. Before the curtain went up for the opening performance, the orchestra played Beethov-en's
Egmont Overture for the first time in Bergen.
The conductor was Ole Bull himself. The play
was "Den Blessed" by Ludvig ▶ Holberg, with
Norwegian speaking actors, and Louise Gulbrandsen in the leading role. A choir of farmers appealed for the renewal of the Norwegian
spirit.

"A great success," noted the critics. "The entire performance was like a miracle", wrote
Ole Bull to his wife, Félicie. She and the child-

▲
*Den Nationale
Scene (The National
Theatre of Bergen)
has, since 1909,
been housed in this
monumental and
now preserved
theatre building
in Engen.*

*Komediehuset
(The House of
Comedy) in Engen
on a postcard from
1930. The house
was destroyed dur-
ing a bombing at-
tack in1944, but
had closed down
as a main stage in
1909.*
        Photo: Teatermuseet.
◄

T

Two major directors at the National Theatre of Bergen, Bjarne Andersen and Per Schwab, follow a rehearsal in 1961.

▶

A dream became reality

Johannes Brun and **Lucie Wolff** – two bright names at the Ole Bull Theatre in Bergen.

ren were "parked" on Andøen outside of Kristiansand. At a dress rehearsal on November 21, Johannes Brun made his debut as Henrik in "Henrik and Pernille". Brun was to become one of the greatest names on the Norwegian stage at the time.

On May 17, 1863, 13 turbulent years later, the theatre company was forced to relinquish its property and assets to the county court. Bergen, with its 25,000 inhabitants was still too small, isolated and immature to be able to give Ole Bull's ideas the impetus they needed. But a dream had become a reality, and the legitimacy of the Norwegian theatre arts was fully documented. In all 339 plays and 947 performances were produced in the theatre.

The gloomy predictions that it would be impossible to find worthy actors were put to shame. Among the many to come forward were talents such as Johannes Brun and Lucie Wolf, the latter known as one of the great comediennes of the Norwegian theatre. Both actors would come to enrich Norwegian theatre arts for many years, and in the country's capital too. Illustrious names during the early years were also Lucie Gulbrandsen, Marie Midling and Georg Krohn. Much of the honour had to be shared with the talented acting teacher Fritz Jensen. The artistic leaders were no less prominent and included Henrik ▶ Ibsen and Bjørnstjerne ▶ Bjørnson.

After a period of 13 years, the theatre curtain would once again be lifted. Meanwhile the theatre life in Bergen was dominated by travelling Danish and Swedish ensembles. The 'reborn' theatre was soon to display a new

T

The popular actors Svend von Düring, Anne Gullestad and Lothar Lindtner are here rehearsing in rural surroundings in 1962 for the play "Du you know the Milk Way?" by Karl Wittinger.

◀

name: Den Nationale Scene (The National Theatre of Bergen). On October 25, 1876, the theatre gave its first performance in the Comedy House. The initiative for the new establishment was taken by Johan Bøgh, and Niels Wickstrøm became the theatre's first artistic director.

The monumental new building for the National Theatre of Bergen (Engen 1) stood completed in 1909. The architect was Einar Oscar Schou. The building was later enlarged and today contains three stages. The "Little Stage" was, in 1967, used as modern theatre and has a maximum capacity of 99 seats. The "Middle Stage" (up to 250 seats) opened in 1982 in an underground building designed by Halfdan B. Grieg. The "Main Stage" had 427 seats. The theatre has been funded by the state since 1993, and the building was protected the same year. It is considered to be one of the great works of art nouveau architecture.

The National Theatre of Bergen has throughout the years offered the public the very best of stage presentations. The repertoire has varied between classical drama and modern theatre, operetta and opera. Several of the plays have been in New Norwegian. The theatre's greatest success is the light comedy "Jan Herwitz", with over 400 performances. (See ▶ Wiers-Jenssen). Theatre history was created with "Our honour and our power" in 1935. (See Nordahl ▶ Grieg.)

Many of the country's most prominent actors have been associated with The National Theatre of Bergen. Several of them have been honoured by paintings or sculptures. Among

Theatre directors at the National Theatre of Bergen

Niels Wickstrøm
1876–79
Johan Bøgh
1879–82
Gunnar Heiberg
1882–89
Johan Irgens Hansen *1890–95*
Olaf Hanson
1895–98
Hans Aanrud
1899–1900
Gustav Thomassen
1900–05
Anton Heiberg
1905–07
Olaf Hansson
1908–09
Ludvig Bergh
1910–24
Christian Sandal
1924–25
Thomas Thomassen
1925–31
KarlBergmann
1931–34
Hans Jacob Nilsen
1934–39
Egil Hjorth-Jensen
1939–46
Stein Bugge
1946–48
Georg Løkkeberg
1948–52

More directors on the following page.

Anne Gullestad portrayed by Arne Vinje Gunnerud. The bust is placed at Stend, by the entrance to the theatre hall which bears her name.

these are Johannes Brun, Magda Blanc, Eilif Armand, Rolf ▶ Berntzen, Svend von Düring, Johann ▶ Dybwad, Joachim Holst-Jensen, Doris Johannessen, Lothar Lindtner, Agnes Mowinckel, Hans Jacob Nilsen and Karin Simonnæs.

Ole Bull Theatre (Ole Bulls plass) was established as an extra stage, the first in Norway, when Hans Jacob Nilsen was director from 1934 to 1939. The locale was used as a cinema from 1937 to 1981.

Komediateatret offered its faithful audience, particularly the rural and coastal people, almost only popular comedy, played in the coastal stril dialect. The theatre opened in an intimate cellar on Vestre Torggate 5/7 in 1933, with director Amund Rydland. Lars Nygard had taken the initiative in the establishment of the theatre, and was its director from 1934 to 1945. His successor was Alv Hordnes, also an eminent actor.

Few theatres in Bergen would have the audience rolling in the aisles like this one. Many therefore were sorry when Komediateatret became homeless in 1964 and had to close down. Throughout the years the theatre had managed without government support.

The Oslo-based review theatre Chat Noir had a Bergen branch in the same locale during the years 1918 to 1920.

Hordaland Theatre established its own stage in ▶ Hordamuseet at Stend in 1988. The theatre was the idea of Anne Gullestad, and she was its artistic leader until her death in 1998. The new 200-seat theatre hall, in use from May the same year, bears her name.

Hordaland Theatre has held status as a professional district theatre from 1995. It has a regular staff of eight employees, including two actors. Extra staff is hired from time to time as needed. Stage language is New Norwegian or in dialect, and performances are aimed at all age groups. Historical plays are the theatre's speciality.

T

The theatre has an extensive tour schedule and visits practically every municipality in the county each year. Some of the tours are carried out on the theatre boat "Innvik". Hordaland Theatre has had the professional responsibility for "Mostraspelet" and the four saga pieces about King Håkon the Good.

The opening performance for the new theatre building was a play by Rolf Losnegård about the patron saint of Bergen, St. Sunniva, entitled "Sunniva and Viking Ravn". In collaboration with the Bergen International Festival, Hordaland Theatre arranges "Barnas Festspill" (The Children's Festival) each year. The theatre is also working to establish an arena for New Norwegian theatre in downtown Bergen. Vera Rostin Wexelsen has been theatre director since 1998.

Fyllingsdalen New Theatre is a family and children's theatre, established in 1976 in a former German military barrack on Folke Bernadottes vei. The building attracts attention in the landscape, since the exterior changes according to the play being presented at the time. The theatre hall has 220 seats – elegant seats that have been taken from the old Logen. The theatre also runs a theatre school.

The theatre is semi-professional and has a regular staff of three people. It is owned and run by Tove Ringereide. There are three plays and about 90 performances per season.

▲
The theatre painter Richard Ringereide paints not only backdrops, but also creates an effective marketing approach by decorating the exterior of the theatre according to the play being shown.

Komedieteatret *did not tempt audiences with its grand façade, but it did present them with a fine spectacle.*

T

Centre for creative performing art in Norway

Bergen International Theatre (BIT) is a professional theatre without a permanent artistic staff. The administration since 1995 has been organised as a foundation. The theatre presents 12 productions per year and has established itself as a centre for creative performing arts in Norway. About 70 performances are given each year in Teatergarasjen (see below) and approximately the same number are presented on tour all over Europe. The institution produces both Norwegian and international performing arts, including plays as well as dance. The objective of the Bergen International Theatre is to challenge, set new standards and break the boundaries of conventional art in order to achieve its goal.

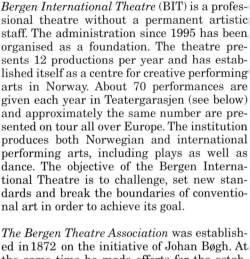

The Bergen Theatre Association was established in 1872 on the initiative of Johan Bøgh. At the same time he made efforts for the establishment of a new national stage in Bergen. The original objective of the association was to support these plans. The association had a strong influence on the theatre's administration, and has supported the theatre through different activities until the government took over in 1972.

Since 1983 the association has awarded two annual prizes, "Rampcløkten" for particularly worthy theatre enterprises, and the "Pernille" statuette for the best acting performance.

The Pernille statuette – The Theatre Association's trophy for best acting performance of the year, is made by Dyre Vaa.

Teatergarasjen (Nøstegaten 54) is a former warehouse, rebuilt and redecorated to form a theatre hall. There is a capacity of 500 seats. The locale is used by Bergen International Theatre (see above). The nine hour long dramatisation of Amalie Skram's "Hellemyrsfolket" was performed in Teatergarasjen by Det Nationale Scene and had its premiere during the International Festival in 1992.

Bergen's Theatre Museum had to close the doors to its building on Villaveien 5 during the summer of 1998 when the University of Bergen was forced to sell the property. It has not yet been possible to find a new locale for the

T

over 6000 registered objects belonging to the collection.

Some of the oldest items date back to Det Dramatiske Selskab and Ole Bull's Norske Theater. Stored for safekeeping is also Johannes Brun's Jeppe costume from 1851 and Adelaide Johannessen's Nora costume from the first performance of "A Doll's House" at Det Nationale Scene in 1880.

Items from Ole Bull's theatre

The Theatre Museum was established in 1919 in the rehearsal hall at Det Nationale Scene, where the "Little Stage" now exists. It was Sigvald Johannessen, the first director of the theatre, who made the first efforts to start the museum based on his private collection of theatre effects. In 1921 the collection was transferred to Det Gamle Teater. During World War II, most of the collection was carried to safety before the theatre was hit by an English bomb and destroyed in 1944. The bomb also killed Johannessen and his wife.

After the war the collection was first exhibited in Manufakturhuset while it was under the direction of Gustav Brosing. From 1980 the exhibition was held in a patrician villa from the 1880s on Villaveien. The Theatre Archives and the Institute for Theatre Studies was housed here as well. At the time, the director was Knut Nygaard, though Kari Gaarder Losnedahl has had responsibility for the collection since 1982. The Theatre Museum is a part of the University's cultural historic collection. In addition to the permanent exhibition, the museum arranges a number of theme exhibits of current interest.

Theme exhibits

T

■ SIGMUND TORSTEINSON

**The father
of the Grieg
museum**

*Sigmund
Torsteinson
in a characteristic
position as a pro-
moter of music at
Troldhaugen. He
changed the artist's
home into a living
Edvard Grieg mu-
seum.*

Music fund

Only one person besides Edvard Grieg himself
has been honoured with a portrait bust in the
composer museum at u Troldhaugen. The bust
shows Sigmund Torsteinson's characteristic
features – the theatre critic, writer and music
mediator. This multi-talented man will primarily be remembered as the father of the Grieg
Museum.

From 1955 to 1977 Torsteinson invited the
public to the first of a series of concerts at Grieg's villa under the title "An Evening at Troldhaugen", where he himself played host. Torsteinson also took the initiative in the building
of Troldsalen. As a result of his efforts he was
awarded the Grieg Prize in 1976.

Torsteinson has published three books:
"Troldhaugen"(1959),"Fifty years of Troldhaugen" (1978) and his autobiography "Thoughts
of Trolls" (1985).

Sigmund Torsteinson's youngest sister,
Rannveig Torstensen, bequeathed in 1997 her
home to Troldhaugen. Profits from the sale
went to a fund for the study of the music of
Grieg and other Norwegian composers. The
fund bears the name of Sigmund Torsteinson.

■ TROLDHAUGEN

**Artist's home
in four
"movements"**

*The welcoming
hosts of Troldhau-
gen.*

"My greatest opus." This was Edvard Grieg's
opinion of his new home at Troldhaugen where
he and his wife, Nina, moved in during the
spring of 1885. One wonders what he would
have said today, when an additional three "movements" of the opus have come to exist: The
Composer's Cottage (1892), Troldsalen (1985)
and finally the Edvard Grieg Museum (1995).
It is hard to imagine a better-composed memorial to the master of melody.

Yearly pilgrimages to Edvard and Nina Grieg's home by Nordås Lake amount to about
200,000 people. Troldhaugen has not just become one of Bergen's most visited tourist attractions, but also the country's decidedly largest forum for chamber music. In Troldsalen,

T

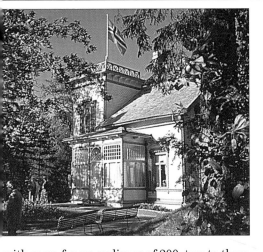

The Villa
at Troldhaugen
was designed by
Grieg's cousin,
architect Schack
Bull. Nina and
Edvard moved into
their home in 1885.

with room for an audience of 200, two to three public concerts are held weekly during the summer and fall season, in addition to several hundred private concerts.

When Grieg's idea of an international festival of music in Bergen became a reality in 1953, Troldhaugen played an important role. Small, intimate concerts are held each day in Grieg's sitting rooms where the music once resounded from the composer's own Steinway grand piano. For fear of spoiling the exclusive quality of the composer's home, four years passed before the public was invited to the first concert here, outside of the International Festival period. This took place in the summer of 1958.

The villa was designed by Grieg's cousin, Schack Bull, and was built according to the Victorian style of the time. The house was not insulated for use in cold weather, but this was unnecessary for Edvard and Nina Grieg – who preferred to fly south for the winter.

Troldhaugen was to be a peaceful place for both work and recreation. The influx of visitors, however, both invited and uninvited, was so large that Grieg soon found it necessary to go into hiding. A composer's studio was created in a small cottage near the edge of the water. Here he wrote a number of "Lyrical Pieces"

Important to the Bergen International Festival

The Grieg Award

The board of directors at Troldhaugen has presented the Grieg Award every year since 1972. The award is the highest distinction in the Norwegian music world and consists of a sum of money and a relief of the composer created by Hans Jacob Meyer. The first to receive the award was pianist Jens Harald Bratlie.

T

Erik Werenskiold's portrait of Grieg was done in the composer's cottage at Troldhaugen. The original hangs in Troldsalen.

Troldhaugen under the hammer

Recreated the artists home

Leif Ove Andsnes at the Steinway grand piano in Troldsalen. In the background the Grieg composer's cottage.

for piano, probably also the song cycle "Haugtussa" from the poem by Arne Garborg. Another great masterpiece was conceived at Troldhaugen: the violin sonata in c-minor, in addition to the "Symphic Dances" for orchestra, "Slåtter" for piano and "Four Psalms" for choir a capella. Troldhaugen, surrounded by natural beauty, has also inspired the great Danish composer, Carl Nielsen. During a summer visit with Nina in 1911, he wrote the first movement of his violin concerto in Grieg's spartan composer's cottage.

Troldhaugen was not just the Grieg couple's home during their lifetime, but also their final resting-place. The urns with their earthly remains are, in accordance with the Griegs' wishes, placed on a ledge of a stone wall just a few metres from the west side of their villa.

When Nina could no longer carry on the traditions of Troldhaugen as a summer home and meeting place for friends and musical pilgrims, the property was placed under the hammer in 1919. Nina saw no other option but to auction off the house, since the government would not place it under protection. Fortunately the new owner of the house and property was the composer's second cousin, Joachim Grieg. In 1923 he offered Fana County the option of taking over Troldhaugen free of charge, on the condition that the place was maintained in the spirit of Grieg.

Most of the inventory had by that time been dispersed, though a persistent group of ladies lead by Aslaug Mohr were able to successfully return it to where it belonged. The composer's cottage, which had ended up at the Folk Museum at Bygdøy was also retrieved. The urns, which were set in St. Jacob's graveyard, were brought to their rightful place in the mountain walls of Troldhaugen. When Troldhaugen was officially opened to the public in 1928, the intendant, Sigmund ▶ Torsteinson, could present the musician's home exactly as it had been when Grieg had lived there – with the original furniture, paintings and numerous treasures and objects, such as his well-used suitcase.

T

The stream of tourists was a heavy strain on the villa, and it was necessary to build a separate concert hall. Troldsalen (architect Peter Helland-Hansen and Sverre Lie) stood completed in 1985, exactly one hundred years after Troldhaugen had become Grieg's home. Another ten years later, the last addition, the museum building (architect Helge Borgen) was opened. Room has been made here for a permanent Grieg exhibition, travelling exhibitions, administration offices and a café.

▲
The composer's cottage at Trold-dalen was accompanied in 1985 by the concert hall, Troldsalen, which may be glimpsed in the background.

Troldhaugens venner (The Friends of Troldhaugen), founded in 1978, is a support group that has contributed to the preservation of the memory of the composer and his musical heritage. The non-profit organization supports their cause through the sale of music records, and for some years also the periodical "Amoroso". In 1996 the International Edvard Grieg Society was officially established at Troldhaugen. Its aim is to create a centre for a worldwide Grieg network in the composer's home.

National and international groups

T

■ THE UNIVERSITY LIBRARY

Books from the 1400s and everything published today

The primary objective of the University Library in Bergen (Universitetsbiblioteket) is to service the University's own research, instruction and educational facilities, but its collections and services are available to the public as well.

The University Library's shelves contain in 1999 about 1.4 million volumes, periodicals and pamphlets. In addition the library has 20,000 newspapers collected through the years and put on microfilm. It also includes 6000 newspapers, 8000 manuscripts, 40,000 maps and almost a half a million photographs. The library receives, according to the law of obligatory delivery, all Norwegian publications and secures international literature needed for research and study.

Since 1621, the University Library has had its own building (architect Kåre Kvilhaug and Jo Svare) on Haakon Sheteligs plass 1. Its construction became possible by a gift from J.L. Mowinckel's shipping company in memory of shipowner and Prime Minister Johan Ludwig Mowinckel (1870–1943). He has also been honoured by a memorial plaque and bust in the entrance hall, created by Cathe Wallendahl.

Significant amount of knowledge

There is a significant amount of knowledge within the walls, but the library also owns many old literary treasures – books, manuscripts, letters and diaries. Christie's diaries from the National Assembly at Eidsvoll in 1814 are here, along with a large collection of notes and rough drafts for the historical works of Christian Magnus Falsen (Regional Com-

◀

Biblia Sacra 1476
is the University Lib-
rary's oldest book.
It was printed in
Venice by the French
book printer Nico-
las Jenson. The first
pages are embellis-
hed with hand-pain-
ted initials. The lib-
rary's oldest manu-
script is a Latin me-
dieval code from the
year 1200.

missioner in Bergen and the "Father of the Constitution", J.C. Dahl's drawings of Norwegian buildings, and works by researchers like D.C. Danielsen and Fridtjof Nansen.

Many literary titbits

The manuscript collection is rich in sources of the city's cultural life. In the collection are 282 letters from Ole Bull, around one hundred letters from painter Nikolai Astrup, and more than 900 letters from the collection of the linguist Gustav Indrebø. Among the literary gems are also 700 letters from Knut Hamsen, a few hundred letters from Hulda and Arne Garborg and around 150 letters from Sigrid Undset to Gøsta of Geijerstam in Sunnfjord. The library also has a Holberg collection of more than 1400 volumes, an Ibsen collection of 950 volumes and a collection of around 2,500 volumes of New Norwegian literature left by Professor Torleif Hanaas. There is a unique Dickens collection comprised of 370 books and pamphlets, 12 manuscripts from Dickens' hand.

Holberg and Dickens

Protocols of the music company Harmonien from the year 1769 have been preserved, as well as handwritten scores from the earliest days of the society. Arne Bjørndal's enormous folk music collection can also be found among the more musical items. (See ▶ Folk Music.)

The first notes of Harmonien

The collection of photographs include the archives of prospectus and landscape photographer Knud Knudsen (1832–1915), the most prominent photographer in Bergen during the 1800s. A separate portrait gallery consists of more than 10,000 portraits of cultural personalities, including numerous photographic visiting cards.

Portraits

V

■ VESTMANNALAGET

Norway's oldest "mållag"

Henrik Krohn, the founder of Vestmannalaget and the editor of the first periodical printed in New Norwegian "Fraa By og Land" (From Town and Country). Krohn was also a merchant and a fruit farmer.

Vestmannalaget in Bergen is Norway's oldest "mållag", which is an association of Norwegians working toward making New Norwegian the predominant language in Norway. Writer Henrik Krohn founded Vestmannalaget in 1968. The primary objective of the association is to "work for the cause of the language, sharpen the national mind and promote Norwegian ethnicity". The association sees it as its duty not only to revive the original Norwegian language, but also to take a stand in matters of national importance.

In addition to publishing the dictionary of Ivar ▶ Aasen (1918) and constributing to the printing of a New Norwegian Bible, the association has become involved in various cultural pursuits. Examples include the restoration of Håkonshallen and the erection of the Snorre Sturlason monument. The association also founded the "Norskt Herbyrge", a Bergen hostel. The Snorre monument was created by Gustav Vigeland, and given to Iceland as a national gift. A replica of the statue was erected at Dreggsalmenning in 1948.

Due to the efforts of the Vestmannalaget, Bergen eventually became the center for the linguistic movement. Mons Litleré's publishing company printed almost all of its earliest books in New Norwegian.

Between 1870 and 1879, the association published the periodical "Fraa By og Bygd" (Town and Country), the first of its kind in the New Norwegian language. "Vestmannen", a magazine in circulation since 1984, comes out ten times a year.

Vestmannalaget has also made an important contribution to Norwegian Folk music. In 1897 the association arranged the first national competition for Hardanger fiddle musicians. The contest, which drew 17 contestants, took place on May 16th in the home of artists Frida and Olav Rusti in Damsgård. The winner, Sjur Helgeland, from Voss, became the very symbol of excellence in Norwegian folk music. The judges were none other than Frantz Beyer, John Grieg and Johan Halvorsen, all well-known personalities in the Norwegian cultural world at the time. In the first row, among the audience, sat composer Edvard Grieg. After the competition, the musicians were cheered by an audience of 1100 at a special performance in Logen, where Per Sivle, also from Voss, excited the crowd with his poetry.

Sjur Helgeland
from Vossestrand
was picked best
musician in the first
Hardanger fiddle
competition in
Bergen 1897.

Photo: The Photo Collection of the University Library.

■ AASMUND OLAVSSON VINJE

"I have never been happier than in a terrible rainstorm in Bergen. The air was so easy to breathe and so exhilarating that I could have danced under my umbrella. And when the weather began to clear, the damp air was so deep and so soft and the sky so blue, she was like a young, blue-eyed mother just after childbirth."

A more poetic description of Bergen's weather would be difficult to find. The author is Aasmund Olavsson Vinje (1818–79). In 1910 a street in Sydnes was named after Vinje, in honour of the great writer.

The New Norwegian poet and journalist visited Bergen only once. He was given a warm welcome by the Vestmannalaget in Bergen while on a lecture tour in the fall of 1869. Vinje wrote of his trip to Bergen in three travelogues published in his own weekly magazine, "Dølen". Vinje's poetry inspired some of the most treasured compositions by Edvard Grieg, such as "At Rondane" and "Spring".

**Inspired
Edvard Grieg**

Aasmund Olavsson
Vinje, ca. 1865.

V

W

■ JOHAN SEBASTIAN WELHAVEN

Warrior in verse

Welhaven is honoured in Bergen by a bust and street name. The bust was made by Per Ung and given to the city by Arild Haaland.

A bust of the poet and philosophy professor Johan Sebastian Cammermeyer Welhaven (1807 –73) was unveiled in 1985 in the kindergarten of St. Jørgen's Hospital. (See ▶ the Leprosy Museum). Here the poet most likely played as a child, since his father was a clergyman for the lepers at Hospitalkirken.

Welhaven was born in Bergen, and already in 1881 had a downtown street named after him. He happily reminisced over his childhood town, where his thoughts "were nourished by the freshest images". He writes: "A spring in Bergen is heavy with rain, but it has March violets, light green meadows, the scent of birch, early bird song and clear streams." His tribute to his hometown was given in the sketches "Images from the Bergen Coast" (1842). In the satirical poem "The Dawning of Norway" (1834) he accuses Bergen of having neglected its cultural duty, and scolds those living in materialism and substituting spiritual life with empty words of freedom and patriotism.

As a student at Bergen Katedralskole, his aesthetic senses were strongly influenced by Lyder ▶ Sagen. In his writing he strove for perfection and beauty – and had a falling out with his literary opponent, "The Wild Apostle", Henrik Wergeland.

Welhaven was more appreciative of Wergeland's sister, Camilla Collett. Sadly, however, the romantic relationship between them dissolved in the fierce battle between Welhaven and Wergeland.

■ WERNERSHOLM

Werner Hosewinckel Christie (1746–1822), the clergyman's son from Tysnes, presiding judge, genius and somewhat of an eccentric.

Cradle of Norway's national anthem

Wernersholm was named after the man who was given this testimonial from his peers. The well-known recreational area was built with money he earned from a stone quarry industry he ran from 1775 on Marmorøya in Nordås Lake.

An elegant mansion was built on Hop Farm, which was bought by Christie in 1784. He also constructed a strange octagon-shaped church covered with a kind of paper maché, with a large round dome and room for 800 people. According to Lyder Sagen it was like a miniature Pantheon. As if this wasn't enough, Christie directed water from Hop Lake into a canal around the property. The property became therefore idyllically isolated on an artificial islet or holm, hence the last part of the name.

Bergen's Pantheon

Wernersholm was elevated to greatness one hundred years later – by none other than master poet Bjørnstjerne ▶ Bjørnson. Inspired by the beautiful surroundings at Wernersholm, Bjørnson wrote a poem during the summer of 1859 which began with the famous words "Ja vi elsker dette landet" (Yes, we love this coun-

Inspired Bjørnson

Here Bjørnstjerne Bjørnson wrote, in 1859, Norway's national anthem "Ja vi elsker dette landet" (Yes, we love this country).

W

try). Ten years later Bjørnson's poem became Norway's official national anthem.

Empire-style building

At this time Wernersholm was owned by merchant Michael Krohn. He had both the church and the old manor building torn down and replaced with a one-story wooden house in Empire-style, the house we know today as Wernersholm.

From the end of May to the beginning of August 1859 the young Bjørnstjerne Bjørnson lived at Wernersholm. The door to the inspiring room was in all probability opened to the poet thanks to his close friendship with Michael Krohn's son, actor Georg Krohn. During his stay Bjørnson put his finishing touches to the rural story "Arne", which the poem "Ja vi elsker" was originally intended for. At Wernersholm he also wrote the beginning to "En glad gutt" (A Happy Boy) and "På Guds veie" (On the Path of God).

"Ja vi elsker" dedicated to King Carl XV

Bjørnson soon found, however, that the poem was not suitable for "Arne". Instead he dedicated it to King Carl XV, who was crowned king that same year. In an extra verse he paid homage to His Majesty. When the king did not keep his promises to Norway, Bjørnson erased the verse in 1863 and changed the poem.

Wernersholm restored

The estate, with its buildings and historic gardens, has gone through a complete restoration during the last few years. The owner since 1993 is the architectural company Wernersholmgruppen Inc., which also has offices inside the manor building. The goal is to restore the property to its original appearance, and in time to make it available to the public.

■ HANS WIERS-JENSSEN

Wrote about Bergen and Bergensians

"There is nothing worse for a genius than to be sentenced to life-long Bergen" – asserts the merchant Herwitz. Throughout generations Wiers-Jenssen's comical merchant characters have made audiences of Bergen roar with laughter, with their elegant, self-ironic remarks and arrogant lashings at the inhabitants east of the mountains. When they haven't been crying tears of laughter at Den Nationale Scene, they may have been singing "Fjellveivisen" (Song of the Mountain) with a tear in the corner of their eye.

Writer, journalist and stage director Hans Wiers-Jenssen (1866–1925) has been honoured by a portrait bust outside Den Nationale Scene and by a street name at Landås.

Few writers have been able to capture the pulse of Bergen in the way Wiers-Jenssen could. He grew up in the heart of the city, in Vågsbunnen. His birthplace was an old house on Hollendergaten where both art craftsmanship and merchant trade were carried on for years. Only a stone's throw away lies Fisketorget (The Fish Market) known as an area of exquisite comic retorts. This must have been a dream come true for a young boy who would later develop into a joyous and passionate master of the written word. In the opposite direction, through Kong Oscar's Street, a couple of blocks away, was the seat of higher learning, ▶ Bergen Katedralskole. There, Wiers-Jenssen soon joined the ranks of famous students.

The young Hans Wiers-Jenssen.

Bergen had a central role in most of Wiers-Jenssen's writing. He is at his best when writing about familiar people and places. His three short story collections are good examples of this. "The Stories of Aunt Mine" (1910), "Chronicles from the Old City" (1916) and "Laurentius and other Chronicles from the Old City" (1923) all contain striking descrip- tions of the environment of both literary and cultural-historical value. The Bergen district also has a central position in his gripping novel "The Vicar of Korshavn and his Wife. A Story from the Seaside" (1907).

Chronicles from the old town

The history of Bergen also provided Wiers-Jenssen with material for his greatest work, the historical drama "Anne Pedersdotter" (1908). The real Anne Pedersdotter was married to the humanist Absalon Pederssøn Beyer, a teacher at the Latin School and palace clergyman at Bergenhus. Anne was tried for witchcraft in 1575 but acquitted. After Ab- salon's

Witch hunt became a play and two operas

A portrait bust of Hans Wiers-Jenssen, made by Per Ung, was unveiled in 1992 outside Den Nationale Scene.

death, Anne was tried again for witchcraft, sentenced and burned to death in 1590. Using the theme of the witch hunt process, the tense drama sheds light on the conflict between the religious and the erotic, the fatigue of age and youth's zest for life.

"Anne Pedersdotter" has inspired two operas

W

– the first by Ottarino Respighi, "La fiamma" (1934). In 1971 Edvard Fliflet Bræin allowed himself to become inspired by the same theme. The result was an opera many believe to be Norway's most significant musical-drama, with a libretto attributed to Hans Kristiansen. The witch drama from Bergen was in 1943 made into a screen version by Carl Th. Dreyer with the title "The Day of Wrath".

National drama of Bergen

In Bergen it is Wiers-Jenssen's comedy "Jan Herwitz" (1913) that surpasses almost any other theatrical production. At Den Nationale Scene the play has been performed over 400 times, but its run is far from over. In 1999 it is scheduled to make a new appearance on stage, to the delight of a new generation of theatre audiences.

This extremely popular comedy has been characterised as the 'national drama' of Bergen and a full figure portrait of a true Bergensian. The figure of merchant Herwitz is fighting for his father's reputation as an inventor. His arrogant attitude toward eastern Norwegians, expressed with an elegant turn of a phrase and a quick retort has always filled the theatre hall with laughter.

Self-irony

In contrast to other local-historical plays that would rather emphasise the positive aspects of the district, Wiers-Jenssen does not see it as his task to glorify his hometown. Quite the contrary. Astonishingly, however, the audience is delighted over the self-irony, even when the merchant from Bergen is mercilessly hanged for his bourgeois ignorance. The lines are often constructed with biting satire. Despite all this, the audiences of Bergen love the play.

As Francis Bull, professor of literature, has stated, the temperament of the Bergen citizen has seldom been more splendidly or more remarkably represented than in Wiers-Jenssen.

Ballad writer

Wiers-Jenssen was also a talented actor and stage director, and will also be remembered as the author of the very popular love song, "På Fjeldveien" (On the Mountain Path), better known as "Fjellveivisen" (The Song of the Mountain Path).

W

■ VALTER AND THORLEIF AAMODT

Musical brothers from Bergen

Brothers Valter Aamodt (1902–89) and Thorleif Aamodt (born 1909) are two of the most prominent musical personalities of our time. Both became composers and enjoyed recognition as conductors for a number of choirs and corps. The eldest of the two was a music publisher, and the youngest a concert organ-ist. In addition, both were diligent music journalists and critics.

With no musical lunchbox brought along from their childhood home at Sydnes, it was the school marching band and the boys' choir that released their musical talents and paved their career paths. When Valter received his salary for a summer job as a trumpet player in the Nordbech Circus, he invested the money in an organ. But it was the younger brother, Thorleif, who became deeply interested in the instrument. This led him eventually to organist positions in Arna, Laksevåg, Sandvikskirken and Johanneskirken, in addition to concert performances both in and outside of the country.

Conductor Valter Aamodt was primarily associated with the marching bands "Fortunen" and "Ulriken", well-known from a number of radio concerts, and with the Follesø Men's Choir. Their singing skills were awarded prizes both at home and abroad, including, among others, the Grieg Prize. When different choirs gathered to sing together Valter was the obvious choice for conductor. Valter Aamodt was editor of the periodical "Norsk Sang" and

Thorleif Aamodt – organist, conductor and composer.

publishing director for the music publishing company "Tonika" in Bergen. From this composer's hand came choir songs, ballads and instrumental pieces, including several cantatas for choir and orchestra. His "Horda Rhapsody" was played at the opening of Grieghallen. Every choir singer knows Aamodt's "Sea Salt", with lyrics by Henrik Rytter.

Brother Thorleif made his mark as a composer, organist and choir conductor. As the conductor for Sandviken's Congregational Choir, he was the first, in 1949, to perform Grieg's "Four Psalms" in its entirety. He later arranged the piece for string orchestra and cello solo. Grieg's opus nr. 33, the Vinje songs, was arranged by Aamodt for a mixed choir. The Bergen Domkantori performed the piece at a premier for the Grieg Anniversary in 1933. The list of works covers also about 30 Biblical psalms or chants, motets, choir pieces and organ music. "Spring Ballad" received first prize for best composition from the Norwegian state television station, NRK in 1970. A major work is "Ego sum" (1964) for mixed choir and orchestra. Both Valter and Thorleif Aamodt were appointed Knights of the Order of St. Olav.

Valter Aamodt
made his debut in 1922 as a composer for the Oslo Philharmonic Orchestra with a piece for strings. He was conductor of Harmonien for six regular concerts.

■ IVAR AASEN

The father of New Norwegian, language researcher and poet Ivar Andreas Aasen from Ørsta in Sunnmøre (1813–96) has given his name to a street between Dokkeveien and Sydnesplass. A large portrait of him, painted by Lars Osa, hangs in the reading room of the Bergen Public Library.

Bergen has a special reason to commemorate this brilliant man. It was here that Ivar Aasen's linguistic marathon seriously began and was encouraged. It all happened in 1841 when he visited Bishop Jacob Neumann in Bergen with his first two scholarly accomplishments, a book of Sunnmøre grammar and a herbarium. The bishop preferred the book of grammar and helped to get it published. He also saw to it that the young, self-taught researcher recei-

Founded New Norwegian – started in Bergen

Ivar Aasen drawn by Oav Rusti.

Aasen portrait in the Library

Lars Osa is probably the only artist who managed to persuade Ivar Aasen to be his model. The poet was very modest and shy. The portrayt is painted at Aasen's place in Oslo 1895, and can now be seen in the reading room of Bergen Public Library.

▶

ved financial support from the Royal Norwegian Scholarly Academy in Trondheim so that he could continue his study of dialects. This made it possible for Aasen to set off on an extensive research journey. He would later harvest the ripe scholarly fruits of his efforts.

Dictionaries, grammars, musical and poetry

With assembly line speed, he turned out new dictionaries and grammar books of "the Norwegian Folk Language", both fundamental works in the field of Norwegian language studies. He also published examples of the usefulness of the rural language in several different areas, such as the musical "Ervingen" (the Heir), which was performed at Det Norske Theater in Bergen. The name was adopted by the country youth club "Ervingen".

Folk songs

Aasen displayed great talent as a poet with his collection of poetry entitled "Symra" from 1863. Several of the poems have later become folk songs. Added to the list of his remarkably productive authorship is a reading book, "Norwegian Proverbs", "Norwegian Plant Names" and "Heimsyn", a book dealing with nature, geography and world history.

Å

■ POSTSCRIPT - REFERENCES

Dear reader. A comprehensive introduction to the culture of Bergen – your expectations for the book you hold in your hand, and may have read, are probably no less than this. The ambitious goal of this project was no less than this either.

Under close scrutiny, Bergen has proven to be a good deal richer in culture than even the most patriotic eyes were at first able to see. Eventually it had to be accepted that every item under the heading of "culture" could not possibly receive the space it deserved within a framework of a book that was meant as a handy and informative guide and not an alphabetical listing of facts. The painful process of sorting out what was, and what was not, to be included was therefore unavoidable. An attempt at a representative selection was made according to the best possible judgement and from a wide assortment of cultural forms. Gunnar Hagen Hartvedt's "Bergen City Encyclopedia" from Kunnskapsforlaget, 1994, has been of inestimable value during this project. The reader is also referred to the following literary sources.

Alver, Brynjulf, Peter Anker og Signy Børsheim (red.). 1987. *Vestlandske Kunstindustrimuseum 100 år.* A.S. John Grieg. Bergen.

Amoroso. Nr. 1-8, 1994-97. Stiftelsen Harmonien og Troldhaugens Venner. Bergen.

Andersson, Espen B. 1985. *Bergenske skulpturer i friluft.* Bergen kommune. Bergen.

Angell, Olav, Jan Erik Vold og Einar Økland (red.). 1974. *Jazz i Norge.* Gyldendal Norsk Forlag. Oslo.

Askeland, Jan og Erling Lauhn. 1971. *Billedhuggeren Sofus Madsen.* F. Beyer Forlag. Bergen.

Balean, Inger Norma (red.). 1998. *Bergen Guide.* Bergen Reiselivslag. *Bergen.*

Benestad, Finn og Dag Schelderup-Ebbe. 1980. *Edvard Grieg, mennesket og kunstneren.* H. Aschehoug & Co. (W. Nygaard). Oslo.

Berg, Adolph og Olav Mosby. 1945. *Musikselskabet Harmonien 1765-1945.* A.S John Grieg Boktrykkeri. Bergen.

Bergens profil. 1944. J.W. Eides Forlag. Bergen.

Beyer, Harald (red.). 1945. *Fra Christie til Nordahl Grieg. XII bergenske kulturpersonligheter.* J.W. Eides Forlag. Bergen.

Bjørkum, Andreas, Magne Myhren og Bjørn Aasland (red.). 1996. *Folkemusikk og folkemusikkutøvarar i Norge.* Notabene. Oslo.

Bull, Francis og Fredrik Paasche. 1923. *Norsk litteraturhistorie.* H. Aschehoug & Co. (W. Nygaard). Oslo.

Bøgh, Gran (red.). 1946. *Et kultursentrum. Bergen og bergensere i norsk kunst og forskning.* John Griegs Forlag. Bergen.

Dagsland, Sissel Hamre og Svein Nord. 1984. *Den gamle by. Om folk og hus i Gamle Bergen.* Universitetsforlaget. Bergen.

Farga, Franz. 1940. *Geigen und Geiger.* Müller. Zürich.

Fasting, Kåre. 1965. *Musikselskabet Harmonien gjennom 200 år 1765-1965.* A.S John Grieg Boktrykkeri. Bergen.

Flaten, Trine Kolderup og Gudrun Gregersen. 1995. *Veier til viten.* Bergen Offentlige Bibliotek. Bergen.

Gatland, Jan Olav (red.). 1996. *Amor Liborum Nos Unit.* Universitetsbiblioteket i

Bergen 1825–1996. Universitetet i Bergen. Bergen.

Gjesdal, Carl O. Gram. 1982. *Byuniversitetet på berget.* Universitetsforlaget. Oslo.

Grieg, Harald. 1963. *Nordahl min bror.* Gyldendal Norsk Forlag. Oslo.

Holmvik, Bjørn F. (red.). 1997. *Handlingsplan for kunst og kunstnere i kulturbyen Bergen.* Bergen kommune. Bergen.

Hoem, Edvard. 1949. *Til ungdommen: Nordahl Griegs liv.* Gyldendal Norsk Forlag. Oslo.

Hopp, Zinken. 1945. *Eventyret om Ole Bull.* John Griegs Forlag. Bergen.

Irgens, Lorentz M. *Guide to the Leprosy Museum.* Lepramuseet. Bergen.

Janson, Kristofer. 1913. *Hvad jeg har oplevet.* Gyldendal. Kristiania.

Jensen, Roald. 1965. *Med fotball i blodet.* Sunnmørsposten. Ålesund.

Johannesen, Ole Rønning. 1963. *For den bildende kunst.* Bergen Kunstforening. Bergen.

Kayser, Jan Henrik. 1997. *Rondo Amoroso. Harald Sæverud og klavermusikken.* Nord 4 Bokverksted. Bergen.

Kortner, Olav, Preben Munthe og Egil Tveiterås (hovedred.). 1993. *Aschehoug og Gyldendals Store Norske Leksikon.* Kunnskapsforlaget. Oslo.

Lexow, Einar. 1929. *King Håkon's Hall and Gerhard Munthe's Decorations.* John Griegs Forlag. Bergen.

Lorentzen, Bernt. 1948. *Den Gode Hensigt gjennom 150 år.* John Griegs Forlag. Bergen.

Laastad, Gerd og Erik Næsgaard (red.). 1995. *Johan Lange og Fjøsanger hovedgård.* Langes Minde/Lange og søskendes legat. Bergen.

Madsen, Alf H. og Arnljot Strømme Svendsen (red.).1988. *Spill, Rolf'en, spill!* Nord 4 Bokverksted. Bergen.

Michelsen, Kari (red.). 1978. *Cappelens musikkleksikon.* J. W. Cappelens Forlag. Oslo.

Midttun, Olav. 1963. *Menn og bøker.* Det Norske Samlaget. Oslo.

Ness, Einar. 1989. *Det var en gang – Norsk skole gjennom tidene.* Universitetsforlaget. Oslo.

Nilsen, Sidsel Marie.1998.*Helst mot urolig vær. Teatermannen Hans Jacob Nilsen.* H. Aschehoug & Co. (W. Nygaard).Oslo.

Nordhagen, Per Jonas.1992. *Bergen Guide & Handbook.* Bergensiana-forlaget. Bergen.

Normann, Axel Otto. 1950. *Johanne Dybwad, liv og kunst.* Gyldendal Norsk Forlag. Oslo.

Pettersen, Egil. 1996. *Ka e' tiss? Bergensmålet slik forfatterne har brukt det.* Alma Mater. Bergen.

Reitan, Lorentz. 1997. *Harald Sæverud. Mannen, musikken, mytene.* Forum / H. Aschehoug & Co. (W. Nygaard). Oslo.

Skarstein, Jakob (red.). 1973. *Den nystemte. En samling Bergensviser.* Gyldendal Norsk Forlag. Oslo.

Smith, Mortimer. 1960. *Ole Bull.* Gyldendal Norsk Forlag. Oslo.

Stang, Ragna. 1989. *Edvard Munch, mennesket og kunstneren.* H. Aschehoug & Co. (W.Nygaard). Oslo.

Steen, Sverre. 1969. *Bergen byen mellom fjellene. Et historisk utsyn.* Bergen kommune. Bergen.

Storaas, Reidar. 1987. *Fest og spill i 35 år.* J.W. Eides Forlag. Bergen.

Tveit, Norvald. 1969. *Ivar Medaas.* Det Norske Samlaget og Troll. Oslo.

Veiteberg, Jorunn. 1985. *Bilethoggaren Ambrosia Tønnesen 1959–1948.* Bergens Kunstforening. Bergen.

Aasen, Elisabeth. 1996. *Dorothe Engelbretsdatter: Tekster i utvalg.* J. W. Eides Forlag. Bergen.

ADDRESSES and TELEPHONE NUMBERS

■ USEFUL TELEPHONE NUMBERS

BERGEN TOURIST INFORMATION
DnB Frescohallen, Vågsallmenningen 1
✆ 55 32 14 80
KULTURBY BERGEN 2000
DnB Frescohallen, Vågsallmenningen 1
✆ 55 55 20 00
BERGEN MUNICIPALITY
Information centre ✆ 55 56 62 04
BERGEN BUSSTATION
✆ 55 55 90 70
GAIA TRAFIKK AS
✆ 55 96 55 00
NORWEGIAN RAILWAYS (NSB)
✆ 815 00 888

DROSJER • TAXI
Bergen Taxi ✆ 55 99 70 00
Reservations: ✆ 55 99 70 10
Taxi Vest ✆ 55 94 80 00
BERGEN AIRPORT, FLESLAND
Braathens ✆ 55 99 82 50
SAS ✆ 55 11 43 00
Widerøe ✆ 55 91 78 60
BERGEN CINEMAS
Ticket reservations ✆ 55 23 23 15
KULTURHUSET USF
✆ 55 31 55 70
GRIEGHALLEN
Ticket office ✆ 55 21 61 50

■ ANTIQUE BOOKSHOPS

HOLBERG ANTIKVARIAT
Lille Øvregt. 2
EIKENS ANTIKVARIAT
Strandkaien 16
HOLLENDERGATEN ANTIKVARIAT
Hollendergaten 13

■ ANTIQUES

AKANTUS
Vetrlidsalmenning 4
ANTIQUARIUS
Skostredet 5
BERGEN BRUKT & ANTIK
Kong Oscars gate 11
BERGEN MARSJANDISE
Kong Oscars gate 18
BESTEMORS KJELLER
Lille Øvregate 5
CECILIE ANTIKK
Kong Oscars gate 32
ELLEN ANTIKK
Vetrlidsalmenning 8
LEINS ANTIK
Holmedalsgården 3, Bryggen
MAGNUSSENS BRUKT OG ANTIKT
Øvregaten 6
SJØ OG LAND
Lars Hilles gt. 26
STEINKJELLEREN ANTIKVITETSHANDEL
Nicolaikirkealmenning 2

■ BALLET • DANCE

NYE CARTE BLANCHE
Danseteatret, Sigurdsgate 6
✆ 55 32 17 10 / 55 23 36 66
BERGEN FOLKLORE Folk dance
Bryggens Museum ✆ 55 31 67 10
FANA FOLKLORE
Rambergtunet, ✆ 55 91 52 40
RISS DANSEKOMPANI
Kulturhuset USF ✆ 55 31 55 70

■ CINEMAS

BERGEN KINO
Ticket sales in Konsertpaleet, *Neumannsgt.*
3 for all cinemas. ✆ 55 23 23 15
CINEMATEKET
Kulturhuset USF, ✆ 55 31 55 70

■ CHURCHES

Churches in downtown Bergen

DOMKIRKEN (Bergen Cathedral)
Domkirkeplass, ✆ 55 31 04 70
JOHANNESKIRKEN (St. John's church)
Sydnesplass, ✆ 55 90 02 25
KORSKIRKEN (Church of the Cross)
Nedre Korskirkeallm./ Kong Oscars gate
✆ 55 31 53 25
MARIAKIRKEN (St. Mary's Church)
Dreggsallmening, ✆ 55 31 59 60
NYKIRKEN (New Church)
Nykirkeallmenning, ✆ 55 32 79 28
ST. PAUL KIRKE
(St. Paul's Catholic Church)
Christies gate / Nygårdsgaten
✆ 55 21 59 50

■ CONCERTS

BERGEN PHILHARMONIC ORCHESTRA
Ticket reservations: ✆ 55 21 61 50
BIT 20
✆ 55 21 61 20
BJØRGVIN CHURCH MUSIC
✆ 55 31 33 20
THE GRIEG ACADEMY
Gunnar Sævigs Sal, ✆ 55 58 69 50
THE HORDALAND CHOIR ASSOCIATION
Komediebakken 9 ✆ 55 56 38 65
JAZZ
Bergen Jazzforum,
Vestnorsk Jazzsenter and
Night Jazz Festival (every year in May)
Kulturhuset USF, *Georgernes Verft 3*
✆ 55 32 09 76
LOGEN *Ole Bulls plass 14*
✆ 55 23 20 15
LYSØEN (Ole Bull's villa)
✆ 56 30 90 77
MARIAKIRKEN (St. Mary's Church)
✆ 55 31 59 60
THE MILITARY MARCHING BAND
Bergenhus ✆ 55 54 62 55
THE NORWEGIAN ASSOCIATION OF MARCHING BANDS
C. Sundtsgt 1, ✆ 55307090
POP AND ROCK
Maxime, Ole Bulls pl. 9/11 ✆ 55 30 71 35
The Academic Quarter
Olav Kyrres gt. 49–53 ✆ 55 30 28 00
Concerts all year round, jazz and classical

SILJUSTØL (The home of Harald Sæverud)
✆ 55 13 60 00 / 55 91 07 10
TROLDSALEN (The home of Edvard Grieg)
✆ 55 91 07 10 / 55 91 17 91
SUMMER CONCERTS – CLASSICAL
Fløien ✆ 55 32 18 75
Schøtstuene,
Bryggen, ✆ 55 31 60 20 / 55 31 41 89
Ulriken ✆ 55 29 86 11

■ FESTIVALS

AUTUNNALE-FESTIVALEN
✆ 55 56 04 44
THE BERGEN INTERNATIONAL FESTIVAL
Bryggen 9, 5. floor
✆ 55 21 06 30 / 55 53 31 33
FORFATTERSLEPPET
✆ 55 96 06 10
OLE BLUES-FESTIVALEN
✆ 55 96 15 35
UKEN *Helleveien 30* ✆ 55 95 98 58

■ GALLERIES

PUBLIC GALLERIES
BERGEN ART MUSEUM
Rasmus Meyers Allé 3
✆ 55 56 80 00
Bergen Billedgalleri
Rasmus Meyers Allé 3
Rasmus Meyer Collections
Rasmus Meyers Allé 7
The Stenersen Collection
Rasmus Meyers Allé 2
THE FJØSANGER COLLECTION
Stamerbakken 7 ✆ 55 91 20 40

PRIVATE GALLERIES
BERGEN ART ASSOCIATION
(Bergens Kunstforening)
Rasmus Meyers Allé 5
✆ 55 32 14 60
FORMAT KUNSTHANDVERK
Vågsalmenningen 12
GALLERI BOUHLOU
Allégaten 22
GALLERI LANGEGÅRDEN
Straumev. 17 A
GALLERI NIKOLAI
Bryggen 13
GALLERI NYGATEN
Nygaten 7
GALLERI PARKEN
Kaigaten 12
GALLERI PROFIL
Sekkegaten 4
GALLERI s.e.
Sandbrogt. 3, Bradbenken
GALLERI SIVERTS
Nedre Korskirkealmenning 3 B
GALLERI URD
Galleriet (6.et.) Torgallmenningen 8
HORDALAND KUNSTSENTER
Galleri 1 – Galleri NK, Klosteret 17
KAFE FINCKEN
Nygårdsgaten 2 A
KONTUR KUNSTHÅNDVERK
Olav Kyrres gate 45
PRIMSTAVEN
Nesttunveien 100
TABLÅ
Marken 26
VIRGO GALLERI OG KUNSTHANDEL
Steinkjellergaten 1A
VISNINGSROMMET
Kulturhuset USF, Georgenes Verft 3

■ LIBRARIES

BERGEN PUBLIC LIBRARY
Strømgaten 6
✆ 55 56 85 60 / 55 56 85 95
THE GRIEG COLLECTION
Grieghallen, ✆ 55 56 85 88
THE MUSIC LIBRARY
Grieghallen, ✆ 55 56 85 80
THE UNIVERSITY LIBRARY
Haakon Sheteligs plass 7
✆ 55 58 25 16 / 55 58 25 39

■ MUSEUMS

ALVØEN MANOR
✆ 55 32 51 08 / 55 93 18 19
THE AQUARIUM
Nordnesbakken 4, ✆ 55 55 71 71
THE ARBORETUM
Mildevegen 240, ✆ 55 98 72 50
BERGEN MUSEUM
✆ 55 58 29 49
Cultural-historical collection
Haakon Sheteligs plass 10
Natural-History collection
Muséplass 3
BERGEN MUSEUM OF TECHNOLOGY
Thormøhlens gate 23, Møhlenpris
✆ 55 96 11 60
BOY'S DRILL CORPS MUSEUM
Murhvelvingen, Østre Muralmenning 23
BRYGGENS MUSEUM
✆ 55 31 67 10
"BULLAHUSET" (Ole Bull's villa)
Valestrand, ✆ 56 39 42 64
DAMSGÅRD ESTATE
✆ 55 94 08 70 / 55 32 51 08
FANTOFT STAVE CHURCH
Paradis, ✆ 55 28 07 10
FJØSANGER ESTATE
✆ 55 91 06 94
GAMLE BERGEN (Old Bergen)
✆ 55 25 78 50
THE HANSEATIC MUSEUM
Bryggen, ✆ 55 31 41 89
HORDAMUSEET
Stend, ✆ 55 91 51 30
HÅKONSHALLEN
Bergenhus, ✆ 55 31 60 67
THE LEPROSY MUSEUM
Kong Oscars gate 59, ✆ 55 97 49 89
THE MARITIME MUSEUM
Haakon Sheteligs plass 15
✆ 55 32 79 80
THE NORWEGIAN MUSEUM OF FISHERIES
Bontelabo 2, ✆ 55 32 12 49

THE NORWEGIAN MUSEUM OF KNITWEAR & TEXTILE CENTRE
Salhus, ✆ 55 19 14 70
THE RAILWAY MUSEUM
Garnes stasjon, ✆ 55 24 91 00
THE ROSENKRANTZ TOWER
Bergenhus, ✆ 55 31 43 80
SCHØTSTUENE
Øvregaten 50, ✆ 55 31 60 20
THETA MUSEUM
Norwegian World War II Resistance
Museum. Enhjørningsgården Bryggen
WESTERN NORWEGIAN MUSEUM OF APPLIED ARTS
Permanenten, Nordahl Bruns gate 9
✆ 55 32 51 08

■ OPERA

BERGEN CHAMBER OPERA
Kulturhuset USF, ✆ 55 31 55 70
OPERA VEST
Grieghallen ✆ 55 21 61 20
WEST NORWAY OPERA
Komediebakken 9 ✆ 55 32 38 56

■ PHILATELY

BRYGGEN COINS AND ANTIQUES
Holmedalsgården, Bryggen
FRIMERKEHUSET A/S (The Postage
Stamp House) Østre Skostræde 2
SIGMUND'S COLLECTORS MARKET
Øvregaten 10

■ THEATRE

BERGEN INTERNATIONALE TEATER
Teatergarasjen, Nøstegaten 54
✆ 55 23 22 35
DEN NATIONALE SCENE
(The National Theatre of Bergen)
Engen 1, ✆ 55 54 97 10
FYLLINGSDALEN NYE TEATER
Folke Bernadottes vei
✆ 55 16 08 80 / 55 16 83 05
HORDALAND TEATER
Stend, ✆ 55 91 60 20
VESTLANDSKE TEATERSENTER
Vestre Strømkaien 1 ✆ 55 31 01 45

MUSICALS AND CABARETS
LOGEN
Ole Bulls plass, ✆ 55 23 20 15
RADISSON SAS HOTEL NORGE
Ole Bulls plass 4, ✆ 55 57 30 00
RICK'S
Veiten 3, ✆ 55 55 31 31